T0353503

Economic Evaluation of Pharmacy Services

Economic Evaluation of Pharmacy Services

Edited by

Zaheer-Ud-Din Babar
University of Auckland, Auckland, New Zealand,
and
Lahore Pharmacy College, Lahore, Pakistan

AMSTERDAM • BOSTON • HEIDELBERG • LONDON
NEW YORK • OXFORD • PARIS • SAN DIEGO
SAN FRANCISCO • SINGAPORE • SYDNEY • TOKYO
Academic Press is an imprint of Elsevier

Academic Press is an imprint of Elsevier
125 London Wall, London EC2Y 5AS, United Kingdom
525 B Street, Suite 1800, San Diego, CA 92101-4495, United States
50 Hampshire Street, 5th Floor, Cambridge, MA 02139, United States
The Boulevard, Langford Lane, Kidlington, Oxford OX5 1GB, United Kingdom

Notices
Knowledge and best practice in this field are constantly changing. As new research and experience broaden
our understanding, changes in research methods, professional practices, or medical treatment may become
necessary.

Practitioners and researchers must always rely on their own experience and knowledge in evaluating and
using any information, methods, compounds, or experiments described herein. In using such information or
methods they should be mindful of their own safety and the safety of others, including parties for whom they
have a professional responsibility.

To the fullest extent of the law, neither the Publisher nor the authors, contributors, or editors, assume any
liability for any injury and/or damage to persons or property as a matter of products liability, negligence or
otherwise, or from any use or operation of any methods, products, instructions, or ideas contained in the
material herein.

British Library Cataloguing-in-Publication Data
A catalogue record for this book is available from the British Library

Library of Congress Cataloging-in-Publication Data
A catalog record for this book is available from the Library of Congress

ISBN: 978-0-12-803659-4

For Information on all Academic Press publications
visit our website at https://www.elsevier.com

Publisher: Nikki Levy
Acquisition Editor: J. Scott Bentley
Editorial Project Manager: Susan Ikeda
Production Project Manager: Nicky Carter
Designer: Mark Rogers

Typeset by MPS Limited, Chennai, India

Dedication

To Danyal

Contents

5. Design Principles for Economic Evaluations in Pharmacy

J.A. Whitty

6. Steps in Conducting an Economic Evaluation

A.A. Shafie, G.N. Chua and Y.V. Yong

7. Evaluation of the Community Pharmacist-led Anticoagulation Management Service (CPAMS) Pilot Program in New Zealand

J. Shaw, J. Harrison and J.E. Harrison

8.   Economic Evaluation of Pharmacy Services in Portugal

S. Costa

9.   Economic Evaluation of Pharmacist-Managed Warfarin Therapy: A Review of Studies

S. Saokaew, N. Samprasit, P. Kulchaitanaroaj and N. Chaiyakunapruk

10. Economic Evaluation of a Medicines Management Model in New Zealand: A Proposal

Z.-U.-D. Babar and R. Edlin

Contributors

Z.-U.-D. Babar University of Auckland, Auckland, New Zealand; Lahore Pharmacy College, Lahore, Pakistan

D.L. Baines Coventry University, Coventry, United Kingdom

N. Chaiyakunapruk Monash University Malaysia, Selangor, Malaysia; Naresuan University, Phitsanulok, Thailand; University of Wisconsin, Madison, WI, United States; University of Queensland, Brisbane, Australia

G.N. Chua Universiti Sains Malaysia, Penang, Malaysia

S. Costa Center for Health Evaluation & Research (CEFAR) of the National Association of Pharmacies (ANF), Lisboa, Portugal

D.M. Dawoud Cairo University, Cairo, Egypt

R. Edlin University of Auckland, Auckland, New Zealand

T. Gammie University of Auckland, Auckland, New Zealand

J. Harrison University of Auckland, Auckland, New Zealand

J.E. Harrison University of Auckland, Auckland, New Zealand

C. Jommi Università del Piemonte Orientale, Novara, Italy; CERGAS Bocconi, Milano, Italy

P. Kulchaitanaroaj University of Iowa, Iowa City, IA, United States

M.I. Mohamed Ibrahim Qatar University, Doha, Qatar

N. Samprasit University of Phayao, Phayao, Thailand

S. Saokaew University of Phayao, Phayao, Thailand; Monash University Malaysia, Selangor, Malaysia

A.A. Shafie Universiti Sains Malaysia, Penang, Malaysia

J. Shaw University of Auckland, Auckland, New Zealand

H.S. Suh Pusan National University, Busan, Korea

S. Vogler Gesundheit Österreich GmbH (Austrian Public Health Institute), Vienna, Austria

J.A. Whitty University of East Anglia, Norwich, United Kingdom

Y.V. Yong Ministry of Health Malaysia, Selangor, Malaysia

Foreword

This book has become available at just the right time. Today in 2016/17, the concept and techniques of pharmacoeconomics have trickled down from a few originator countries in North America and Western Europe to nearly all countries and territories in the world. While the formulae and calculations are now widely known, what are badly needed are examples and knowledge of how these principles might be employed under different circumstances in a variety of countries where we find diverse political, economic, and regulatory systems.

This book fills that void. Dr. Babar and his chapter authors have provided us with a valuable array of diverse uses and modifications of the four basic pharmacoeconomic formulae that may be applied and modified for application in the least developed country to the most industrialized and wealthy ones. The chapter on methodologies for community and hospital pharmacies is a good introduction to the content found in the subsequent chapters. Chapter 3, Economic Evaluation of Pharmacy Services: Review of Studies from Asia, Africa, and South America, offers us a glimpse of the activities in this domain in examples from Africa, Asia, and South America. It is not intended to be all-inclusive, but the book's structure allows the reader to pick and choose what pieces he or she wants to incorporate into a specific, customized procedure for a single country. This will, of course, differ, depending on the wealth, resources, degree of privatization or government control, etc. in each country.

Chapter 4, Economic Evaluation and its Types, provides more specifics in the methodology arena. When one decides upon conducting a pharmacoeconomic evaluation of a certain medicine, it is wise to review this chapter to make certain that one's study is comprehensive and follows general policies to prevent and avoid preventable study design flaws. Fortunately, the precision of a pharmacoeconomics study is not equal to that required in a randomized clinical trial, where much greater accuracy is necessary. This permits us to use smaller than ideal sample sizes, when expedient or necessary.

Chapter 5, Design Principles for Economic Evaluations in Pharmacy, is very similar to Chapter 4, but that is no problem, as the approach in each chapter is different and repetition of important, key points is usually desirable. If one has a study in mind, the review of Chapter 4, Economic Evaluation and its Types and Chapter 5, Design Principles for Economic

Evaluations in Pharmacy, should stop one until critical questions can be answered based on the study design. In Chapter 6, Steps in Conducting an Economic Evaluation, we find what in its most fundamental form is a checklist. Just as the pilot uses a checklist to make certain that all switches and levers are in the correct position before takeoff, this chapter can serve as a type of checklist with the same purpose.

In Chapter 7, Evaluation of the Community Pharmacist-led Anticoagulation Management Service (CPAMS) Pilot Program in New Zealand, we find an excellent example of a well-designed, conducted, and reported pharmacoeconomics study. It can serve as a fine template for one about to conduct their first pharmacoeconomics study. Obviously, the details will be different, but it is an excellent copy that may be copied. Even the report is really good, an often neglected point, but a most important one always. The best study that is not easy to follow or understand is not much better than no study at all.

The last two Chapter 8, Economic Evaluation of Pharmacy Services in Portugal and Chapter 9, Economic Evaluation of Pharmacist-Managed Warfarin Therapy: A Review of Studies, are additional examples of pharmacoeconomics studies: one conducted in Portugal and the other, a literature-based retrospective study conducted at no particular location. With these examples or templates, the reader should have sufficient tools to perform an acceptable pharmacoeconomics study.

After using this book, one should be able to produce pharmacoeconomics work of an acceptable quality. One of the positive features of the book is the ability to use only 1 or 2 or 3 chapters as needed for a reference purpose. If one has studied in this discipline, but feels uncomfortable about performing a real study alone, Chapters 5 through 8 or 9 may be the only contact with the book that is needed. This book can be used as a textbook in its entirety or as a reference work for people in the health policy area. In any event, its use should result in more persons knowledgeable about selecting the optimal drug product for patients in national health schemes, or with private insurers or other payers. That is a fine result.

Professor Albert Wertheimer
Philadelphia, PA, USA

Preface

Services managed by pharmacists in both hospital and community pharmacy settings are vital and can improve the quality use of medicines significantly. Pharmacists are the most accessible health care professionals and are well placed to manage cases of high blood pressure, diabetes, stroke, smoking cessation, weight loss, contraception, anticoagulation, etc. Also community private retail pharmacies are considered a key route to deliver health care programs. The pharmacies also serve as a place to access services for those patient groups, who are not registered with the general practitioners.

Though governments in the United States, Australia, the United Kingdom, and Canada are increasingly investing in these services; however, there is no clear evidence whether these pharmacy services are cost-effective or otherwise.

There is an enthusiasm that pharmacists can contribute toward wider role in health care, however well-defined research is needed to support this argument, as most of the evidence is based on small studies. These studies assume that pharmacist's role is effective; for example, pharmacist can play a key role in improving patient's medicines regime or increasing patient's adherence to medical programs.

However, critiques argue that the majority of these studies are being conducted by pharmacists themselves, generally with little insight into the increasingly sophisticated methodological approaches used in health services research. In this context and also with the increasing cost in health care, having an economic evaluation of a pharmacy service could demonstrate its true value.

This book presents a mix of topics; ranging from synthesis of research, case studies as well as application of economic methodologies on pharmacy services and programs. The book highlights economic evaluation studies in high-income western countries as well in the context of low- and middle-income countries. The book also narrates commonly used economic evaluation methodologies and how an economic evaluation could be undertaken in practice setting.

This book would be useful for pharmacists, academics, researchers, funders, policy makers, and for health services researcher who are working in this area.

I hope that the information provided would be helpful to build cost-effective approaches toward pharmacy and health care.

Zaheer-Ud-Din Babar
August 2016

Chapter 1

An Introduction to Economic Evaluation of Health Care Programs

C. Jommi[1,2]
[1]Università del Piemonte Orientale, Novara, Italy, [2]CERGAS Bocconi, Milano, Italy

Chapter Outline

RATIONALE FOR ECONOMIC EVALUATION

Health market is characterized by an unbalance between supply of health services (resources used to deliver services, including people, time, facilities, equipment, and knowledge) and demand for health services, which is driven by economic growth, increase in life expectancy, technological innovation, and rising health expectations.

This unbalance may be found in other markets as well. In these markets, the excess of demand over the supply is managed by market mechanisms. In a purely competitive environment, suppliers will be forced to reduce prices to absorb the demand excess. In a monopolistic market, consumers who are not willing to pay for services will be excluded from the market. In health care markets, market mechanisms do not work well (information are incomplete and asymmetric, consumers are not rational, demand may be induced by the supply) or their consequences are not acceptable (e.g., access to services would depend on consumer income).

On the one hand, if this unbalance is not managed, there is a risk that health expenditure would increase exponentially. In fact, health care expenditure has been growing faster than the gross domestic product (GDP) in all main OECD countries in the last 25 years (Fig. 1.1). The incidence of health care expenditure over GDP has grown on average from 7.3% in 1990 to 10.8% in 2015.

On the other side, in the last 5 years (2010−15) the increase of ratio of total health expenditure to GDP dropped. It is obvious that cost-containment has dominated the agenda of public health care payers and economic crisis has negatively influenced private expenditure (Table 1.1).

In this context, a systematic and appropriate evaluation of economic consequences is necessary. Otherwise there is a risk that scarce resources are not efficiently allocated, when decisions are taken on long-term programs (e.g., Should we invest in a scoliosis screening program in secondary school? Is it worth investing in a clinical pharmacy service? Should public payers cover vaccines against Human Papillomavirus? Should a new drug at the price required by the pharmaceutical company be listed on the formulary?) or day-by-day action (Is it worth treating a patient with a new drug instead of an older one?). Economic analysis may support this decision-making process.

Economic evaluation, comparing costs and consequences of different courses of action, provides an answer to the following question: Does the new course of action (compared with the existing one) provide value for money (i.e., do added benefits justify added costs)? [1]. Budget impact estimates the impact on payers budget of a new course of action, thus providing evidence on its sustainability [2]. Integrating economic evaluation with budget impact, decision-makers are expected to take more rational decisions that incorporate economic arguments.

ECONOMIC EVALUATION: COSTS, OUTCOMES, TECHNIQUES

A full economic evaluation stands for a comparative analysis of costs and consequences of alternative courses of action (alternative ways of using scarce resources). Courses of action include different products (e.g., two drugs for the same therapeutic indication), different pathways (e.g., two different drug sequences), and different programs (implementing a community pharmacist-led diabetes management education program compared to the standard of care). In brief, two features characterize a full economic evaluation: (1) costs and consequences are simultaneously estimated and (2) to take decisions on alternative ways of using scarce resources.

Costs included into an economic evaluation analysis depend on the perspective used. The perspective may range from one of the health care payers (only health care services are included), other payers (e.g., payers of social care), the patient/family (out-of-pocket expenses, transportation costs, informal care provided by the family to patients are considered), and the society as a whole (this perspective includes also productivity lost due to temporary or permanent absence from work, premature mortality, and presenteeism, i.e., working while sick). The ideal perspective is the societal one.

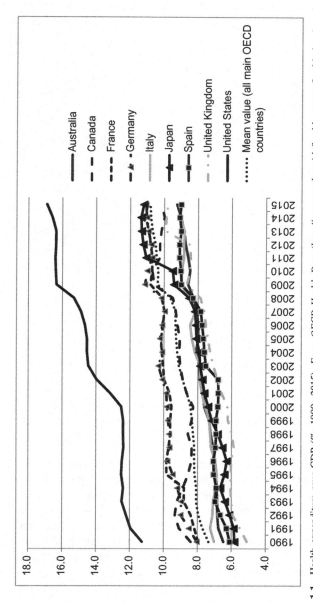

FIGURE 1.1 Health expenditure over GDP (%; 1990–2015). *From OECD Health Data (http://www.oecd.org/els/health-systems/health-data.htm, last access 11/7/2016).*

TABLE 1.1 Health Expenditure Over GDP (%, Absolute Variation—Δ)

Country	Δ 1990–95	Δ 1995–2000	Δ 2000–05	Δ 2005–10	Δ 2010–15
Australia	0.4	0.7	0.4	0.5	0.8
Austria	1.2	0.3	0.4	0.5	0.2
Belgium	0.4	0.5	1.1	0.9	0.4
Canada	0.2	− 0.3	0.8	1.6	− 0.5
Denmark	− 0.3	0.3	1.0	1.4	0.1
Finland	0.1	− 0.5	1.2	0.9	0.8
France	1.9	− 0.3	0.6	0.5	0.3
Germany	1.4	0.3	0.4	0.8	0.1
Greece	1.9	− 0.7	1.8	0.9	− 1.6
Ireland	0.5	− 0.2	1.8	2.9	− 1.3
Italy	− 0.1	0.7	0.8	0.6	0.1
Japan	0.6	1.0	0.7	1.4	1.7
Netherlands	0.3	− 0.3	2.4	1.0	0.3
Norway	0.2	0.4	0.6	0.6	1.0
Spain	0.9	− 0.2	0.9	1.3	− 0.0
Sweden	0.0	0.1	0.9	0.2	2.6
Switzerland	1.5	0.5	0.9	0.2	1.1
United Kingdom	1.0	0.2	1.2	1.0	1.3
Mean value	0.7	0.1	1.0	1.0	0.4
United States	1.2	0.0	2.0	1.8	0.5

Source: OECD Health Data (http://www.oecd.org/els/health-systems/health-data.htm, last access 11/7/2016).

It includes all costs, it drives intersector optimal resource allocation, and it is more consistent with the principles of welfare economics, which places emphasis on the principles that what counts is the value attached by individuals [1]. However, in many studies a narrower perspective is used because health care payers often require this perspective. For example, the National Institute for Health and Care Excellence, which uses economic evaluation to recommend new drugs/health technologies in England, requires that the perspective of health and social care payers is used.

The two main consequences of a health program are its impact on patient's health state (life-years gained; quality of life gained) and the costs saved, i.e., the costs that would have been incurred if the program would have not been implemented. A third consequence is represented by the value

TABLE 1.2 Different Economic Evaluation Techniques

Economic Evaluation Technique	Indicator
Cost-effectiveness	ICER[a] = (Δ Costs[b])/(Δ Effect[c])
Cost–utility	ICER[a] = (Δ Costs[b])/(Δ QALY)
Cost–benefit	Net Monetary Benefit (Monetary Value of Benefit—Costs)

[a]Incremental cost-effectiveness ratio.
[b]Including saved costs.
[c]Effect in physical units (e.g., life years gained, avoided hospitalization).

created by a heath care program, which does not directly affect the patient's health state (e.g., the value of patient's reassurance of a screening program).

Consequences of health care programs drive the economic evaluation technique used in the analysis. A cost-effectiveness analysis is performed if the consequences of alternative courses of actions are measurable in a common physical unit (e.g., life of years saved, avoided hospitalization, number of relapses avoided, number of adherent patients). If the quality of life is an important dimension of patient's health state, a cost–utility analysis is carried out: the increase in life expectancy and the impact on quality of life are integrated into a common outcome indicator, named QALY (Quality Adjusted Life Years saved). Outcomes are monetized through a cost–benefit analysis if the consequences are different and either cannot be represented using a single indicator or they go beyond QALYs (Table 1.2).

Cost-effectiveness analysis supports the allocation of scarce resources within the same health problem. For example a recent study [3] compared tocilizumab with adalimumab in patients with rheumatoid arthritis. The impact of drugs was measured using improvement criteria suggested by the American College of Rheumatology (ACR Score). The ACR Score integrates different criteria used to measure rheumatoid arthritis severity, including tender joints, swollen joints, results of test for inflammation (erythrocyte sedimentation rate or C-reactive protein blood test). The authors estimated a 6-month incremental cost (from the US payer perspective) using tocilizumab instead of adalimumab ranging from $6570 per additional low disease activity score achiever (ACR) with 20% improvement to $14,265 per additional ACR with 70% improvement. This ICER cannot be compared with economic evaluation studies carried out for other diseases.

Cost–utility analysis allows for comparisons across different health problems, because it relies on a parameter (QALY), which is comparable across health areas. The study mentioned before used a patient-level simulation to estimate the lifetime incremental cost per QALY of tocilizumab versus adalimumab. The authors converted ACR responses into Health

Assessment Questionnaire (HAQ) score and mapped the HAQ score to utility to estimate QALYs, finding a lifetime $36,944/QALY ICER. This result can be compared with the ones from drugs with different indications and/or possible thresholds for ICER set by payers.

Cost—benefit analysis allows for intersector (health and others) evaluation, because it converts all possible consequences into monetary values.

ECONOMIC EVALUATION: METHODOLOGICAL ISSUES AND RECENT DEVELOPMENTS

Despite economic evaluation has been applied to health care for a long time, there are many methodological aspects that are still under discussion and are shaping the agenda of the latest developments in this discipline.

The first is represented by the study design. An economic evaluation can be trial-based or rely on models [4]. Trial-based studies have the advantage of minimizing bias in comparison. Furthermore, the possible access to individual patient data offers useful insight regarding the information (e.g., examining heterogeneity in treatment response). However, a trial does not correspond to real practice, alternatives used may be not appropriate, the follow-up is often too short, and the sample size is not necessarily adequate for economic analysis. Models are more flexible and are necessary if trial data are not available. They are also useful to integrate trial data (e.g., to extrapolate long-term impact on health from trial results). However, in many circumstances models rely on assumptions and leave analysts a huge discretion in designing and populating them. For this reason transparency is often required by payers, when the results from models are presented by the industry. This is to sustain the value proposition and to get a required price.

Challenges are also related to health and economic effects measurement. As for health effects, the surrogacy of nonfinal endpoints, the indirect comparison if head-to-head trials are not available, and the long-term extrapolation of future benefits (projections are needed for maintenance of treatment effects, rates of withdrawal from therapy, implications of withdrawal) are the most discussed issues. As for economic benefits, the main challenges include the existence and measurement of benefits other than health (e.g., productivity changes, costs and benefits on other sectors of the economy, consumption benefits from health care) and whether QALY is a complete indicator of value.

In fact, some approaches to health state preference measurement may not adequately capture all the quality of life changes and aspects such as convenience and access may be disregarded by QALYs [1]. Other elements of value for the patient should be estimated. In such situations, the analysis should move from cost—utility to cost—benefit, because different benefits should be taken into account and summarized in a monetary value.

Methods used to evaluate monetary value of benefits moved from the traditional human capital approach (where healthy time is measured by the production in the market place) to others, i.e., contingent valuation (willingness-to-pay (WTP) for a given bundle of attributes) and conjoint analysis (e.g., discrete choice experiments) where respondents are asked to choose between different scenarios where the various attributes are achieved to varying degrees [5]. These approaches may allow to value benefits such as convenience and access. However, despite the growing number of studies that use these methods, there is still a quite limited use of these studies in economic evaluations. Most of the studies indicated that, although these items are valuable to patients, they are usually ranked below the traditional measures of health gain. Furthermore, these benefits beyond health are generally disregarded by payers as they focus more on "hard" benefits. In fact, most of the recent contributions on patients' preferences using contingent evaluation or conjoint analysis have not been incorporated in a broader cost−benefit analysis [6].

Another challenge is thresholds for ICER. Despite some countries use unofficial or transparent thresholds to manage listing policies or recommendation for use [7], there is still a huge debate on whether (1) ICERs should be defined as a punctual value or a range of values (the latter option would permit a higher discretion in decision making, avoiding that some technologies, like orphan drugs, are systematically excluded from reimbursement because on average they are priced far higher than other drugs); (2) it should be set considering the WTP or the WTP under budget constraint; or (3) they should be used as the unique criteria to decide [8].

ECONOMIC EVALUATION AND PHARMACY SERVICES

The number of economic evaluations of hospital and community pharmacy services has increased in the last years. This is evident from the increasing number of systematic and descriptive reviews of the relevant studies ([9−13], and Chapter 2).

However, these studies are still few compared with economic evaluations applied to health products.

First because economic evaluation is playing quite an important role in evaluating health care technologies including medicines. While the origin of economic evaluation can be traced to cost−benefit analysis applied to public programs, in the last years its application has been more frequent for health care products (pharmaceuticals, devices, and other health technologies) rather than on services/programs. The reason is its use to list new products (or new indications) into formularies and to support actions aimed at governing clinical behavior.

The second reason is that whereas economic evaluation of new technologies is quite standardized (despite methodological issues illustrated before) and may rely on the evidence provided by clinical studies, evaluating hospital and community pharmacy services usually requires further efforts in (1) the identification of the intended consequence(s) and (2) the evaluation of impact.

As for the identification of consequences, most recent studies (identified in Chapter 2) rely more on QALYs. However, in many cases multiple consequences (e.g., reduction in medical visits, change in medication errors, reductions in adverse events) are expected from the implementation of these programs and a cost–benefit analysis seems to be more appropriate to incorporate all these outcomes.

The second major issue is the impact evaluation. Economic evaluation applied to health technologies (particularly drugs) may rely on experimental studies (clinical trials). Interventions of pharmacists in real life scenarios and pure experiments (trials) are quite rare.

The main challenge of an impact evaluation in real life is to determine what would have happened to the beneficiaries if the program had not existed (counterfactual issue), i.e., creating a convincing and reasonable control group (not-treated group) for beneficiaries and avoiding selection bias [14].

The easiest way is to consider treated population before treatment as the control group (pre–post or before–after method). The risk of this method is that it might not provide an accurate assessment of the impact, because it does not control for possible confounding factors.

If a prospective study is carried out, a statistical option is to do randomization: individuals are randomly allocated across treatment and control group, thus avoiding selection bias in randomization.

Retrospective methods include (1) propensity score matching, i.e., ex-post comparison of the effects on treatment group with matched control group, with the matching being conducted on a range of observed characteristics (which are expected to be the only or prevalent confounding factors); (2) difference-in-difference analysis, which assumes a time invariant unobserved selection and measures the impact of a program as the difference in consequences (benefits) across treatment and control group before and after the program intervention. Other more complex methods (e.g., instrumental variable applied to panel data) allow for correcting a selection bias on unobserved characteristics varying with time.

In this respect, economic evaluations applied to hospital and community pharmacy services have not been always well designed. A systematic review focused on clinical pharmacy interventions reported that only 35% of the selected studies relied on a randomized trial or a prospective/retrospective cohort study. The others were conducted on the grounds of a before and after method and even on a case-series approach [12]. The review presented in Chapter 2 shows that trials and cohort studies are more frequent in most recent studies: This is a clear signal that methods are improving.

Despite these methodological issues and that many studies are still partial, economic evaluation (either on costs or on consequences [10]), the evidence on the economic impact of clinical and community pharmacies is growing. It is expected that this trend would grow in the future and methodological approach in these studies would be enhanced as well.

REFERENCES

[1] Drummond MF, Sculpher MJ, Claxton K, et al. Methods for the economic evaluation of health care programmes. 4th ed. New York: Oxford University Press; 2015.

[2] Sullivan SD, Mauskopf JA, Augustovski F, et al. Budget impact analysis-principles of good practice: report of the ISPOR 2012 Budget Impact Analysis Good Practice II Task Force. Value Health 2014;17(1):5−14.

[3] Carlson JJ, Ogale S, Dejonckheere F, Sullivan SD. Economic evaluation of tocilizumab monotherapy compared to adalimumab monotherapy in the treatment of severe active rheumatoid arthritis. Value Health 2015;18(2):173−9.

[4] Roberts M, Russell LB, Paltiel AD, et al. Conceptualizing a model: a report of the ISPOR-SMDM Modeling Good Research Practices Task Force-2. Value Health 2012;15(6):804−11.

[5] Hauber AB, González JM, Groothuis-Oudshoorn CG, et al. Statistical methods for the analysis of discrete choice experiments: a report of the ISPOR Conjoint Analysis Good Research Practices Task Force. Value Health 2016;19(4):300−15.

[6] Higgins A, Barnett J, Meads C, et al. Does convenience matter in health care delivery? A systematic review of convenience-based aspects of process utility. Value Health 2014;17(8):877−87.

[7] Cleemput I, Neyt M, Thiri N, et al. Using threshold values for cost per quality-adjusted life-year gained in healthcare decisions. Int J Technol Assess Health Care 2011;27:71−6.

[8] Claxton M, Martin S, Soaves M. Methods for the estimation of the NICE cost effectiveness threshold. CHE Research Paper 81. York: 2013.

[9] Perez A, Doloresco F, Hoffman JM, et al. ACCP (American College of Clinical Pharmacy): economic evaluations of clinical pharmacy services: 2001−2005. Pharmacotherapy. 2009;29(1):128.

[10] Schumock GT, Butler MG, Meek PD, et al. Task Force on Economic Evaluation of Clinical Pharmacy Services of the American College of Clinical Pharmacy. Evidence of the economic benefit of clinical pharmacy services: 1996−2000. Pharmacotherapy. 2003;23(1):113−32.

[11] Touchette DR, Doloresco F, Suda KJ, et al. Economic evaluations of clinical pharmacy services: 2006−2010. Pharmacotherapy 2014;34(8):771−93.

[12] De Rijdt T, Willems L, Simoens S. Economic effects of clinical pharmacy interventions: a literature review. Am J Health Syst Pharm 2008;65(12):1161−72.

[13] Kaboli PJ, Hoth AB, McClimon BJ, Schnipper JL. Clinical pharmacists and inpatient medical care: a systematic review. Arch Intern Med 2006;166(9):955−64.

[14] Khandker SR, Koolwal GB, Samad HA. Handbook of impact evaluation. Quantitative methods and practices. World Bank; 2010.

Chapter 2

Economic Evaluation of Community and Hospital Pharmacy Services: An Introductory Review

T. Gammie[1], S. Vogler[2] and Z.-U.-D. Babar[1,3]

[1]University of Auckland, Auckland, New Zealand, [2]Gesundheit Österreich GmbH (Austrian Public Health Institute), Vienna, Austria, [3]Lahore Pharmacy College, Lahore, Pakistan

Chapter Outline

INTRODUCTION

Research consistently demonstrates the clinical and socioeconomic benefits of pharmacy and pharmacist directed care of patients in hospital and community settings [1]. Considering that both the clinical benefit and cost of medicines continue to show extensive differences, economic evaluation of pharmacy services has become increasingly commonplace to evaluate the value for money that these services provide [1]. These evaluations most often look to evaluate the clinical "cost-effectiveness" of medicines with the aim of distributing limited health resources to those medicines that show sufficient levels of clinical efficacy and value for money [1,2]. Health economics methodologies and economic evaluations are increasingly utilized in choosing between the most clinically cost-effective programs and technologies in health care. Growing pressure to get the best value for money has pressured policy makers and governments to utilize health economic evaluation tools. This has contributed to the increasing number of evaluations regarding the efficacy and effectiveness of pharmacy services [2,3]. Within the passing years, pharmacy services have transformed from a role primarily focused in medicine dispensing and delivery to involving pharmacists in providing individualized expert care as an important part of health care teams [1]. It is of increasing importance to evaluate the efficacy and effectiveness of such services in pharmacy based research and practice.

Economic evaluations of pharmacy services most commonly involve four types of pharmacoeconomic analyses: cost-minimization analysis (CMA), cost-effectiveness analysis (CEA), cost−benefit analysis (CBA), and cost−utility analysis (CUA) [4]. Techniques for the economic evaluation of health care interventions are designed to compare alternate interventions in terms of consequences (benefits) and costs [5,6]. It is noted that while a number of previous studies have included the cost related with community and hospital pharmacy services, the vigorous use of pharmacoeconomic analysis for these services is limited [2]. It has become increasingly important to conduct and evaluate well-designed economic studies of these services to obtain a clear scenario regarding their economic impact. Well-designed pharmacoeconomic studies further enable to rationalize limited health care resources [3]. The primary objective of this chapter is to provide a review synthesizing the updated international body of literature from 2010 to 2015 concerning various methods of health economic evaluations used in hospital and community based studies of pharmacy services, their clinical outcomes, and cost-effectiveness.

METHODS

Search Strategy

The PRISMA guidelines for conducting systematic reviews were employed [7]. The literature search was undertaken between May 2, 2015 and September 4, 2015 to identify published peer-reviewed articles in English. A search strategy was developed and implemented under the leadership of ZB and SV. Keywords included the following: "Health economics" and "Evaluation," "Assessment" or "Appraisal," "Methods," "Hospital" or "Community" or "residential care," "Pharmacy" or "Pharmacy Services" and "Cost minimization analysis" or "Cost utility analysis" or "Cost effectiveness analysis" or "Cost benefit analysis." The keywords were combined and incorporated in database and journal searches.

The databases searched (by TG) included: Medline (2010−15), PubMed (2010−15), Google Scholar (2010−15), Science Direct (2010−15), Springer Links (2010−15), and Scopus (2010−15). We also searched the following journals: *PLoS One* (2010−15), *PLoS Medicine* (2010−15), *Nature* (2010−15), *Health Policy* (2010−15), *Pharmacoeconomics* (2010−15), *The European Journal of Health Economics* (2010−15), *Expert Review of Pharmacoeconomics and Outcomes Research* (2010−15), and *Journal of Health Economics* (2010−15). Search results are detailed in Table 2.1 by database and journal. References of retrieved articles were considered for relevant articles that may have been missed.

In the search process, "Boolean Operator" rules were employed. The terms used were searched utilizing "AND" to combine the keywords listed and using "OR" to remove search duplication where possible.

Article Selection and Data Collection

The title and abstract of all retrieved articles were reviewed by lead author (TG) for relevance. If there was any uncertainty about the paper, the full-text article was retrieved and read for relevance. Articles were included if they detailed and/or utilized health economic evaluation methods in either a hospital or community based pharmacy setting. We only included articles published in peer-reviewed journals in English. Studies were also limited to countries with a publically funded health care system; this was to ensure applicability of results to this type of health system and funding.

From the database/journal searches, 34,865 titles/abstracts were retrieved (Table 2.1). After removing 34,804 duplicates and titles/abstracts unrelated to health economic evaluations of hospital and pharmacy services (and methodologies utilized), we identified 55 peer-reviewed articles in English. Six more articles were identified from references of the retrieved articles, therefore 61 articles were considered against our study inclusion/exclusion criteria provided in Table 2.2. Thus TG and ZB have read these articles in full, with contribution from SV. We aimed to include only studies that were published in the last 5 years (2010−15), for this reason, two studies were excluded based upon year of publication and eight studies were excluded based upon article type, that is, these studies were not original (primary) research. Of these, only 14 articles were relevant to health economic evaluations and hospital and/or community based pharmacy services therefore based on these criteria, 14 articles were included for analysis (Fig. 2.1).

Data collected on individual articles included: author, objective or aim if any, setting (hospital, community or residential care based), dates of data collection or article publication, health economic evaluation methodology

TABLE 2.1 Number of Search Results ("Hits") by Database or Journal

Databases	("Economic Evaluation") AND ("Pharmacy" or "Pharmacy Services")	("Health economic") AND ("Evaluation" or "Assessment" or "Appraisal") AND ("Hospital" or "Community" or "residential care") AND ("Pharmacy" or "Pharmacy Services")	("Health economic") AND ("Evaluation") AND ("Methods") AND ("Hospital," "residential care" or "Community") AND ("Pharmacy" or "Pharmacy Services")	("Health" or "Health-care") AND ("Economic") AND ("Evaluation" or "Assessment" or "Appraisal") AND ("Hospital," "residential care" or "Community") AND ("Pharmacy" or "Pharmacy Services")	("Economic Evaluation") AND ("Health" or "Health-care") AND ("Pharmacy" or "Pharmacy Services") AND ("Cost minimization analysis" or "Cost utility analysis" or "Cost effectiveness analysis" or "Cost benefit analysis")
Google Scholar	149,000	5920	16,700	3130	16,700
Medline	480	–	–	–	–
PubMed	1098	–	299	–	3
Science Direct	5889	1681	1817	–	–
Springer Links	5807	431	391	320	262
Scopus	258	156	89	157	131
Journals					
PLoS One	533	32	–	31	508
PLoS Medicine	62	9	–	9	69
Nature	146	–	–	–	–

Health Policy	133	–	3	–	–
Pharmacoeconomics	223	132	–	3	37
The European Journal of Health Economics	92	39	32	–	–
Expert Review of Pharmacoeconomics and Outcomes Research	3406	–	–	–	–
Journal of Health Economics	38	–	–	–	–

TABLE 2.2 Study Inclusion and Exclusion Criteria

No.	Category	Inclusion Criteria
1	Year of release	2010–15
2	Publication type	Full text original research articles in peer-reviewed scientific journals and in English
3	Countries covered	Countries with a publicly funded health system and those that undertake (various) heath economic methodologies and evaluations of hospital and/or community-based pharmacy services
4	Health care setting	Hospital, community, residential, and aged care–based pharmacy service
5	Methodologies of economic evaluation	Any utilized in the evaluation of hospital and/or community-based pharmacy services. Including, but not limited to: CMA, CEA, CBA, and CUA
6	Definitions and issues to include	Health economics, pharmacoeconomics, pharmacy practice, economic evaluation, hospital pharmacy services, community pharmacy services. Definition of pharmacoeconomics, economic evaluation, costs, benefits, outcome measures discounting, sensitivity analysis, CMA, CEA, CBA, CUA
7	Methodology and topic of research	Systematic review of peer-reviewed journal articles investigating and/or utilizing methods of economic evaluations used for hospital and/or community-based studies
Exclusion Criteria		
1		Articles that are not published in the English language
2		News Reports, Editorials, Commentaries, Opinions

utilized/discussed, research methodology if any, collected data if any, and outcome measures if any. Studies were analyzed for bias, including internal and external validity measures, bias due to confounding, bias in selection of participants into the study, bias in measurements of interventions, bias due to departures of intended interventions, bias due to missing data, bias in measurement of outcomes, and bias in the selection of the reported result. No significant bias that would affect the cumulative results reported was found.

After the extraction of relevant information, a narrative synthesis was undertaken.

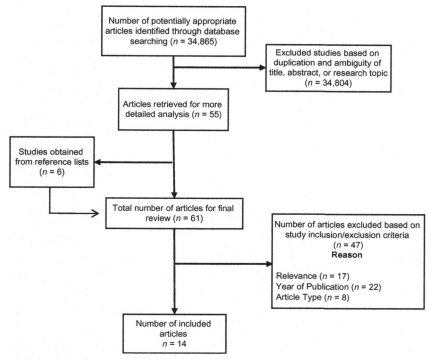

FIGURE 2.1   Study selection flow diagram (based on PRISMA guidelines).

Analysis

A systematic literature review was undertaken to ensure that the narrative synthesis developed within based upon the most complete base of literature regarding health economic evaluation of hospital and community pharmacy based services. Furthermore, a systematic review enabled the literature gathered to be sourced in the most vigorous and complete manner possible. Narrative synthesis of the articles was conducted, with the addition of new categories as needed, and relevant subcategories created for examination until no more themes were identified and saturation was deemed to be reached. Through consideration of methodologies of evaluation utilized, we were able to identify the primary methods of health economic evaluations used in hospital and community based studies of pharmacy services as well as the clinical outcomes and cost-effectiveness of these services through descriptive analysis. Table 2.3 provides a general overview of the characteristics of the included studies.

TABLE 2.3 General Characteristics of Studies

Study (First Author's Name)	Method of Economic Evaluation	Setting	Clinical Outcomes	Economic Outcome	Overall Outcome
Wright [10]	CUA	Community	Improvements in patient reported adherence, utilization of rescue packs, quality of life, and a reduction in routine GP visits were identified	As the intervention was estimated to be associated with a cost saving (from both an NHS and a societal perspective) and a QALY gain, the intervention was estimated to dominate no intervention. According to the CEAC, the estimated probability of the intervention being cost-effective at the λ of £20,000 per QALY was 96.7% and 97.2%, respectively	Results suggest that the service improved patient's medicine-taking behaviors and that it was cost-effective
Carnevale [3]	CBA	Hospital	At 6 months, the intervention group contained higher percentages of patients without coinfections and of patients with CD4+ >500 cells/mm^3. None of the differences between intervention group and control group considering clinical outcomes and costs were statistically significant. However, at 1 year, the intervention group showed higher percentage of better clinical outcomes	The care program generated lower spending (not to procedures). An additional health care system daily investment of US$1.45, 1.09, 2.13, 4.35, 1.09, and 0.87 would be required for each additional outcome of viral load <50 copies/mL, absence of coinfection, CD4+ >200, 350, and 500 cells/mm^3, and optimal immune response, respectively	The clinical outcomes and the costs did not have statistical difference but showed higher percentage of better clinical outcomes and lower costs for some items

Elliott [11]	CUA	Community	The pharmacist-led information technology based intervention (PINCER) was significantly more effective in reducing medication errors in general practices than providing simple feedback on errors	The PINCER intervention generated £2679 less cost and 0.81 more QALYs per practice (ICER: −£3037 per QALY) in the deterministic analysis. At a ceiling "willingness-to-pay" of £20,000 per QALY (NICE), PINCER reaches 59% probability of being cost-effective	PINCER produced marginal health gain at slightly reduced overall cost. Results are uncertain due to the poor quality of data to inform the effect of avoiding errors
Hendrie [5]	CEA	Community	Significantly greater reductions in number of hyperglycemic and hypoglycemic episodes occurred in the intervention relative to the control group respectively, with a net reduction of 1.86 days with glycemic episodes per patient per month	The cost-effectiveness of DMEP relative to standard pharmacy care was AU$43 (US$39) per day of glycemic symptoms avoided. Patients with type 2 diabetes in three surveys were willing to pay an average of 1.9 times that amount to avoid a hypoglycemic day	DMEP decreased days with glycemic symptoms at a reasonable cost
Bojke [12]	CUA	Community	The intervention led to an average improvement of 0.019 QALYs	The incremental cost per additional QALY was estimated at £10,000. In making decisions about value for money of treatments, NICE generally uses a threshold of between £20,000 and £30,000 per QALY. This suggests that, on average, pharmaceutical care is cost-effective. However, the uncertainty in differential costs and QALYs means that the	Although pharmaceutical care is estimated to be cost-effective in the United Kingdom, the results are uncertain and further research into its long-term benefits may be worthwhile

(Continued)

TABLE 2.3 (Continued)

Study (First Author's Name)	Method of Economic Evaluation	Setting	Clinical Outcomes	Economic Outcome	Overall Outcome
				probability of the intervention being cost-effective is between 78% and 81% for this threshold range	
Khdour [8]	CUA	Hospital	Statistically significantly lower unscheduled GP visits, ED visits, hospital bed days (60% less in intervention group), and oral steroid and antibiotic courses were observed in the intervention group compared to usual care over the 12-month study period	The mean differences in costs and effects between the self-management and education program and usual care were −£671.59 and 0.065. Thus, the intervention was the dominant strategy as it was both less costly and more effective than usual care. The probability of the intervention being cost-effective was 95% at a threshold of £20,000 per QALY gained	The self-management and education program was found to be highly cost-effective compared to usual care
Rubio-Valera [13]	CUA	Community	No statistically significant differences were observed between groups in clinical outcomes	From a societal perspective, the ICER for the community pharmacist intervention compared with usual care was €1866 for extra adherent patient and €9872 per extra QALY. In terms of remission of depressive symptoms, the usual care dominated the community	A brief community pharmacist intervention addressed to depressed patients initiating antidepressant treatment showed a probability of being cost-effective of 0.71 and 0.75 in terms of improvement of adherence and QALYs, respectively, when compared to

			pharmacist intervention. If willingness to pay is £30,000 per extra adherent patient, remission of symptoms or QALYs, the probability of the community pharmacist intervention being cost-effective was 0.71, 0.46, and 0.75, respectively (societal perspective)	usual care. Regular implementation of the community pharmacist intervention is not recommended
Perraudin [14]	CUA	Community	Patients with untreated and treated obstructive sleep apnea (OSAS) had utility values of 0.32 and 0.55, respectively. Continuous positive airway pressure (CPAP) treatment was associated with an improvement in utility of 0.23	The probabilistic sensitivity analysis showed that the "screening strategy with CP" was dominant in 80% of cases. It was more effective and less costly in 47% of cases, and within the cost-effective range (maximum ICER at £6186.67/QALY) in 33% of cases	CP involvement in OSAS screening is a cost-effective strategy. This proposal is consistent with the trend in Europe and the United States to extend the practices and responsibilities of the pharmacist in primary care
Jodar-Sanchez [15]	CUA	Community	By the end of the follow-up, both groups had reduced the mean number of prescribed medications they took, although this reduction was greater in the intervention group (0.28 ± 1.25 drugs; $p < 0.001$) than in the control group (0.07 ± 0.95 drugs; $p = 0.063$). Older adults in the intervention group saw their quality of life improved by 0.0528 ± 0.20 ($p < 0.001$). In	The mean total cost was €977.57 $\pm$ 1455.88 for the intervention group and €1173.44 $\pm$ 3671.65 for the control group. In order to estimate the ICER, we used the costs adjusted for baseline medications and QALYs adjusted for baseline utility score, resulting in a mean incremental total cost of -€250.51 $\pm$ 148.61 (95% CI	The MRF service is an effective intervention for optimizing prescribed medication and improving quality of life in older adults with polypharmacy in community pharmacies. The results from the CUA suggest that the MRF service is cost-effective

(Continued)

TABLE 2.3 (Continued)

Study (First Author's Name)	Method of Economic Evaluation	Setting	Clinical Outcomes	Economic Outcome	Overall Outcome
			contrast, the control group experienced a slight reduction in their quality of life: 0.0022 ± 0.24 ($p = 0.815$)	−541.79 to 40.76) and a mean incremental QALY of 0.0156 ± 0.004 (95% CI 0.008–0.023)	
Adibe [6]	CUA	Hospital	The medical and educational content of the training course was rated positively by the 17 physicians and 29 nurses; the majority 38 (82.6%) rated the content as "excellent" and the remaining 8 rated the content as "very good" or "good"; only 3 (6.5%) of them suggested little modification or changes	The PC intervention led to incremental cost and effect of NGN 10,623 ($69) and 0.12 QALY gained, respectively, with an associated incremental cost–utility ratio of NGN 88,525 ($571) per QALY gained	The PC intervention was very cost-effective among patients with type 2 diabetes at the NGN 88,525 ($571.13) per QALY gained threshold, although considerable uncertainty surrounds these estimates
Obreli-Neto [16]	CUA	Community	Every clinical parameter evaluated improved for the pharmaceutical care group, whereas these clinical parameters remained unchanged in the usual care group	No statistically significant difference was found between the intervention and control groups in total direct health care costs ($281.97 ± $49.73 per patient vs $212.28 ± $43.49 per patient, respectively; $p = 0.089$); pharmaceutical care added incremental costs of $69.60 (± $7.90) per patient. The ICER per QALY was $53.50 (95% CI = $51.60–$54.00); monetary amounts are given in US dollars	While pharmaceutical care did not significantly increase total direct health care costs, significantly improved health outcomes were seen. The mean ICER per QALY gained suggests a favorable cost-effectiveness

Borges [17]	CEA	Community	A statistically significant reduction in glycosylated hemoglobin (HbA1C) levels of patients in the PC group was observed; even these patients showed a statistically significant reduction in the prescribed dose of metformin On the other hand, the only significant result in the control group concerning the parameters presented in Table 2.2 was the increase in drug prescription	The pharmaceutical care group had a statistically significant reduction in costs of metformin and ED visits, and increased costs with their family physicians. On the other hand, the control group had a statistically significant increase of 21.3% in the general costs of treatment and visits. For the control group, there was a statistically significant increase in the total cost of treatment, including drugs and visits. Besides, this group had an increase of 0.7% in HbA1c levels, and there is an increase in the general cost of drug treatment and visits of $ 22.8	The pharmaceutical care group maintained the same costs related to drugs and visits, while the control group showed a significant increase in general costs
Claus [9]	CBA	Hospital	In half of cases, therapy was reinitiated without any further adverse drug event	Cost difference (cost value) between that of the avoided toxicity and that of the intervention where a positive cost value is cost saving. Per annum, pharmacists performed interventions for valproic acid ($n = 18$) and digoxin ($n = 21$); the annual cost value of interventions for valproic acid was €18,853.7 with a standard deviation of €15,020.6; for digoxin it was €41,832.0 ± €15,348.5	Interventions that prevent digoxin and valproic acid toxicity were cost-effective in this setting. The routine advice to switch the antibiotic class for every reported penicillin allergy is unlikely to avoid adverse drug events and challenges the cost value of this intervention

(Continued)

TABLE 2.3 (Continued)

Study (First Author's Name)	Method of Economic Evaluation	Setting	Clinical Outcomes	Economic Outcome	Overall Outcome
Bauld [18]	CUA	Community	The proportion of carbon monoxide–validated quitters from both services combined fell from 22.5% at 4-week follow-up to 3.6% at 52 weeks. The group service achieved a higher quit rate (6.3%) than the pharmacy service (2.8%)	The lifetime analysis resulted in an incremental cost per QALY of £4800 for the group support and £2600 for pharmacy one-to-one counseling. The group service was more intensive and required greater overhead costs	Despite disappointing 1-year quit rates, both services were considered to be highly cost-effective

RESULTS

Setting and Methods of Economic Evaluations of Hospital and Community Pharmacy Services

Fourteen articles utilized various methods of health economic evaluations in hospital- and/or community-based studies of pharmacy services (Table 2.4). Studies were organized by setting of intervention; hospital ($n = 4$) [3,6,8,9] and

TABLE 2.4 Common Methods of Pharmacoeconomic Analysis and Economic Evaluation [2,4]

Method	Description	Example of Practical Applications
CMA	Analysis deals only with costs. In particular, this analysis is utilized to recognize the most inexpensive option when effectiveness of appraisals is identical	May be applied when comparing generics of the same medicine or selecting medicines from the same class
CEA	Method of analysis is utilized to compare options when effectiveness is not identical. CEA considers a single measure of output with results often expressed in a cost-effectiveness ratio, i.e., $1000 per life-year gained or as natural units such as years of life gained. CEA also requires utilization of the same unit for comparison of the health interventions or programs	Identification of most economical option in comparing a pharmacist-led diabetes management education program (DMEP) compared to standard care [5]
CBA	Method of analysis is utilized to compare options when effectiveness is not identical. Values consequences (benefits) of programs in monetary terms in order to allow comparison with costs. Outcomes are measured as net or total dollar benefit	Identification of most economical option in evaluating the clinical and economic impact of pharmaceutical care (pharmacist presence at each physician appointment) of HIV-infected patients compared to standard care [6]
CUA	Analysis to identify the most cost-effective option or course of action. CUA measures the benefits or consequences of interventions by utility weights or measures such as the Quality Adjusted Life Year (QALY) for every dollar invested	CUA of a pharmaceutical care intervention versus usual care in management of patients with diabetes [8]

community ($n = 10$) [5,10−18], as well as method of economic evaluation; CMA ($n = 0$), CEA ($n = 2$) [5,17], CBA ($n = 2$) [3,9], and CUA ($n = 10$) [6,8,10−16,18]. There were a number of studies which focused on economic evaluations of hospital pharmacy services. This included utilization of a clinical pharmacist as part of a health care team (i.e., supplementing physicians to reduce risk of adverse events) or pharmacists providing education regarding medications and self-care [3,6,8,9]. Community based studies focused upon medication or disease specific education (often for chronic disease such as type 2 diabetes), medication management programs, medication review or follow-up support [5,10−18].

Methods of economic evaluation such as CMA, CEA, CBA, and CUA were developed to assist decision makers in comparing the value of alternative interventions in health care. CUA was the most widely utilized methodology. All other methods were also utilized in included studies [6,8,9], except CMA.

CUA facilitates the comparison of health care interventions without placing monetary values on health states. As such, CUA addresses problems with conventional CEAs, which do not allow comparisons across different health problems [6]. Considering the increasing number of multiattribute utility instruments, which can generate health utilities for CUA, CUA is increasingly emerging as the preferred method of economic evaluation of health care interventions and was noted as the most common methodology of pharmacoeconomic analysis in the 14 studies included in this review. A brief summary of common methods of economic evaluation and pharmacoeconomic analyses are provided in Table 2.4.

Clinical Outcomes and Cost-Effectiveness of Community and Hospital Pharmacy Services

Clinical outcomes and cost-effectiveness of pharmacy services were assessed by including the following inclusion/exclusion criteria.

Clinical benefits of community and hospital pharmacy services included but were not limited to: improvements in patient health outcomes (e.g., reductions in the number of hyperglycemic and hypoglycemic episodes in type 2 diabetes patients), lower unscheduled general practitioner (GP) visits, emergency department (ED) visits, hospital bed days, medication errors, reductions in adverse events, and increases in health-related quality of life for patients [3,5,6,8−18]. Many studies suggested that hospital and community pharmacy services were cost-effective and that pharmacy service programs were likely to be considered cost-effective when considered against the usual method of care [3,5,6,8,10,12,14−18].

Hospital Pharmacy Services

Four studies provided an economic evaluation of hospital pharmacy services. These studies focused on the utilization of a clinical pharmacist on broad health care teams or pharmacists providing education regarding medications and self-care [3,6,8,9]. Carnevale et al. [3] conducted a CBA investigating the clinical and economic impact of pharmaceutical care of HIV-infected patients in a Sao Paulo Hospital. They found that, at a 6-month period, the intervention group contained higher percentages of patients without coin-fections and patients with CD4 cell counts of greater than 500 cells/mm^3. The care program generated a benefit of $2.51 per day for every $1.00 spent [3]. Another study by Khdour et al. [8] undertook a CUA of a pharmacy-led self-management program for patients with chronic obstructive pulmonary disorder (COPD). Statistically significantly lower ED visits, hospital bed days (60% less in the intervention group), oral steroid and antibiotic courses were observed within the intervention group as compared to the control group receiving usual care. An ICER of £3278 per QALY was generated with a 95% probability of being cost-effective at a threshold of £20,000 per QALY gained.

Adibe et al. [6] conducted a CUA of pharmaceutical care intervention versus usual care in the management of patients with type 2 diabetes. It was discovered that the medical and educational content of the training course was rated positively by the 17 physicians and 29 nurses. Moreover, the phar-maceutical care intervention led to incremental cost and effect of Nigerian naira (NGN) 10,623 ($69) and 0.12 QALY gained, respectively, with an associated incremental cost−utility ratio of NGN 88,525 ($571) per QALY gained. At the NGN per QALY gain threshold of NGN 88,525 or ($571.13) per QALY, the hospital pharmacy service intervention was considered cost-effective [6]. Finally, Claus et al. [9] piloted a CBA of pharmacist-led inter-ventions at a University hospital where pharmacists provided bedside therapy recommendations. Cost difference between avoided toxicity and that of the intervention was the main outcome measure where a positive cost value (in terms of costs saving) was observed. The pharmacist interventions remained cost-effective after correcting for toxicity [9]. We recognized that hospital pharmacy services and interventions provided several clinical benefits including improvements in patient health outcomes and a reduction in adverse medication use and that all studies were considered cost-effective due to meeting a cost−utility (per QALY) threshold or were acknowledged as cost-saving. Pharmacy services in hospital settings constitute educating prescribers around medication use and pharmacotherapy as well as providing education regarding medicines use in patients [3,6,8,9].

Community Pharmacy Services

The 10 remaining studies in this review undertook economic evaluations of community pharmacy services. These studies most often involved pharmacists providing medication or disease specific education, medication management programs, medication review or follow-up support [5,10−18]. Moreover, these studies tended to be multicentered and included larger number of patients. Eight out of ten studies utilized CUAs while the other two studies utilized CEA in their evaluations of these pharmacy services. A shift in economic evaluation methods from CEA to CUA in economic evaluations of health care was noted in this review. Many studies indicated the relative cost-effectiveness of community pharmacy services. Wright et al. [10] evaluated the effect of a community pharmacy based COPD service on patient outcomes. The study involved a pharmacist-led intervention where a pharmacist discussed an initial COPD assessment with patients who smoked and provided medication counseling, lifestyle advice, information regarding a stop smoking service, and a referral letter to the patients GP to obtain a COPD rescue pack [10]. Patients reported improvements in adherence, utilization of rescue packs, quality of life, and reductions in GP visits. The intervention was estimated to be cost saving and to include a QALY gain, to dominate no pharmacist intervention, and to be 96.7% cost-effective at the threshold of £20,000 per QALY [10].

Another study by Bojke et al. [12] evaluated the cost-effectiveness of community pharmacy services and pharmaceutical care for older people as compared to usual care in the United Kingdom. Bojke et al. revealed that these services and care led to an average improvement of 0.019 QALYs and an incremental cost per QALY was calculated at £10,000 per QALY. At a cost-effectiveness threshold of £20,000−£30,000, community pharmacy services and pharmaceutical care was estimated to be cost-effective in the United Kingdom, however further research was suggested [12]. Jodar Sanchez et al. [15] estimated the incremental cost-effectiveness ratio (ICER) of a pharmacist-led medication review with follow-up (MRF) service for older adults with polypharmacy against the standard of usual care. At the end of follow-up, both groups had reduced the number of mean prescribed medications they received; however, this number was higher in the intervention group. Moreover, quality of life improvements were seen in the intervention group of 0.0528 ± 20, whereas the control group experienced a slight quality of life reduction 0.0022 ± 0.24. The mean incremental, total cost of the service was €250.51 ± 148.61 and a mean incremental QALY of 0.0156 ± 0.004 suggesting the service was cost-effective [15].

Obreli-Neto et al. [16] evaluated the economic cost and ICER per QALY while evaluating pharmaceutical care in the management of diabetes and hypertension in elderly patients. The service involved pharmaceutical care in addition to usual care where by individual pharmacotherapy follow-ups and educational group activities were provided by pharmacists to patients. The researchers reported that clinical parameters improved in the group receiving pharmaceutical care while these parameters remained unchanged in the control group. Moreover, the ICER per QALY of the service was $53.50 (USD) with this mean ICER suggesting a favorable cost-effectiveness [16]. Bauld et al. [18] conducted a CUA for smokers accessing group based and pharmacist-led smoking cessation services. The group service involved

7 weeks of group based support while the pharmacist-led service involved one-to-one counseling with pharmacists. The proportion of carbon monoxide−validated quitters from both services fell from 22.5% to 3.6% at 4- and 52-week follow-up, respectively. The group services achieved a higher quit rate than the pharmacy service. However, the ICER per QALY for the group service was £4800 and £2600 for the pharmacy service due to higher overhead costs for the group service. Both services were considered highly cost-effective [18].

Additional studies reported similar findings of community pharmacy service cost-effectiveness and improvements in clinical outcomes [5,11,14,15,17]. Two examples were Elliott et al. [11] and Perraudin et al. [14]. Elliott et al. conducted a CUA of a pharmacist-led information technology based intervention (PINCER) to reduce rates of clinically important errors in medicines management. The analysis discovered that PINCER was considerably more effective in reducing errors in medications management than providing simple feedback on errors in general practices. The intervention also generated £2679 less cost and 0.81 more QALYs per practice with an ICER per QALY of £3037. Elliot et al. [11] noted that at a willingness to pay of £20,000, the intervention reaches 59% probability of being cost-effective. Perraudin et al. [14] undertook a CUA of a community pharmacist-led sleep apnea screening service. A screening strategy with a community pharmacist was evaluated for cost-effectiveness. The screening strategy with community pharmacists were dominant in 80% of cases, were more effective, and less costly in 47% of cares. An ICER of £6186.67 per QALY was reported in 33% of cases and the intervention was considered cost-effective [14].

Some studies of community pharmacy services included in this review did however report minimal cost-effectiveness. Rubio-Valera et al. [13] explored the cost-effectiveness of a community pharmacist intervention service in patients with depression. The community pharmacist intervention was compared with usual care and involved an educational program provided by pharmacists to improve patient knowledge regarding antidepressant medicines as well as compliance and side-effect advice. The study noted that no statistically significant differences were seen between groups in clinical outcomes, and the probability of the service being cost-effective was 0.71 and 0.75 in terms of improvements of adherence and QALYs (at a willingness to pay of £30,000) and that regular implementation of the service was not recommended [13].

We recognized that community pharmacy services were considered relatively cost-effective in 8 out of 10 studies. These services illustrated several and significant benefits in clinical outcomes and patient quality of life, as well as improvements in patient's medicine-taking practices and adherence as well as increased clinical education provided to patients regarding medicine use [5,10−18]. Economic evaluations of community pharmacy services, much like hospital services, were most often conducted through

CUAs and were most often reported cost-effectiveness relative to a threshold value between £20,000 and £30,000. This is as per the recommendations of the UK National Institute of Clinical Excellence (NICE). Nine of ten evaluations of community pharmacy services reported cost-effectiveness, most often utilizing ICERs (cost per QALY) in this analysis. We thus noted that community pharmacy services appear to illustrate minor to significant clinical benefits and cost-effectiveness in this review.

DISCUSSION

This chapter reports a systematic literature review of the current literature from 2010 to 2015 on the international body of literature concerning various methods of health economic evaluations used in hospital and community based studies of pharmacy service as well as their clinical outcomes and cost-effectiveness. Studies included in this review utilized three main methodologies of economic evaluation: CBA, CEA, and CUA while no study based on CMA was found in this review. CMA as a method of economic evaluation is becoming less common, as the method assumes identical benefits for both interventions or services (i.e., usual care versus pharmacy services/care) and is most likely to be utilized in in-house projects within hospitals or community pharmacy organizations [2,4]. The limited use of CBAs when compared with cost-effectiveness and more explicitly, CUA is likely due to the technical challenges in quantifying the cost of clinical benefits, risks, and outcomes [2] However, it should be noted that with the rise of the "willingness to pay" method, this analysis is being increasingly used.

We noted that the use of CUA was most common [6,8,10−16,18] when compared with CBA [3,9] and CEA [5,17]. CUA is commonly considered to be a variant of general CEA which utilizes assessment of the quality of life years gained as a measure of benefit, not merely the number of life years or a single disease outcome, as well as allowing comparisons with multiple, as well as differing, health problems within the study [2,4,6]. In addition, CUAs allow comparisons across studies. It also allows evaluation between services on their relative cost-effectiveness when compared to one another [2,4,6]. In the literature, CUAs commonly reported ICERs where the cost per QALY was reported and compared to a threshold to determine the cost-effectiveness of the service. The most commonly reported threshold was a threshold value between £20,000 and £30,000 as per the recommendations of the UK NICE but it can vary by the country. There are concerns in the literature that the use of an ICER may limit the availability of treatments or interventions to patients that do not meet this ratio. This is experienced in cases such as orphan medicines for rare diseases, which often do not provide a high ICER due to the small patient market.

Hospital and community pharmacy services were considered by the majority of studies to indicate minor to significant clinical benefits and to be cost-effective. Hospital pharmacy services most often included the pharmacist acting as part of a general health team and providing education to physicians and nurses regarding medicine usage, education around medicines to patients, avoidance of adverse events and outcomes through the checking of pharmaceutical care plans. Pharmacists also provided therapy recommendations in some cases.

Economic evaluations of hospital pharmacy services were generally conducted to assess and to justify the inclusion of a clinical pharmacist as part of these teams or in providing independent education and advice [3,6,8,9]. All hospital studies indicated that hospital pharmacy services were generally cost-effective and provided several clinical benefits including reductions in adverse events and improvements in patient (health-related) quality of life [3,6,8,9]. Community pharmacy services and pharmaceutical care most often included pharmacist-led services where pharmacists provided medication or disease specific education to patients and GPs, medication management programs, review of physician implemented medicine plans, or follow-up support for patients with regard to medicine use [5,10−18]. Studies assessing the cost-effectiveness of these services utilizing economic evaluation analyses were most often implemented to assess the clinical benefit and cost-effectiveness of pharmacist-led services and programs in the community when compared with the usual standard of care. Nearly all studies indicated clinical benefit including: medication adherence, reductions in the number of unnecessary medication prescriptions and use, improvements in smoking cessation rates, reducing errors in medication management, improvements in multiple disease specific clinical parameters, and improvement in general patient (health related) quality of life [5,10−18].

We saw a wide range of countries conducting economic evaluations of community and pharmacy services. These countries included the United Kingdom [8,10−12,18], Australia [5], Brazil [3,16,17], Spain [13,15], France [14], Nigeria [6], and Belgium [9]. Interestingly, methods of economic evaluation worldwide were similar, with most studies, regardless of countries utilizing CUA and evaluating cost-effectiveness based upon NICE directed or general cost-effectiveness ICER per QALY thresholds. We consider that this may reflect an increasing consensus in the literature on applicable methodologies for conducting economic evaluations of pharmacy services and health care more broadly. We also consider the introduction of the Consolidated Health Economic Evaluation Reporting Standards (CHEERS), a 24-item checklist to improve reporting of economic evaluations by the international society for Pharmacoeconomics and Outcomes Research (ISPOR) may have also played a role in this similarity in the methods of economic evaluation worldwide. CHEERS was published in 2013 and is endorsed by a variety of health and health economics journals including *BMJ, Pharmacoeconomics, Value in Health* and *The European Journal of Health Economics*, among others. The impact of economic evaluation in global health care practice has enabled the development and use of the scientific discipline of health economics to value hospital and pharmacy services and base funding decisions upon objective data [2]. Promising results regarding the cost-effectiveness of hospital and pharmacy services in this review may reflect the need for consensus regarding methodologies of economic evaluations of these services as well as an increasing need for economic evaluation of these services to indicate their cost-effectiveness to policy makers.

Existing reviews in this field predominately summarized studies undertaking economic evaluation of clinical pharmacy services and interventions and not those of community studies or only provided a discussion of the economic methods utilized. Our review provides important insights regarding the clinical benefit of hospital and community based pharmacy services as well as their value for money with particular consideration of studies published in the last five years while many other reviews have considered the literature up to the year 2010. Our study has several limitations. First, outcome reporting bias and/or publication bias may have led to publication or nonpublication of studies depending on their reported findings [1]. Second, researchers only included studies in the English language and we only included peer-reviewed articles; gray literature was excluded. This step was undertaken to ensure academic accuracy however, we may have missed several important reports or economic evaluations conducted by organizations such as Ministries of Health or NICE that have reported on the cost-effectiveness of hospital or community pharmacy services. Future research on economic evaluations of hospital and community pharmacy services is needed to increase the relatively limited available literature on the topic. This will enable an understanding of which health care services provide value for money and to inform policy makers as to which services will be cost-effective in light of limited health care resources.

CONCLUSIONS

Economic evaluations of hospital and community pharmacy services are becoming increasingly commonplace to enable an understanding of which health care services provide value for money and to inform policy makers as to which services will be cost-effective in light of limited health care resources. CUA provides a critical advantage over other measures in allowing comparisons across different health care problems and does not encounter technical challenges seen in CBA in quantifying the cost of clinical benefits, risks, and outcomes. Hospital and community pharmacy services provided several important clinical benefits including increased medication adherence, reductions in adverse events, and improvements in patient quality of life.

REFERENCES

[1]   Touchette DR, Doloresco F, Suda KJ, Perez A, Turner S, Jalundhwala Y, et al. Economic evaluations of clinical pharmacy services: 2006−2010. Pharmacotherapy 2014;34 (8):771−93.

[2]   Zaidi ST. Applying pharmacoeconomics in community and hospital pharmacy research. In: Pharmacy Practice Research Methods. Springer International Publishing; 2015. p. 157−73.

[3] Carnevale RC, Molino CD, Visacri MB, Mazzola PG, Moriel P. Cost analysis of pharmaceutical care provided to HIV-infected patients: an ambispective controlled study. Daru 2015;23(1):13.

[4] Drummond MF. Methods for the economic evaluation of health care programmes. Oxford University Press; 2005.

[5] Hendrie D, Miller TR, Woodman RJ, Hoti K, Hughes J. Cost-effectiveness of reducing glycaemic episodes through community pharmacy management of patients with type 2 diabetes mellitus. J Prim Prev 2014;35(6):439—49.

[6] Adibe MO, Aguwa CN, Ukwe CV. Cost-utility analysis of pharmaceutical care intervention versus usual care in management of Nigerian patients with type 2 diabetes. Value Health Reg Issues 2013;2(2):189—98.

[7] Moher D, Liberati A, Tetzlaff J, Altman DG. The PRISMA Group preferred reporting items for systematic reviews and meta-analyses: the PRISMA statement. PLoS Med 2009;6(6):1—6.

[8] Khdour MR, Agus AM, Kidney JC, Smyth BM, Elnay JC, Crealey GE. Cost-utility analysis of a pharmacy-led self-management programme for patients with COPD. Int J Clin Pharm 2011;33(4):665—73.

[9] Claus BO, Vandeputte FM, Robays H. Epidemiology and cost analysis of pharmacist interventions at Ghent University Hospital. Int J Clin Pharm 2012;34(5):773—8.

[10] Wright D, Twigg M, Barton G, Thornley T, Kerr C. An evaluation of a multi-site community pharmacy—based chronic obstructive pulmonary disease support service. Int J Pharm Pract 2015;23(1):36—43.

[11] Elliott RA, Putman KD, Franklin M, Annemans L, Verhaeghe N, Eden M, et al. Cost effectiveness of a pharmacist-led information technology intervention for reducing rates of clinically important errors in medicines management in general practices (PINCER). Pharmacoeconomics 2014;32(6):573—90.

[12] Bojke C, Philips Z, Sculpher M, Campion P, Chrystyn H, Coulton S, et al. Cost-effectiveness of shared pharmaceutical care for older patients: RESPECT trial findings. Br J Gen Pract 2010;60(570):e20—7.

[13] Rubio-Valera M, Bosmans J, Fernández A, Peñarrubia-María M, March M, Travé P, et al. Cost-effectiveness of a community pharmacist intervention in patients with depression: a randomized controlled trial (PRODEFAR Study). PLoS One 2013;8(8):e70588.

[14] Perraudin C, Le Vaillant M, Pelletier-Fleury N. Cost-effectiveness of a community pharmacist-led sleep apnea screening program—a Markov model. PLoS One 2013;8(6): e63894.

[15] Jódar-Sánchez F, Malet-Larrea A, Martín JJ, García-Mochón L, del Amo MP, Martínez-Martínez F, et al. Cost-utility analysis of a medication review with follow-up service for older adults with polypharmacy in community pharmacies in Spain: the conSIGUE program. Pharmacoeconomics 2015;33(6):599—610.

[16] Obreli-Neto PR, Marusic S, Guidoni CM, de Oliveira Baldoni A, Renovato RD, Pilger D, et al. Economic evaluation of a pharmaceutical care program for elderly diabetic and hypertensive patients in primary health care: a 36-month randomized controlled clinical trial. J Manag Care Pharm 2015;21(1):66—75.

[17] Borges AP, Guidoni CM, Freitas OD, Pereira LR. Economic evaluation of outpatients with type 2 diabetes mellitus assisted by a pharmaceutical care service. Arq Bras Endocrinol Metabol 2011;55(9):686—91.

[18] Bauld L, Boyd KA, Briggs AH, Chesterman J, Ferguson J, Judge K, et al. One-year outcomes and a cost-effectiveness analysis for smokers accessing group-based and pharmacy-led cessation services. Nicotine Tob Res 2011;13(2):135—45.

Chapter 3

Economic Evaluation of Pharmacy Services: Review of Studies From Asia, Africa, and South America

M.I. Mohamed Ibrahim[1] and H.S. Suh[2]
[1]*Qatar University, Doha, Qatar,* [2]*Pusan National University, Busan, Korea*

Chapter Outline

INTRODUCTION

Pharmaceutical management is characterized by a complex series of processes from research and discovery up to utilization. Pharmacists especially in developing countries (e.g., low- and middle-income countries (LMICs)) do have the capability to provide pharmacy services to patients and family members. Cost is an important element along the chain of processes of medicines and services utilization. The selection of medicines and pharmacy services, plus quantifying the benefits of both, could benefit from the use of health and pharmaceutical economics methods.

Economics can help pharmacy managers and policy makers in the developing countries to make difficult decisions by providing a framework and a set of concepts and tools for assessing options in terms of costs and benefits [1]. Morbidity, mortality, and cost of care in many developing countries increase due to lack of sufficient access and expensive essential medicines and health technologies. These forces people and families into poverty and leads to disability and out-of-pocket expenses. Enabling the development of quality cost-effectiveness studies can encourage the sharing of critical assets, resources, skills, and capabilities to make better patient's health outcomes [2].

There is enough evidence to show that developing countries consider cost as a major barrier to provide medicines and pharmacy services and to ensure the affordability, availability, and accessibility of medicines and services. For developing countries, building up strong health systems is a main challenge to improve the delivery of cost-effective interventions in primary health care and achieving the vision of the Alma-Ata Declaration [3]. Health policy makers require information about values, costs, availability of resources, and the local needs, in addition to the information on effects on health outcomes.

A number of economic evaluation studies are performed to examine the value of pharmaceutical services, but to what extent does economic evaluation of pharmacy services has been carried out in developing countries? What types of hospital and community pharmacy services were implemented and evaluated? What methods were applied and from whose perspective? How robust were these studies? What were the outcomes of these evaluations?

International Pharmaceutical Federation (FIP) [4] reported that LMICs tend to have lower number of pharmacists and pharmacies per population ratio compared to the developed nations. According to the FIP [4], the average density of pharmacists per 10,000 population of around 82 countries in the world is about 6.02. In some situations, there are no or few registered pharmacists at hospitals and at community pharmacies. These problems negatively affect the access to pharmacist, as well as getting the services and medicines [5]. Cornia [6] stated that in developing countries, the period prior to the 1990s has resulted in a slow, unstable, and unequal pattern of growth and stagnation in health indicators. Even though some countries have improved but others are still experiencing challenges. The rise of inequalities among and within countries negatively affects access to health care [7]. Doloresco and Vermeulen [8] mentioned that countries with low and medium Health Development Index category reported a shortage of qualified pharmacists in the hospital setting. This does hinder a nation's ability to provide even simple basic pharmacy services. In addition, there is lack of evidence in the developing countries regarding the impact of pharmacists on patient's health outcomes in the health care system.

Why This Topic Is Important?

Most of the studies used for reference were conducted in the high-income countries and not many were from LMICs. Findings from the developed countries cannot easily be translated and generalized to developing countries due to several fundamental factors. These two sets of countries are different in many aspects; from political, cultural, socioeconomic perspectives, which to a certain extent influence the practice of pharmacy in the country or the region. This chapter aims to explore the economic evaluation methods used to evaluate pharmacy services specifically in the less developed regions of the world, objectives of those studies, countries where these studies were conducted, pharmacy setting involved, type of interventions, key outcomes measures, and other aspects which will be beneficial for the readers.

What Is the Purpose of This Chapter?

This chapter will focus on studies on economic evaluation of pharmacy services provided in developing countries setting, i.e., Latin (South) America, Africa, Middle East (part of the Western Asia), and other Asia regions (East-Asia and Southeast Asia, Southwest Asia, South Asia). Few countries might not be proper to be classified as LMICs (i.e., Japan, Korea, Taiwan, Qatar, and Singapore); they are high-income countries based on the World Bank classification, however most countries included in these regions are developing countries.

Specifically, we would like to determine the relationship between pharmacy interventions and its benefit in terms of cost outcomes in public and private health care institutions, i.e., hospital, community pharmacy, and primary health care clinics in developing countries.

How the Findings Will Benefit Others?

The chapter will:

1. provide a quick overview on the scope of studies conducted;
2. provide an evidence regarding the extent of economic evaluations conducted in pharmaceutical sector in relation to pharmacy interventions;
3. determine the strength and quality of evidence compiled in terms of the study design; and
4. identify the gaps of economic evaluation research conducted between LMICs and high-income countries (including Japan, Korea, Taiwan, and Singapore).

Based on the four points mentioned above, future research could be planned and carried out by researchers.

What Is Known About This Topic?

- Economic evaluations are more popular and more applied in the developed countries especially in North America and Europe.
- Results from economic evaluations in developed countries including North America and Europe are used as evidence base in pharmaceutical practice and policy improvement.
- Though studies were conducted in LMICs setting, there were variations in pharmacy interventions.

MATERIALS AND METHODS

The authors have critically evaluated hospital and community pharmacy-based studies through a mix of quasi-systematic review [9] and systematic search methods, in which health economic evaluation tools were applied on pharmacy interventions. Literature search was done through various databases, i.e., PubMed, Science Direct, Scopus, EMBASE, Cochrane Library, Ovid MEDLINE, and Google Scholar to find published studies on economic evaluation (cost analysis, cost-effectiveness analysis, cost-minimization analysis, cost−benefit analysis, cost−utility analysis) of hospital, community pharmacy, and primary care clinic services, programs, or systems performed in each country located in the regions mentioned above. The database search was also supplemented with electronic searches in relevant journals and/or publications or using the author's name. The period specified was from 1990 till 2015. The whole review was based upon full-text original research articles written in English.

In addition, several domestic search databases (http://kmbase.medric.or.kr, http://www.ndsl.kr, http://kiss.kstudy.com, http://society.kisti.re.kr) and clinical pharmacy journals (http://www.kshp.or.kr, http://www.kccp.or.kr) in Korean were searched. Other domestic search databases and clinical pharmacy journals were not searched due to language barrier. Conference proceedings or abstracts were also included. This review was based upon full-text original research articles and conference proceedings written in English or Korean.

Search terms used keywords such as: cost, cost analysis, economic evaluation, economic analysis, cost-effectiveness, cost−benefit, cost−utility, pharmacy, pharmacy services, hospital pharmacy, community pharmacy, in combination with region (South America, Africa, Middle East, East Asia, Southeast Asia, and South Asia) or developing countries or individual country name in each region/continent. If the intervention included pharmacy services as part such as multifaceted intervention or as multidisciplinary team, studies with this intervention were considered eligible for the review. Titles were extracted, abstracts were reviewed, relevant abstracts were further screened for full-text articles, and lastly each article was critically analyzed. Selected studies were evaluated based on the following aspects: country where the study was conducted, pharmacy setting, i.e., hospital or community pharmacy or primary care settings, type of services and pharmacy initiatives, type of economic evaluation, objectives of the study, outcome measures, target group, and key findings.

Countries Which Were Considered in This Section

Countries classification was based on the definition of the World Bank; it classifies countries according to income. According to the World Bank, LMICs are considered to be "developing" [10].

We included 12 countries in South America (Argentina, Bolivia, Brazil, Chile, Colombia, Ecuador, Guyana, Paraguay, Peru, Suriname, Uruguay, and Venezuela—and two non-sovereign areas—French Guiana, an overseas department of France, and the Falkland Islands), 54 countries in Africa (Algeria, Angola, Benin, Botswana, Burkina Faso, Burundi, Cameroon, Cape Verde, Central African Republic, Chad, Comoros, Congo, Democratic Republic of Congo, Djibouti, Egypt, Equatorial Guinea, Eritrea, Ethiopia, Gabon, Gambia, Ghana, Guinea, Guinea-Bissau, Ivory Coast, Kenya, Lesotho, Liberia, Libya, Madagascar, Malawi, Mali, Mauritania, Mauritius, Morocco, Mozambique, Namibia, Niger, Nigeria, Rwanda, Sao Tome and Principe, Senegal, Seychelles, Sierra Leone, Somalia, South Africa, South Sudan, Sudan, Swaziland, Tanzania, Togo, Tunisia, Uganda, Zambia, and Zimbabwe), and 17 countries in the Middle East (major part of the Western Asia region) regions (Turkey, Syria, Lebanon, Iraq, Iran, Palestine, Jordan, Egypt, Sudan, Libya, Yemen, Saudi Arabia, Kuwait, Oman, Bahrain, Qatar, and United Arab Emirates).

From the other parts of Asia, four countries in East Asia (China, Japan, Korea, and Taiwan), six countries (Bangladesh, Bhutan, India, Nepal, Pakistan, and Sri Lanka) in South Asia, and nine countries (Brunei, Burma, Indonesia, Laos, Malaysia, Philippines, Singapore, Thailand, and Vietnam) in Southeast Asia regions were included.

Screening and Analysis

Duplicate articles were screened and removed. After excluding some articles, the full-text articles were assessed for eligibility. Articles were excluded with the following reasons: published in non-English language, a full-text article was not accessible, in different practice settings, evaluating pharmacy intervention effectiveness but without taking into consideration cost factor, i.e., economic outcome, and economic studies conducted on pharmaceuticals.

Two reviewers independently scanned the abstract, title, or both sections of every record retrieved. The full-text articles or conference abstracts were independently investigated for all potentially relevant articles. If there were any disagreement between reviewers, a third party intervened and resolved the issue by discussion. Articles were excluded with the following reasons: the absence of pharmacy intervention, no comparison, inappropriate outcomes, patients in countries other than listed above, review articles, editorials, and published in non-English language except Korean.

To examine the study trend and interest in outcomes evaluation of pharmacy services, we analyzed the number of studies by 5-year period (<1999, 2000–04, 2005–09, 2010–14, 2015). The types of pharmacy services were categorized employing a criteria used in Perez et al. study [11] which were: (1) general pharmacotherapeutic monitoring service, (2) targeted drug program service, (3) disease management service, (4) medication therapy management service, (5) wellness program or immunization service, (6) pharmacokinetic monitoring service, (7) health screening or laboratory testing service, (8) patient education program or cognitive service, and (9) others. Two reviewers independently categorized the type of pharmacy intervention and reached consensus for each eligible study. Studies with full text were only evaluated as it was perhaps difficult to categorize the intervention type in studies by just only reading the abstracts.

Data and information were presented descriptively based on the qualitative approach taken when evaluating every article based on the following aspects: country where the study was conducted; pharmacy setting, i.e., hospital or community pharmacy or primary care settings; types of services and pharmacy initiatives; types of economic evaluation; objectives of the studies; outcome measures; target group; and key findings.

ANALYSIS, FINDINGS, AND DISCUSSION

We divided this section into two parts: Part A: South America, Africa, and Middle East, and Part B: East Asia, Southeast Asia, and South Asia.

We aimed to assess and summarize original studies of the economic impact of clinical pharmacy services in the hospital and community pharmacy settings in developing countries. Articles were published as far as from 1990s to 2015. At the end, we provide recommendations for future activities.

Part A: South America, Africa, and Middle East

Based on the articles searched and reviewed, there were very few articles from the three regions, which were included in the final analysis. First, there was lack of articles from developing countries, which studied on economic aspects of pharmacy services. Many articles, if any, were focused on medicines or pharmaceuticals, rather than services. If services were evaluated, unfortunately, the economic aspect was not part of the evaluation criteria. There were many articles, which applied economic analysis, but were not in the pharmacy field; many were related to health care in general.

Around 13,000 articles were screened based on the search terms used without specifying the geographical location or countries. Then, it was narrowed down to the specific countries. After screening, 108 articles were related to South America, 552 for Africa, and 245 for the Middle East. Out of these articles, the numbers of usable articles related to the focus areas were only 10 for South America, 13 for Africa, and 16 for the Middle East regions, i.e., a total of 39 studies. The studies were published from 1992 till 2015. Only 3 studies were published prior to 2000, while 24 studies were published in 2010 and beyond (Table 3.1, Refs. [12−50]).

Out of 39 studies, 10 studies were from South America (7 from Brazil, 1 Columbia, 1 Peru, 1 Argentina), 13 from Africa (7 from South Africa, 1 Uganda, 1 Gambia, 1 Malawi, 1 Kenya, 1 Nigeria, 1 Sierra Leone), and 16 from the Middle East (4 from Saudi Arabia, 4 Iran, 3 Turkey, 1 Jordan, 1 Lebanon, 1 Oman, 1 Egypt, 1 Qatar).

In all regions, most of the studies were conducted in the hospital setting (79.5%; 31/39). Unfortunately, only a few were done in the community pharmacy setting or at primary health care clinics. This is due to the issue as community pharmacy practice in the LMICs is not well established or advanced. Nunan and Duke [51] mentioned that generally, the quantity and quality of evidence was scarce and recommended that there is a need for more systematic studies of multifaceted pharmaceutical interventions.

Most of the pharmacy interventions were focused on the use of antimicrobial, and then perhaps followed by clinical pharmacy services. The target groups in most studies were patients, around 11/39 (28.2%) of the studies did not directly target the patients; and around 13/39 (33.3%) of the studies were on chronic diseases. The studies focused on broad range of pharmacy services. According to Rotta et al. [52], positive impact of pharmacists' interventions on patient outcomes has been shown by clinical pharmacy services that focused on specific medical conditions, such as hypertension or diabetes mellitus. This perhaps shows that based on evidence-based practice standards, more studies are needed to show the added value of clinical pharmacy services.

There were only 6 (out of 39; 15.4%) studies which applied full economic evaluation methods, i.e., cost-effectiveness analysis, where both aspects, cost and outcome, were considered in the analysis; however, two studies were incomplete as only study methodology was published (Table 3.2). Other studies only focused on simple cost analysis, cost reduction, or cost savings. It is also interesting to note that no study was conducted by using full economic evaluation technique in the Middle Eastern region. Most studies reported positive economic advantages of the pharmacy intervention evaluated, i.e., more cost-effective, reduced cost, or saved cost. Only in two studies, patient's QoL was taken into consideration. Lack of expertise, resources, reliable data or the system, and process of practice are some of the reasons which could have contributed to lack of rigorous studies in the region.

It is also important to point out that three review articles and article with proposed framework were found and extracted (Table 3.3, Refs. [53−56]). These articles published between 2011 and 2014 explored the use of economic

TABLE 3.1 Key Characteristics of Studies

Author	Country Where Study Done	Setting	Intervention	Target Group	Primary Outcome
Latin America					
Prado et al. [12]	Brazil	Hospital	Perioperative antibiotic prophylaxis protocol	Surgical patients	Cost of the prophylactic antibiotic per surgical procedure
Magedanz et al. [13]	Brazil	Hospital	Antimicrobial stewardship programs (ASPs)	Infectious disease physician	Antimicrobials consumption and cost
Carnevale et al. [14]	Brazil	Hospital	Pharmaceutical care	HIV-infected patients	CD4+ count, viral load, absence of coinfections and optimal immune response, and economic outcomes
Marin et al. [15]	Brazil	Hospital	Internal manufacture of pharmaceutical formulations	Manufacturing service of the central pharmacy	Cost of drugs and savings
Rosselli et al. [16]	Columbia	Hospital	IV drug administration system	Intensive care unit (ICU) patients	Medical errors, drug administration cost, error cost
Obreli-Neto et al. [17]	Brazil	Primary health care	Pharmaceutical care program	Elderly diabetes mellitus and hypertension patients	Quality of life (QoL), CE, and incremental cost-effectiveness ratio (ICER)

de Sá Borges et al. [18]	Brazil	Public health service	Pharmaceutical care service	Outpatients with type 2 diabetes mellitus	Cost of drugs and visits
Bantar et al. [19]	Argentina	Hospital	Pharmacists as part of the multidisciplinary antimicrobial treatment committee	Hospital-wide	Quality of use and cost savings
Adams et al. [20]	Peru	Community pharmacy	Training pharmacy workers (PWs) in syndromic management of sexually transmitted diseases (STDs)	PWs in private pharmacies	Cost-effective of the program and number of cases adequately managed
Queiroz et al. [21]	Brazil	Hospital	Antibiotic prophylaxis protocol	Physicians	Adherence to treatment protocol, consumption, and cost reduction
Africa					
Rosen et al. [22]	South Africa	Hospital	Different models of treatment delivery	HIV/AIDS patients	Viral load, CD4 counts, and outpatient cost per patient
Babigumira et al. [23]	Uganda	HIV/AIDS clinic, Infectious Diseases Institute	Pharmacy-only Refill Program (PRP)	HIV–AIDS patients	Favorable immune response, i.e., CD4 lymphocyte count
Foster and McIntyre [24]	South Africa	District health care facilities	Pharmaceutical care models	AIDS patients	Cost
Dreyer et al. [25]	South Africa	Community pharmacy	Pharmacotherapeutic service	Doctor's prescriptions	Cost of pharmaco-therapeutic service

(Continued)

TABLE 3.1 (Continued)

Author	Country Where Study Done	Setting	Intervention	Target Group	Primary Outcome
Leiva et al. [26]	Gambia	Community pharmacy	STD case management	PWs	Quality and cost of case management
Lubinga et al. [27]	Malawi	District hospitals	Pharmacy assistants training and deployment	Children, patients	Medicines supply management, DALYs, cost and CE of training, and deployment
Strother et al. [28]	Kenya	Hospital	Oncology pharmacy service	Cancer patients	Cost containment, cost saving
Thuray et al. [29]	Sierra Leone	Hospital	Cost recovery system	Obstetric patients	Drug supply and cost improvement
Oshikoya et al. [30]	Nigeria	Hospital	ADR monitoring	Children in pediatric wards	Incidence of ADR and cost
Gaziano et al. [31]	South Africa	Hospital	Microsimulation model	Adult with CVD	Lives per million adults, annual cost per patient
Boyles et al. [32]	South Africa	Hospital	Web-based educational material, antibiotic prescription chart, and antibiotic stewardship ward rounds	Inpatient	Antibiotic usage and cost, inpatient mortality, and readmission rates

Study	Country	Setting	Service/Intervention	Population	Outcome
Muller et al. [33]	South Africa	Primary care facility	Objective and subjective measures of adherence	Pediatric and caregiver	Adherence rate and cost
Pillans et al. [34]	South Africa	Hospital	Cost containment strategy	Hospital-wide	Medicine usage and medicine expenditure; cost recovery
Middle East					
Aljbouri et al. [35]	Jordan	Hospital	Clinical pharmacy practices (patient data collection and evaluation, documentation, identifying and solving DRPs and reactive clinical interventions)	ICU patients	Cost of drug therapy
Khalili et al. [36]	Iran	Hospital	Clinical pharmacy services (medical chart review, prevention and management of medication error and ADRs)	Infectious disease patients	Medication error and cost
Gharekhani et al. [37]	Iran	Hospital	Clinical pharmacy services (detected, managed, and recorded the medication errors)	Nephrology patients	Medication error and cost
Nasser et al. [38]	Lebanon	Hospital	Policy restriction on IV drug usage	Inpatient drug orders	Cost

(Continued)

TABLE 3.1 (Continued)

Author	Country Where Study Done	Setting	Intervention	Target Group	Primary Outcome
Saddique [39]	Saudi Arabia	Hospital	Various clinical pharmacy services (e.g., therapeutic and dosing administration, pharmacokinetics, and total parenteral nutrition)	Patients in different wards	Quality of the services provided, therapeutic merits, direct cost of the clinical intervention
Mousavi et al. [40]	Iran	Hospital	Clinical pharmacist intervention (providing local stress ulcer prophylaxis protocol and educational classes for physicians)	Chronic kidney disease patients	Appropriateness of acid suppression therapy and related cost
Dashti-Khavidaki et al. [41]	Iran	Hospital	Clinical pharmacy services (e.g., drug discontinuation, changing the frequency, duration and dose of drugs, adding a drug to treatment regimen)	Nephrology and infectious disease patients	Clinical significance, acceptance rate of clinical pharmacy services, and cost reduction
Sabry et al. [42]	Egypt	Hospital	Evidence-based prescribing protocol	Physicians	Cost of drugs, trend of utilization
Al-Siyabi and Al-Riyami [43]	Oman	Hospital	Awareness campaigns on unused medicines	Outpatients	Value and type of medicines returned

Study	Country	Setting	Program/Intervention	Population	Outcomes
Amer et al. [44]	Saudi Arabia	Hospital	ASP	ICU adult patients	Prescribing appropriateness rate, physicians' acceptance rate, antibiotic use and cost
Nurgat et al. [45]	Saudi Arabia	Hospital	Web-based tool to document clinical pharmacist intervention	Hospital pharmacists	Number and types of interventions recorded by pharmacists, data mining of archived data, efficiency, cost savings, and the accuracy of the data generated
Al-Ghamdi [46]	Saudi Arabia	Community pharmacy	Rational dispensing	Community pharmacists	Type, number, and cost of drugs dispensed for acute urinary tract infection (UTI)
Bozat et al. [47]	Turkey	Hospital	Formulations for parenteral nutrition	Patients on nutrition support	Cost
Altunsoy et al. [48]	Turkey	Hospital	National antibiotic restriction program (NARP)	Hospitalized patients	Antibiotic consumption, antimicrobial resistance, and cost
Ozkurt et al. [49]	Turkey	Hospital	Antibiotic restriction policy	Hospitalized patients in medical and surgical wards	Antibiotic use, cost, and consumption
El Hajj et al. [50]	Qatar	Hospital	Smoking cessation program	Adult smokers	Confirmed by an exhaled carbon monoxide test, HRQoL, and cost per patient case, per patient outcome, and CEA

TABLE 3.2 Objectives, Type of Economic Analysis, and Key Findings of the Selected Studies

Author	Objective	Economic Analysis Method	Key Findings
Latin America			
Prado et al. [12]	To describe the implementation of a perioperative antibiotic prophylaxis protocol that emphasizes the contribution of the pharmacist	Cost analysis	The appropriateness of the indication for prophylaxis rose from 56.4% to 100% and that of the postoperative maintenance prophylactic antibiotics rose from 21.9% to 95.7%. The cost of the perioperative antibiotic prophylaxis per surgery decreased 40.5%
Magedanz et al. [13]	To assess the impact of ASP, with and without the presence of a pharmacist, in a cardiology hospital in Brazil	Cost analysis	The pharmacist contributed to the significant reduction in consumption of antibiotics. Adherence rate to the ASP team recommendations was 64.1%. There was a significant reduction of 69% in hospital antibiotics costs
Carnevale et al. [14]	To evaluate the clinical and economic impact of pharmaceutical care of HIV-infected patients	Cost analysis	Pharmaceutical care of HIV-infected patients, for a 1-year period was able to decrease the number of pharmacotherapy problems. However, the clinical outcomes and the costs did not have statistical difference but showed higher percentage of better clinical outcomes and lower costs for some items
Marin et al. [15]	To assess the entire physical and economical manufacturing output of the Central Pharmacy and compare with the alternative of purchasing the same products from commercial sources	Cost analysis	Direct comparison of internal and external costs confirmed savings of 63.5% for commercially available formulations. If computed for the entire production, a yearly balance of over US $5,000,000 in favor of the hospital would have been reached

Rosselli et al. [16]	To evaluate four medication administration systems: conventional preparation by nursing staff, MINIBAG Plus delivery system, compounding center preparation, and premix drugs	Cost saving	Average costs for each dopamine dose delivered were $46,995 for premix, $47,625 for compounding center, $101,934 for MINIBAG Plus, and $108,870 for drug prepared in the ICU. The variability of these results is higher for compounding center than for premix, and even higher for MINIBAG Plus and nurse delivery
Obreli-Neto et al. [17]	To evaluate the economic cost and the ICER per quality-adjusted life year (QALY) of pharmaceutical care in the management of diabetes and hypertension in elderly patients in a primary public health care system in a developing country	Cost-effectiveness	Pharmaceutical care did not significantly increase total direct health care costs, but significantly improved health outcomes. The mean ICER per QALY gained suggests a favorable cost-effectiveness
de Sá Borges et al. [18]	To analyze the costs related to visits and drug prescription in outpatients with type 2 diabetes mellitus assisted by a pharmaceutical care service	Cost analysis	The pharmaceutical care group had a statistically significant reduction in costs of metformin and emergency department visits, and increased costs with their family physicians. On the other hand, the control group had a statistically significant increase of 21.3% in the general costs of treatment and visits
Bantar et al. [19]	To optimize antibiotic use in our hospital and to report the impact of this program on prescribing practice, antibiotic use, cost savings, and bacterial resistance	Cost saving	The systematic program executed by a multidisciplinary team is a cost-effective strategy for optimizing antibiotic use in a hospital and has an evident impact on prescribing practice, antibiotic use, cost savings, and bacterial resistance
Adams et al. [20]	To assess the cost-effectiveness of training PWs in syndromic management of STDs	Cost-effectiveness	Under base-case assumptions, from the societal perspective the intervention saved an estimated US $1.51 per case adequately managed; from the program perspective, it cost an estimated US $3.67 per case adequately managed. Training pharmacists in syndromic management of STDs appears to be cost-effective when only program costs are used

(Continued)

TABLE 3.2 (Continued)

Author	Objective	Economic Analysis Method	Key Findings
Queiroz et al. [21]	To promote rational antibiotic surgical prophylaxis, through the implementation of a protocol for the use of these drugs in a surgical unit, to evaluate the adhesion of the health team to the protocol and to define the consumption of antimicrobials used, measured as daily defined dose	Cost analysis	There were significant differences in the prophylactic antibiotic prescriptions after the implantation of the protocol, particularly in the dosages, the intraoperative repetition of the antibiotic, and the number of postoperative doses. There was also marked reduction in the cost of the antibiotic prophylaxis
Africa			
Rosen et al. [22]	To estimate the average outpatient cost per patient in care and responding to treatment 1 year after initiation of antiretroviral therapy (ART) under different models of treatment delivery in South Africa	Cost analysis	If all ART patients remain in care and responding, total costs will increase but the average cost to produce an IC patient will fall. The cost per ART patient treated varies moderately among sites. Cost differences increase markedly when patient outcomes are taken into account
Babigumira et al. [23]	To estimate the cost-effectiveness of the PRP—a form of task-shifting—as compared to Standard of Care (SOC)	Cost-effectiveness	The PRP is more cost-effective than the SOC
Foster and McIntyre [24]	To compare two task-shifting approaches to the dispensing of ART: Indirectly Supervised Pharmacist's Assistants (ISPA) and Nurse-based pharmaceutical care models against the SOC which involves a pharmacist dispensing ART	Cost analysis	The ISPA model was found to be the least costly task-shifting pharmaceutical model. However, patients preferred receiving medication from the nurse

Dreyer et al. [25]	To determine the incidence, extent, and outcomes of interventions by community pharmacists in the supply of prescription and nonprescription medication and to estimate, where possible, the benefits in economic and health care terms of these endeavors	Cost-effectiveness	Interventions by a national random sample of community pharmacists indicate the provision of a cost-effective pharmacotherapeutic service and considerable contribution to the detection, prevention, and resolution of drug-related problems when reviewing doctors' prescriptions
Leiva et al. [26]	To describe the quality and costs of STD case management in urban pharmacies in the Gambia, and explore PWs willingness to improve the STD care they provide	Cost analysis	Fifteen (63%) pharmacies were equipped for treatment of urethral discharge syndrome (UDS), pelvic inflammatory disease (PID), and genital ulcer syndrome (GUS), according to national guidelines. The reported costs for treatment of UDS, PID, and GUS ranged from $2.5 to $15.0. The cost of treatment actually purchased by the SC averaged $3.5 (range $1.5–$9.6) for UDS. Excluding the pharmacy sector from interventions will limit the impact of STD control measures
Lubinga et al. [27]	To assess the impact of pharmacy assistant training and deployment on operational efficiency at health centers, access to medicines, mortality, DALYs, and to estimate cost-effectiveness of training	Cost-effectiveness	Study is still ongoing
Strother et al. [28]	To describe the experience and lessons learned in establishing a chemotherapy pharmacy in western Kenya	Cost saving and containment	The chemotherapy pharmacy services have improved the supply management of pharmaceuticals, environment safety, reduced risks to patients, controlled therapy protocols, and managed to provide cost-containing measures

(Continued)

TABLE 3.2 (Continued)

Author	Objective	Economic Analysis Method	Key Findings
Thuray et al. [29]	To study the impact of cost-recovery system on the supply of obstetric drugs and cost recovery	Cost analysis	There were no shortages of obstetric drugs after the intervention and significant improvement in cost recovery
Oshikoya et al. [30]	To determine the incidence of ADRs as a cause of pediatric admissions at the Lagos State University Teaching Hospital over an 18-month period and to estimate the cost of treating these patients	Cost analysis	Twelve children (0.6%) were admitted because of ADRs and 23 (1.2%) developed ADR(s) during admission. Forty ADRs were suspected in these 35 patients and involved 53 medicines. Antibiotics (50%) were the most suspected medicines. Approximately 1.83 million naira (USD 15,466.60) was expended to manage all the patients admitted due to ADRs
Gaziano et al. [31]	To investigate the health and economic impacts of increasing prescription length	Cost analysis	Increasing prescription length prove to be cost saving in terms of annual per patient costs related to cardiovascular disease
Boyles et al. [32]	To measure the volume and cost of overall antibiotic consumption, inpatient mortality, and readmission rate	Cost reduction	Introduction of antibiotic stewardship ward rounds and a dedicated prescription chart can achieve reduction in antibiotic consumption without harm to patients
Muller et al. [33]	To compare the use and cost of objective and subjective measures of adherence to pediatric antiretroviral treatment in a primary care facility	Cost analysis, cost comparison	PR and VAS would give an inexpensive assessment of objective and subjective adherence, but only VAS showed any correlation with MEMS usage. MEMS gave realistic adherence data but MEMS caps are not affordable in most RLS

Pillans et al. [34]	To study the impact of cost-containment strategies on medicines expenditure	Cost saving; cost containment	The 20 pharmaceuticals making the greatest contribution to the drug bill declined from R7.4 million to R5.7 million, a decrease of 23%. A decrease in expenditure was realized in 14 of the 15 categories reviewed. Overall a 20% saving, or R3.3 million, was achieved for these categories
Middle East (West Asia)			
Aljbouri et al. [35]	To determine whether the presence of Clinical Pharmacist affects the cost of drug therapy for patients admitted to the ICU at Al-Hussein hospital at Royal Medical Services in Amman, Jordan	Cost saving	The total reduction of drug therapy cost after applying Clinical Pharmacy practices in the ICU over a period of 10 months was 149,946.80 JD (211,574.90 USD), which represents an average saving of 35.8% when compared to the first period in this study
Khalili et al. [36]	To determine the frequency and type of medication errors, the type of clinical pharmacy interventions, acceptance of pharmacist interventions by health-care provider team, nursing staff satisfaction with clinical pharmacy services, and the probable impact of clinical pharmacy interventions on decreasing direct medication costs at an infectious diseases ward in Iran	Cost analysis	Incorrect dose was the most frequent medication error in the infectious diseases ward. Thirty-nine percent of clinical pharmacist's interventions had moderate to major financial benefits in present study. The direct medication cost per patient was decreased about 3.8% following clinical pharmacist's interventions
Gharekhani et al. [37]	To evaluate the frequency, types, and direct related cost of medication errors in nephrology ward and the role played by clinical pharmacists	Cost analysis	More than 85% of patients experienced medication error. The rate of medication errors was 3.5 errors per patient and 0.18 errors per ordered medication. Clinical pharmacists' interventions decreased patients' direct medication costs by 4.3%. About 22% of medication errors led to patients' harm

(Continued)

TABLE 3.2 (Continued)

Author	Objective	Economic Analysis Method	Key Findings
Nasser et al. [38]	To assess the impact of the pharmacist on cost through simple implementation of restriction policy on IV drug usage during pharmacy dispensing procedure	Cost reduction	The average monthly consumption of IV esomeprazole was 1439 vials in the prerestriction period as compared to 346 vials in the postrestriction period. Therefore, the associated cost was reduced by an average of $21,233 per month
Saddique [39]	To evaluate the impact of our Clinical Pharmacy program on the patients' care as well as its perception by the Medical staff who came from different parts of the world	Cost analysis	The study provides evidence of the economic value of Clinical Pharmacy services, and the appreciation of the Medical staff of this unique service. A clinical pharmacist is a very efficient decision-maker both in terms of therapeutics and in minimizing cost
Mousavi et al. [40]	To evaluate appropriateness of acid suppression therapy in kidney disease patients and to assess the role of clinical pharmacists to decrease inappropriate stress ulcer prophylaxis prescribing and related costs for these patients	Cost analysis	The results showed significant relative reduction in inappropriate stress ulcer prophylaxis prescribing and related cost in patients with renal insufficiency by about 44% and 67%, respectively
Dashti-Khavidaki et al. [41]	To understand the types of services provided by Iranian clinical pharmacists in nephrology and infectious disease wards, the acceptance rate of clinical pharmacy services in these wards by physicians, and the clinical significance of these services in the main teaching hospital in Iran	Cost reduction	During 1 year, clinical pharmacists contributed to 1386 services for 1105 patients who were admitted in these two wards; of these services, about 95% were accepted by the physicians and about half of them were of moderate-to-life saving clinical significance. Also at least 32% of services were considered to reduce the cost of drug therapy

Sabry et al. [42]	To evaluate the impact of a multifaceted intervention to promote timely switching from IV to oral paracetamol in the postoperative setting	Cost reduction	There was an immediate decrease in utilization and costs and a trend change over the follow-up period with an average monthly reduction of 26%
Al-Siyabi and Al-Riyami [43]	To examine the value and types of medicines returned by patients at a tertiary care unit in Oman	Cost saving	Medications used for cardiovascular and infectious diseases appeared as the most frequent and the most expensive returned medicines. The patients returned a total of 1071 drugs (mean per patient 3.1 per month) corresponding to a total cost of Omani Rial (OR) 20,140 (mean per patient OR 10.6) (1 OR = 2.58 US dollar). Potential cost saving was OR 5550 (mean per patient OR 2.9)
Amer et al. [44]	To compare the prescribing appropriateness rate of the empirical antibiotic therapy before and after the ASP implementation in a tertiary care hospital and physicians' acceptance rate, patient's ICU course, total utilization, and total direct cost of antibiotics	Cost analysis	The ASP implementation in the medical ICU improved appropriateness of empirical antibiotics utilization. Physician's acceptance rate was 96.3%. ASP also reduced direct cost and antibiotic consumption
Nurgat et al. [45]	To develop a database for documenting pharmacist intervention through a web-based application and to determine if the new, web-based application provides any benefits with regard to documentation compliance by clinical pharmacists and ease of calculating cost savings	Cost saving	The web-based application is an efficient system for documenting pharmacist interventions. The number of documented clinical interventions increased. Using the web-based application, 29.06% of documented interventions resulted in cost savings
Al-Ghamdi [46]	To document attitude of community pharmacists to fulfill the concept of pharmaceutical care, to evaluate how they manage a case of acute uncomplicated UTI	Cost analysis	Fluoroquinolones over the counter were highly dispensed and there was lack of pharmacist's adherence to pharmaceutical law

(Continued)

TABLE 3.2 (Continued)

Author	Objective	Economic Analysis Method	Key Findings
Bozat et al. [47]	To compare the cost of premixed multichamber bags versus compounded parenteral nutrition	Cost analysis, cost comparison	Usage of hospital-compounded parenteral nutrition bags showed a cost advantage in hospitals that treat more than 15 patients per day. In small volume hospitals, premixed multichamber bags may be more beneficial
Altunsoy et al. [48]	To evaluate the effect of NARP on antibiotic consumption, antimicrobial resistance, and cost	Cost analysis	An amount of $5,389,155.82 saving occurred after 2 years of NARP. It also indicated that NARP was effective in lowering antibiotic used and resistance
Ozkurt et al. [49]	To compare antibiotic use, cost, and consumption before and after an initiation of an antibiotic-restriction policy	Cost saving	The rate of antibiotic use decreased, the appropriate use increased, culture-based treatment increased, consumption of restricted antibiotics decreased, and total expenditure of all antibiotics decreased with a cost saving of $332,000 per year
El Hajj et al. [50]	To test the effect of a structured smoking cessation program delivered by trained ambulatory pharmacists in Qatar	Cost-effectiveness	Study is still ongoing

TABLE 3.3 Findings From Review Articles on Economic Outcomes of Pharmacists' Interventions in LMICs

Author	Objective	Economic Analysis Method	Key Findings
Faden et al. [53]	To study the impact of insurance system strategies on cost-effective use of medicines in LMICs	Systematic review	There is a lack of published evidence on the impact of insurance system strategies on improving the use of medicines in LMIC, i.e., very little evidence on medicines selection, purchasing, or utilization management strategies, and furthermore majority of the published studies utilize weak study designs
Mori et al. [54]	To study the extent to which pharmacoeconomic analysis is employed to influence in the selection of essential medicines	Systematic review	Country-specific pharmacoeconomic analyses are too scarce and inconsistently used to have had a significant influence on the selection of essential medicines in Tanzania
Pande et al. [55]	To examine the effect of pharmacist-provided nondispensing services on patient outcomes, health service utilization, and costs in LMICs	Review	Twelve studies comparing pharmacist-provided services versus usual care were included in this review. A single study examined the effect of patient targeted pharmacist interventions on medical expenses and the cost was found to be reduced. No studies

(Continued)

TABLE 3.3 (Continued)

Author	Objective	Economic Analysis Method	Key Findings
			assessing the impact of pharmacist-provided nondispensing services that targeted health care professionals reported health service utilization and cost outcomes
Babigumira et al. [56]	To propose a framework that can be used to estimate the costs of pharmacovigilance (PV) (including the value of investments to increase PV capacity and the costs of managing medicines-related problems (MRPs)) and outcomes associated with PV (including improvements in morbidity, mortality, and QoL as a result of the reduction in MRPs)	Pharmacoeconomic analysis (opinion and recommendation)	A framework was proposed for assessing the economic value of PV programs. Evidence generated using this framework could assist stakeholders in evaluating investments to increase the capacity and efficiency of PV and contribute to improving population health

evaluation in various pharmacy interventions in LMICs; one study looked at impact of insurance system strategies on the use of medicines, another one evaluated the utilization of pharmacoeconomic evaluation on medicines selection, and the third one screened the effect of non-dispensing pharmacy services. The fourth paper provided framework for economic evaluation of PV program in LMICs.

Part B: East Asia, Southeast Asia, and South Asia

Starting from 7047 studies from initial search, a total of 79 studies were identified after the systematic process to identify, screen, and review the papers (Fig. 3.1). Out of 79 studies, 49 studies were from East Asia (13 from

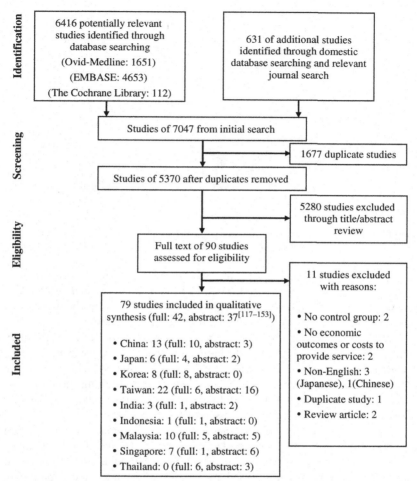

FIGURE 3.1 Literature search method and screening results of identifying studies evaluating outcomes* of pharmacy services in East Asia, Southeast Asia, and South Asia [117−153]. *Overall outcomes not limited to economic outcomes only.

China, 6 from Japan, 8 from Korea, and 22 from Taiwan), 3 studies were from South Asia (3 from India), and 27 were from Southeast Asia (1 from Indonesia, 10 from Malaysia, 7 from Singapore, and 9 from Thailand).

As can be seen in Fig. 3.1, 11 studies were excluded in the last stage of screening for eligible studies. There were two studies without control group [57,58], two studies were without economic outcomes or costs [59,61], three studies were in Japanese [62,63], one study was in Chinese [64], one duplicate study [65], and there were two review articles [55,66]. Before-and-after studies were considered to have control group.

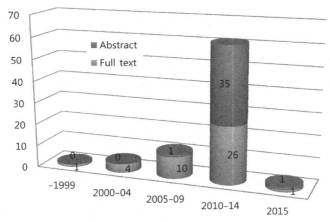

FIGURE 3.2 The number of studies (full texts plus conference abstracts) published by year examining the economic outcomes of pharmacy services in East Asia, Southeast Asia, and South Asia.

As can be seen from Fig. 3.2, the number of studies examining the outcomes of pharmacy services in East Asia, Southeast Asia, and South Asia increased in the recent years (Fig. 3.2). The number of studies between 2010 and 2014 were 61 whereas those between 2000 and 2004 were 4.

Among the types of pharmacy services suggested in Perez et al. study (2009), the most common types of pharmacy services were the general pharmacotherapeutic monitoring services (46%) and pharmacokinetic monitoring service (15%). There was a paucity of evidence in examining the outcomes of disease management services, wellness programs, immunization services, and medication therapy management services (Table 3.4).

Most of the studies examining the outcomes of pharmacists' intervention were performed in hospital setting (Table 3.5, Refs. [67−107]). The majority of target groups in these studies were patients. Although the definition of pharmaceutical care slightly varied by studies, it included participating in daily clinical rounds, providing review of medication orders/consultations with physicians or nurses, therapeutic drug monitoring in critically ill patients, delivering lectures related to rational usage of drugs, detecting and reporting of adverse drug reaction (ADR), and participating in consultations and treatment in cases of emergencies with regard to drug safety. Out of 42 studies with the full-text material, 18 studies have before-after criteria. Eight studies were randomized controlled trials although two studies were not clear whether groups were randomized or not. The rest of the studies were retrospective or cohort studies. Among studies using retrospective data, studies without comparison group were classified as retrospective studies whereas studies with comparison group were categorized as retrospective cohort studies. There were four modeling studies, using Markov and decision analytic modeling techniques.

TABLE 3.4 Types of Pharmacy Services[a] (Part B: East Asia, Southeast Asia, and South Asia)

Types of Intervention	Number of Studies (%)
General pharmacotherapeutic monitoring service	27 (45.8%)
Pharmacokinetic monitoring service	9 (15.3%)
Targeted drug program service	7 (11.9%)
Patient education program or cognitive service	7 (11.9%)
Health screening or laboratory testing service	4 (6.8%)
Disease management service	1 (1.7%)
Wellness program or immunization service	1 (1.7%)
Medication therapy management service	0 (0.0%)
Other	3 (5.1%)
Total	59 (100.0%)

[a]Criteria used in Perez et al. [11]. Only studies with full texts examining the economic outcomes of pharmacy services were analyzed (n = 42). One study could have several types of pharmacy services.

Among 42 studies with full text, most studies (33 studies, 72.1%) examined the costs only (Table 3.6). Among 33 studies, 2 studies only evaluated the input costs, which were needed to perform pharmacists' intervention. These two studies did not measure the impact of pharmacy services in economic terms. Only one study performed a cost—utility analysis reporting ICER as incremental cost per QALYs, which is the gold standard for the economic analysis. Out of 42 studies, 5 studies (11.6%) used cost-effectiveness analysis and four studies (9.3%) were conducted by using cost—benefit analysis technique. These studies were conducted between 2004 and 2014. Most studies reported positive economic outcomes of the pharmacists' intervention, i.e., reduced cost, saved cost, cost-effective, or cost-beneficial (Table 3.7).

There was one study performed in Taiwan [90] which evaluated the QoL using Short-Form 36 (SF-36). The SF-36 was used to measure the impact of pharmacists' intervention on patients' QoL. In addition, the findings clearly indicated that 54% of the studies were from Japan, Korea, Taiwan, and Singapore.

Both hospital and community pharmacy settings (and other primary care settings) are important institutions for people in all parts including South America, Africa, Middle East, East Asia, Southeast Asia, and South Asia. Our study indicated that studies were conducted in both settings but more in the public sector; more in hospital setting as compared to other settings. According to Laing [108], patients frequently access each of the different

TABLE 3.5 Key Study Characteristics in Studies Examining Economic Outcomes of Pharmacy Services Which Were Published in Full Texts (Part B: East Asia, Southeast Asia, and South Asia)

Author	Country Where Study Done	Setting (Study Design)	Intervention	Target Group	Primary Outcome (Not All Outcomes Are Listed)
East Asia (China, Japan, Korea, Taiwan)					
Jiang et al. [67]	China	Hospital (before-after study)	Pharmaceutical care for 3 months (pharmacists participated in daily clinical rounds, provided review of medication orders, consultations with physicians or nurses, therapeutic drug monitoring in critically ill patients, conducting of lectures for rational usage of drugs, detection and reporting of ADR, and participation in consultations and treatment in cases of emergencies with regard to drug safety)	Patients in the ICU of a university-affiliated hospital	Drug cost per patient
Jiang et al. [68]	China	Hospital (before-after study)	Specialized antimicrobial dosing service from critical care pharmacists	Septic patients receiving continuous renal replacement therapy	Costs occurred in the ICU

Jiang et al. [66]	China	Hospital (before-after study)	Dosing adjustment recommendations for patients receiving continuous renal replacement therapy	Patients receiving continuous renal replacement therapy	Cost savings per critically ill patient in the ICU
Shen et al. [70]	China	Hospital (randomized controlled trial)	Direct interactions between physicians and pharmacists at ward level	Patients hospitalized with respiratory tract infections	Total cost of hospitalization and costs of antibiotic drugs
Xin et al. [71]	China	Hospital (before-after study)	Pharmaceutical care (pharmacists made rounds with the doctors, face-to-face counseling, monitoring, goal setting, and drug therapy management, contributes to the management team by making medication and laboratory recommendations to help manage comorbidities, and by assisting patients in obtaining and properly using their prescribed medications)	Patient with diabetes	Drug cost per patient day
Zhang et al. [72]	China	Hospital (randomized controlled trial)	Pharmaceutical care (pharmacists answering questions of physicians and nurses, giving advice on treating patients, checking prescriptions, and patient counseling at discharge)	Pediatric patients	Cost of drugs, cost of hospitalization

(Continued)

TABLE 3.5 (Continued)

Author	Country Where Study Done	Setting (Study Design)	Intervention	Target Group	Primary Outcome (Not All Outcomes Are Listed)
Zhang et al. [73]	China	Hospital (before-after study)	Real-time monitoring of medical records and controlling of the prescriptions by pharmacists	Surgical patients who use antibiotic for prophylactic in a tertiary hospital	Cost saving, benefit to cost ratio
Zhou et al. [74]	China	Hospital (before-after study)	Pharmacists participation in antibiotic stewardship programs of the hospital and conduction of real-time interventions	Patients using antibiotics for prevention of incision infection in urology	Average antibiotic cost, the cost of antibiotics as a percentage of total drug cost
Chung et al. [75]	China (Hong Kong)	Hospital (randomized clinical trial)	Pharmaceutical care (clinical pharmacist assessed LDL-C levels, medication compliance and the proper use of drugs and provided recommendations, education and monthly telephone follow-ups)	Outpatients visiting lipid clinic	Input cost, the percentage of patients achieved LDL-C goals
Ko et al. [76]	China (Hong Kong)	Hospital (randomized clinical trial)	Structure care (using a protocol with predefined treatment targets by pharmacist–diabetologist team)	Patients with diabetes	Cost savings

Reference	Country	Study design	Intervention	Population	Outcome
Iihara et al. [77]	Japan	Hospital (before-after study)	Pharmaceutical care (verification of prescription orders, mixing of anticancer injections, monitoring ADRs, implementation of supportive care) and provision of information about cancer chemotherapy to medical staff and patients	Patients with cancer chemotherapy	Cost savings of antiemesis
Ise et al. [78]	Japan	Hospital (before-after study)	Change of prescription medication by pharmacists	Hospital-wide	Cost saving, cost avoidance
Tachi et al. [60]	Japan	Hospital (prospective controlled study; uncertain whether randomized or not)	Pharmacists activity by evaluating the patients' kidney function and adjusting the appropriate dosage at the time of dispensation	Elderly patients receiving levofloxacin	Cost of reduced levofloxacin, cost for treatment and examination related to the ADRs, total costs difference between two groups
Yagi et al. [79]	Japan	Hospital (retrospective cohort study)	Pharmacists' intervention on administration of meropenem based on its pharmacokinetics and pharmacodynamics	Patients admitted with serious infections who were successfully treated with meropenem for three or more days	Total reduction in drug cost
Ahn et al. [80]	Korea	Hospital (randomized controlled trial)	Regimen adjustment by pharmacists (10 min before meal vs immediately after meal)	Adult outpatients with type 2 diabetes mellitus	Average daily drug price

(Continued)

TABLE 3.5 (Continued)

Author	Country Where Study Done	Setting (Study Design)	Intervention	Target Group	Primary Outcome (Not All Outcomes Are Listed)
Cho et al. [81]	Korea	Hospital (retrospective cohort study)	Anticoagulation service by pharmacists	Patients visiting physicians having higher proportion of patients with anticoagulation service	Patient satisfaction, drug adherence, length of stay, profit due to reduced medical examination time
Han [82]	Korea	Hospital (retrospective study)	Prescription monitoring and intervention by pharmacists	Patients receiving chemotherapy	Cost savings, cost avoidance
Lee et al. [83]	Korea	Hospital (before-after study)	Prescription monitoring, overall evaluation, rounding by pharmacists	Elderly patients who are hospitalized	Cost avoidance, number of inappropriate medication prescribed
Mo et al. [84]	Korea	Hospital (before-after study)	Expanded nutritional support team services	Patients with parenteral or enteral nutrition support in ICU	Parenteral nutrition costs

Park et al. [85]	Korea	Hospital (retrospective study, modeling study)	Pharmacy consultation activity	Patients with pneumonia receiving vancomycin	Prevention effect of nephrotoxicity, costs of treating nephrotoxicity, ICER
Park et al. [86]	Korea	Hospital (retrospective study)	Intervention by unit pharmacist in charge (designated-pharmacist)	Hospital-wide	Acceptance rate of intervention, prevention of adverse drug event, cost avoidance by preventing adverse drug event
Sohn and Shin [87]	Korea	Community pharmacy (modeling study)	Pharmaceutical care	Elderly patients visiting community pharmacy	Drug-related morbidity and mortality, hospitalization, outpatient visit, drug adherence, inappropriate medication discontinuation, cost–benefit ratio, net benefit, ICER
Chan et al. [88]	Taiwan	Hospital (retrospective cohort study)	Ongoing evaluation of the appropriateness of activated protein C therapy use	Hospitalized patients with severe sepsis	Total direct medical costs

(Continued)

TABLE 3.5 (Continued)

Author	Country Where Study Done	Setting (Study Design)	Intervention	Target Group	Primary Outcome (Not All Outcomes Are Listed)
Chan and Wang [89]	Taiwan	Hospital (before-after study)	Pharmacist provided the patients with an explanatory booklet and brochure (containing information about the etiology of asthma, drugs used to treat asthma, and the application technique of inhalation)	Patients with moderate to severe asthma in outpatient clinics	Total cost per patient, ICER
Lee et al. [90]	Taiwan	Hospital (randomized controlled study)	Cyclosporine therapeutic drug monitoring by pharmacists	Stable patients receiving cyclosporine with renal transplant age greater than 1 year	SF-36 score, cost of intervention
Lin et al. [91]	Taiwan	Hospital (before-after study)	Antimicrobial stewardship (education, clinical pharmacists-based intervention, and regular outcome announcement) as a multidisciplinary team	Hospital-wide	Cost saving in the costs of antibiotics
Lu et al. [92]	Taiwan	Hospital (retrospective study)	Pharmacists' intervention (screening of patients medication uses and communicating with the physicians to solve drug-related problems)	Patients in ICUs, neurology, cardiology, and nephrology wards	Potential cost saving, benefit to cost ratio

Yen et al. [93]	Taiwan	Hospital (before-after study)	Pharmacists determined if the patients were ready to switch from intravenous levofloxacin to the oral form by assessing patients' vital signs and body condition	Hospitalized adult patients receiving intravenous levofloxacin	Cost of drug, inpatient expenditures
South Asia (India)					
Lucca et al. [94]	India	Hospital (retrospective study)	Pharmacists reviewed drug prescriptions, discussed with a physician, and provided suggestions	Patients who stayed at least overnight in ICUs	Total net cost savings
Southeast Asia (Indonesia, Malaysia, Singapore, Thailand)					
Nasution et al. [95]	Indonesia	Hospital (before-after study)	Clinical pharmacy education on drug-related problems and dose adjustment	Patients with chronic kidney disease stages 4 and 5	ICER
Hassan et al. [96]	Malaysia	Hospital (before-after study)	Clinical pharmacists rounding with the nephrology unit team and providing dosing adjustment recommendations	Patients with creatinine clearance ≤ 50	Cost savings
Jing et al. [97]	Malaysia	Hospital (before-after study)	Pharmacists review of the appropriateness in using activated vitamin D based on guideline	Patients who were prescribed with activated vitamin D	Drug expenditure

(Continued)

TABLE 3.5 (Continued)

Author	Country Where Study Done	Setting (Study Design)	Intervention	Target Group	Primary Outcome (Not All Outcomes Are Listed)
Ping et al. [98]	Malaysia	Community pharmacy (cross-sectional study, before-after study)	Generic substitution practice by community pharmacist	Patients visiting community pharmacy	Total drug expenditure of patients
Zahari [99]	Malaysia	Hospital (retrospective study)	Making an assessment on the application of rosuvastatin based on the patient's clinical condition by pharmacists	Hospital-wide	Cost savings
Zaidi et al. [100]	Malaysia	Hospital (retrospective study)	Pharmacist reviewing the patient's progress charts, and documented drug-related problems if any	Patients in the ICU	Total net cost saving, cost addition per intervention
Lim et al. [101]	Singapore	Hospital (randomized controlled trial)	Pharmacist consultation (identification of MRPs such as therapeutic duplication and ADRs)	Elderly outpatients	Cost avoidance
Ratanajamit et al. [102]	Thailand	Hospital (before-after study)	Pharmacist assessment of the appropriateness of therapeutic drug monitoring process	Patients diagnosed with epilepsy or seizures	Cost avoidance

Saokaew et al. [103]	Thailand	Hospital (randomized controlled trial)	Patient care team including a clinical pharmacist	Patients in the ICU	Overall drug cost per patient, length of ICU stay, cost saving, cost avoidance
Saokaew et al. [104]	Thailand	Hospital (Markov modeling study)	Pharmacist-participated warfarin therapy management	Patients with warfarin therapy aged 45 years	ICER
Sookaneknun et al. [105]	Thailand	Community (prospective cohort study)	Community pharmacy-based screening program for diabetes and hypertension	Patients aged 40 years and over who were not known to have diabetes or hypertension	Referral rate, model unit costs per screened person
Tasila and Permsuwan [106]	Thailand	Hospital (retrospective study)	Intensive adverse products reactions monitoring program by pharmacists	Hospitalized patients	Net benefit cost, benefit to cost ratio
Thavorn and Chaiyakunapruk [107]	Thailand	Community pharmacy (modeling study)	Community pharmacist-based smoking cessation program	Adults with regular smoking	Cost saving, ICER

TABLE 3.6 Types of Outcomes Used in Studies Evaluating the Economic Outcomes of Pharmacy Services (Part B: East Asia, Southeast Asia, and South Asia)[a]

Types of Analysis or Outcomes	Number of Studies (%)
Cost−utility analysis	1 (2.3%)
Cost−benefit analysis	4 (9.3%)
Cost-effectiveness analysis	5(11.6%)
Costs (input) only	2 (4.7%)
Costs (output) only	31 (72.1%)
Total	43 (100.0%)

[a]Only studies with full texts examining the economic outcomes of pharmacy services were analyzed (n = 42). One study could have several types of outcomes.

systems concurrently or one after the other. These systems include the traditional systems, the public sector, and the private sector. The public sector often provides some preventive services and attempts to be a curative service to those, who are too poor to access private services. Unfortunately, due to other demands, in some countries, the governments have reduced its spending on health. As resources become limited, practitioners and stakeholders must find cost-effective ways to utilize these resources.

Several studies [109−111] reported that the majority of the studies reviewed described positive financial benefits from the clinical services evaluated; however, many did not include the input costs of providing the clinical service. The studies also noted that the evaluations of ambulatory practices were increasingly common. Our studies indicated that less than one-fourth were conducted in the ambulatory setting. Clinical pharmacy services were generally considered cost-effective or provided a good cost−benefit ratio. Their findings also found that a greater proportion of studies used rigorous study designs [109−111]. Their study findings were similar to our study findings where the cost-effectiveness, cost−benefit, or cost−utility studies were conducted more after 2010.

According to Singer [112], developing countries lag behind in the development of economic evaluation methods. Our findings from all studied regions confirmed this views point as pharmacoeconomic studies lack in all regions. It was observed that there is serious lack of studies conducted in the developing countries context; especially the least or none in the low-income countries (in the countries with the low Human Development Index). These gaps to a certain extent will affect negatively on pharmacy practice and policy development and implementation. In nutshell, lack of economic studies

TABLE 3.7 Objectives, Type of Economic Analysis, and Key Findings of the Studies Published in Full Texts (East Asia, Southeast Asia, and South Asia)

Author	Objective	Economic Analysis Method	Key Findings
East Asia (China, Japan, Korea, Taiwan)			
China			
Jiang et al. [67]	To evaluate fulltime clinical pharmacy services in ICU	Cost analysis	The drug cost per patient day was US $347.43 in the intervention group versus US $307.36 in the control group. Although the difference was not significant ($p = 0.095$), the presence of the pharmacist in the ICU had potential drug-cost saving effects
Jiang et al. [68]	To evaluate the effects of dosing adjustments performed by pharmacists	Cost analysis	The costs occurred in the ICU were US $9938 and US $13,463 in the intervention group and the control group, respectively ($p = 0.038$). The involvement of pharmacists in antimicrobial dosing adjustments in septic patients receiving continuous renal replacement therapy is associated with lower ICU costs
Jiang et al. [69]	To examine the effectiveness of pharmacist interventions of dosing adjustment for critically ill patients receiving continuous renal replacement therapy	Cost analysis	The cost saving per critically ill patient was US $2345.98 after implementing pharmacist dosing adjustment in the ICU. The intervention was also associated with lower adverse drug event rates, though the length of ICU stay and mortality were not significantly affected

(Continued)

TABLE 3.7 (Continued)

Author	Objective	Economic Analysis Method	Key Findings
Shen et al. [70]	To evaluate the impact of pharmacist interventions on antibiotic use in inpatients with respiratory tract infections	Cost analysis	The significant cost savings in the total cost of hospitalization (US $1422.3 in the intervention group vs US $1729.6 in the control group with standard treatment strategies without pharmacist involvement, $p = 0.001$) and cost of antibiotic drugs (US $832.0 vs US $943.9, $p = 0.01$) have resulted from the pharmacist interventions (direct interaction with physicians at ward level). Pharmacist interventions lead to the reduction in health care costs
Xin et al. [71]	To evaluate the effectiveness of pharmaceutical care services	Cost analysis	Including a pharmacist as a part of the diabetes management team might result in direct drug cost saving ($p = 0.095$)
Zhang et al. [72]	To determine the effectiveness of clinical pharmacists	Cost analysis	There was no significant effect of clinical pharmacists on reduction of cost of drugs and hospitalization
Zhang et al. [73]	To evaluate the impact and cost–benefit value of pharmacist interventions	Cost–benefit	The net mean cost savings was US $239.64 and the benefit to cost ratio was 18.79:1. The real-time interventions provided by a clinical pharmacist led to favorable economic outcomes among surgical patients who used antibiotic for prophylactic purpose

Zhou et al. [74]	To examine the impacts of pharmacist intervention on the use of antibiotics	Cost analysis	The average antibiotic cost decreased by US $24,694 and the cost of antibiotics as a percentage of total drug cost decreased by 27.7%. Antibiotic stewardship program with pharmacist participation including real-time interventions can significantly decrease costs
Chung et al. [75]	To assess the clinical and economic outcomes of a clinical pharmacy service in dyslipidemic management	Cost (input) analysis	A better clinical effect was observed in the intervention group with pharmacist intervention versus the usual medical care group (the percentage of patients achieved LDL-C goals, 58.7% vs 4.3%, $p < 0.05$). The input cost for this clinical service was estimated to be US $385 per month. Positive impact of clinical pharmacy service on achieving treatment goals in lipid management was observed
Ko et al. [76]	To evaluate the effects of structured care by pharmacist as a diabetologist team	Cost analysis	Cost savings in the intervention group with pharmacist intervention showed a cost saving by HK $154,564 compared with the control group with usual care. Structured care performed by pharmacist as a multidisciplinary team had reduced treatment costs
Japan			
Iihara et al. [77]	To evaluate the outcomes of pharmacists' activities	Cost analysis	Costs for antiemesis treatments were US $124.5 versus US $147.7 after the intervention with pharmaceutical care and before the intervention, respectively. Pharmacists contributed to the improved efficiency of medical practices

(Continued)

TABLE 3.7 (Continued)

Author	Objective	Economic Analysis Method	Key Findings
Ise et al. [78]	To evaluate the contributions of pharmacists	Cost analysis	The cost saving (defined as the difference of the prescription medication expenses after and before the intervention implemented) was estimated to be ¥440,639. The cost avoidance (defined as the amount of medical expense avoided due to pharmacists' activities to avoid ADR) was estimated to be ¥1,941,847–3,883,695. Pharmacists contribute to hospital management through cost savings and avoidance
Tachi et al. [60]	To investigate the effectiveness of pharmacists' interventions in minimizing ADRs resulting from levofloxacin administration in elderly patients	Cost analysis	The costs of reduced levofloxacin per patient were ¥191.1 and 0 for the intervention group and control group, respectively. Similarly, the costs for treatments and examinations related to the ADRs per patient were ¥15.5 and ¥290.0, respectively. The intergroup difference in the total cost per patient was ¥465.6. Dose adjustment of levofloxacin at the time of dispensation by the pharmacist resulted in a decrease in cost
Yagi et al. [79]	To evaluate a plan of administration of meropenem	Cost analysis	The total decrease in drug cost in the intervention group was US $17,490 over 3 years. Pharmacist intervention on administration of meropenem based on pharmacokinetics and pharmacodynamics was associated with lower drug costs

Korea

Ahn et al. [80]	To assess the cost-effectiveness of pharmacists intervention (improved dosing schedules) to patients with type 2 diabetes	Cost analysis	No significant differences in the cost between two groups were found
Cho et al. [81]	To evaluate the impact of anticoagulation service on patient satisfaction, length of stay, and hospital profit	Cost analysis	The number of patients increased by 489 per month (due to the decreased consultation time by physicians, 31.6 h per month) and the treatment income increased by 47,409,500 Korean won per month. It was estimated to have an increase in hospital profit by 568,914,000 won per year
Han [82]	To evaluate the clinical and economic impact of pharmacists' interventions at chemotherapy preparation unit	Cost analysis	The amount of cost avoidance (estimated by the reduction in potential adverse drug events by pharmacists' intervention) was US $88,244 and cost saving (estimated by the reduction in anticancer treatment wastage which was mainly the ample breakage and the reduction of additional use of treatment) was US $92,483
Lee et al. [83]	To evaluate medications for geriatric inpatients based on revised inappropriate medication criteria and cost avoidance by pharmacists' intervention	Cost analysis	The cost avoidance (estimated by reduction in length of stay due the intervention) of the pharmacists' intervention was estimated to be 52,216,666 Korean won. The most frequent types of intervention were related with the identification of potential drug adverse events and drug–drug interaction in geriatric patients

(Continued)

TABLE 3.7 (Continued)

Author	Objective	Economic Analysis Method	Key Findings
Mo et al. [84]	To examine the effects of nutrition support team services on nutrition supply type and patients outcomes in the ICU	Cost analysis	The average parenteral nutrition costs per patient decreased from 114,193 Korean won in 2008 to 93,837 Korean won in 2009 (about 20% cost reduction). Providing nutrition support team services in the ICU saved parenteral nutrition costs
Park et al. [85]	To evaluate the economic effect of clinical pharmacokinetic consultation service for vancomycin by pharmacists in hospital	Cost-effectiveness	The ICER was 184,602 Korean won of providing consultation service. Comparing with the treatment cost of nephrotoxicity (986,536 won), pharmacokinetic monitoring and dosage adjustment to prevent nephrotoxicity are cost-effective
Park et al. [86]	To measure the effect of designated pharmacists on intervention in hospital	Cost analysis	The cost avoidance (estimated by reduction in drug adverse event due the intervention multiplied by the incremental medical costs due to drug adverse event) of the pharmacists' intervention was estimated to be 10,030,000 Korean won. The designated-pharmacist policy has a positive effect on pharmacotherapy
Sohn and Shin [87]	To evaluate economic impact of comprehensive pharmaceutical care intervention provided by community pharmacists for elderly outpatients	Cost–benefit, cost-effectiveness	Benefit to cost ratio was 4.8:1 and net benefit was 73,816 Korean won per year for individual elderly patient. ICER of pharmaceutical care versus usual care was approximately 4900 million Korean won. The comprehensive pharmaceutical care by community pharmacists has a positive economic effect

Taiwan

Chan et al. [88]	To assess the cost outcomes of pharmacist intervention	Cost analysis	The total direct medical costs were US $20,632.3 and US $24,785.8 in the intervention group and control group, respectively. The pharmacist intervention in prescribing activated protein C for patients with severe sepsis might reduce direct medical costs
Chan and Wang [89]	To assess the economic outcomes of clinical pharmacist interventions	Cost-effectiveness	The total cost per patient at baseline was statistically different from the total cost per patient at 3-month ($NT2880 vs $NT1683, respectively). The ICER for the decrease in drug cost per visit was 0.93. Pharmacist intervention for the education of asthma patients was cost-effective in patients with moderate to severe asthma
Lee et al. [90]	To evaluate the impact of cyclosporine therapeutic drug monitoring service using the pharmaceutical care concept on the health-related QoL in patients with stable renal transplant recipients and to assure the value of the pharmacist performance	Cost (input) analysis	The total cost per year for pharmacists' intervention was estimated to be $NT84,360. The input costs of the therapeutic drug monitoring service included on the time spent on training, chart reviewing, and working patients. The implementation of this service could have a positive result on the QoL (based on the findings of SF-36 score)
Lin et al. [91]	To assess the effectiveness of an ASP	Cost analysis	The cost savings in antibiotics were US $607,140 and US $2,495,954 at 1 year and 3 years, respectively, after implementing the program. The multidisciplinary ASP was beneficial to reduce antibiotic cost and consumption

(Continued)

TABLE 3.7 (Continued)

Author	Objective	Economic Analysis Method	Key Findings
Lu et al. [92]	To evaluate the cost implication after preventing drug adverse events by pharmacists' interventions	Cost–benefit	The overall potential cost saving was estimated to be between US $126,970 and US $313,330. The pharmacists' intervention (of screening patients' medication uses and communicating with physicians to solve drug-related problems) resulted in a benefit to cost ratio between 3.4:1 and 8.4:1. The benefit was estimated based on the probability value of an adverse drug event without the pharmacists' intervention. Interventions provided by hospital clinical pharmacists were cost-beneficial
Yen et al. [93]	To evaluate the economic impacts of a pharmacist's intervention	Cost analysis	The cost of drug significantly decreased after implementing pharmacists' intervention (US $449.0 vs US $568.9 after and before implementing the service, respectively, $p = 0.044$). The inpatient costs also significantly decreased ($p = 0.017$). The pharmacist-managed intravenous levofloxacin to oral conversion service produced cost savings, both on medication costs and the total inpatient expenditures

South Asia (India)

Lucca et al. [94]	To assess the pharmacoeconomic impact of drug-related problems identified by clinical pharmacists	Cost analysis	Pharmacists identified the drug-related problems and the potential cost savings were estimated based on the direct drug cost (i.e., discontinuation of medication due to inappropriate use) and the probability of readmission, length of stay, laboratory monitoring changes, and medical procedures. The total net cost savings by pharmacists' intervention was estimated to be US $1796. Clinical pharmacist interventions had a significant impact on the cost of drug therapy

Southeast Asia (Indonesia, Malaysia, Singapore, Thailand)

Indonesia

Nasution et al. [95]	To evaluate the clinical and economic impacts of clinical pharmacy education	Cost-effectiveness	ICER in stage 4 patients with chronic kidney disease was Rp 2,045,341. That in stage 5 was Rp 1,767,585. The pharmacist intervention of chronic kidney disease stage 4 and 5 was cost-effective

Malaysia

Hassan et al. [96]	To evaluate the impact on drug cost of having a pharmacist accompanying a team of physicians on their rounds	Cost analysis	The cost savings of pharmacists' intervention was estimated to be US $2250. The pharmacists' intervention can save drug costs
Jing et al. [97]	To determine the effects of a clinical pharmacist's intervention in reducing the inappropriate use of activated vitamin D	Cost analysis	A significant reduction in drug expenditure due to reduced use of activated vitamin D was found (US $221,777 vs US $110,495 after and before the intervention, respectively, $p = 0.002$). Pharmacist intervention on the use of activated vitamin D resulted in cost saving

(Continued)

TABLE 3.7 (Continued)

Author	Objective	Economic Analysis Method	Key Findings
Ping et al. [98]	To evaluate the generic substitution practice undertaken by community pharmacist	Cost analysis	Total drug costs of patients decreased from US $2643 to US $1028 after pharmacists' intervention (cost saving of 61.1%). Consumer can save the drug expenditures through the generic substitution recommended by community pharmacists
Zahari [99]	To examine whether there was a potential drug cost savings from the pharmacists' intervention making an assessment on the rosuvastatin use based on the patient's condition and clinical evidence available	Cost analysis	The overall cost reduction was estimated to be 84.5% when the pharmacist intervention on recommending the use of rosuvastatin was accepted. Pharmacist is expected to play an important role in reviewing the need of rosuvastatin and suggest an appropriate alternative providing similar lipid lowering effect
Zaidi et al. [100]	To assess the pharmacoeconomic impact of clinical pharmacists' interventions	Cost analysis	The total net cost saving was US $4014. Pharmacists' intervention in the ICU resulted in a significant cost savings in terms of drug expenditure

Singapore

Lim et al. [101]	To evaluate the impact of a pharmacist consult clinic on health-related outcomes of elderly outpatients	Cost analysis	The cost avoidance over 2 months was US $387.28. This was estimated based on the deducted cost if the pharmacists' recommendation was accepted

Thailand

Ratanajamit et al. [102]	To compare the proportions of appropriate therapeutic drug monitoring utilization for antiepileptic drugs	Cost analysis	Unnecessary costs were reduced by 90% due to the pharmacist intervention. Pharmacist intervention significantly improved the appropriateness of therapeutic drug monitoring use and resulted in reduced unnecessary costs
Saokaew et al. [103]	To evaluate whether pharmacists' interventions led to change in cost saving and cost avoidance in ICU	Cost analysis	The overall drug costs per patient were US $1076.37 and US $1258.38 in the intervention group and control group, respectively, $p = 0.138$). Pharmacists' intervention resulted in drug cost saving of US $1971.43 and adverse drug event cost avoidance of US $294.62. Involving pharmacist in the patient care team at ICU led to a reduced overall drug cost, cost saving, and cost avoidance, though the difference between the intervention group and control group was not statistically significant
Saokaew et al. [104]	To evaluate the incremental costs and health benefits of pharmacist-participated warfarin therapy management	Cost–utility	ICER was US $3882.3 per QALYs which was lower than the willingness to pay for 1 QALY. The pharmacist-participated warfarin therapy management is a cost-effective intervention

(Continued)

TABLE 3.7 (Continued)

Author	Objective	Economic Analysis Method	Key Findings
Sookaneknun et al. [105]	To evaluate models for collaboration between community pharmacies and a government primary care unit	Cost analysis	Two models carrying out a screening program for diabetes and hypertension were compared. One model was involved with community pharmacies and the other model was involved with streets communities. Pharmacy-based screening was more costly, but the success rate for referral was higher than a community-based service
Tasila and Permsuwan [106]	To examine the benefit of adverse product reaction monitoring	Cost–benefit	The net benefit cost was estimated to be US $1664.48 and the benefit to cost ratio was 2.17:1. The intensive adverse product reactions monitoring program is a cost beneficial program
Thavorn and Chaiyakunapruk [107]	To estimate the cost-effectiveness of a structured community pharmacist-based smoking cessation program	Cost-effectiveness	The program resulted in cost savings of US $500 to the health system in men. The ICER was US $17,503.53 per life years gained. The community pharmacist-based smoking cessation program leads to cost savings and life year gains

may hinder optimal allocation of resources to improve the effectiveness, efficiency, and equity [113] of pharmacy services in the developing countries.

Babar et al. [114] proposed that "pharmacoeconomic theory and modelling should not be 'hyped-up' but should be realistic according to country's health status, academic capacity and pharmaceutical situation." Babar et al. [114] also argued that the health system needs to be strengthened before economic evaluation of services to be conducted. Nevertheless, there is great potential for health technology assessment to be adopted in LMICs. But despite a strong need for the efficient allocation of relatively scarce health budgets; many LMICs have not adopted health technology assessment processes. The evidence concurs readily that health technology assessment could be used to meet this "value for money" objective [115].

Although our study showed that the strong evidence is available on the effectiveness of pharmacy programs for certain health issues and outcomes, in most of LMICs, most of the studies found did not report data on costs or cost-effectiveness. Individuals should be well informed that integration may not improve service delivery or health status, and if policy makers and health care managers consider incorporating health care services they should monitor and assess these economic evaluation studies by using quality study designs [116]. It will be difficult to justify rational resource allocation if proper and robust economic evaluation is not used. The evidence of the effect of pharmacy services is needed for policy makers. Recognizing that if the governments would fund these pharmacy services, there is an increased interest to conduct economic evaluation of pharmacy services in a proper and robust manner. For example, there are several randomized controlled trials ongoing in South Korea to evaluate the economic outcomes of clinical pharmacy services provided to patients with diabetes, renal failure, and cardiovascular disease.

LIMITATIONS OF STUDIES IN SOUTH AMERICA, AFRICA, MIDDLE EAST, EAST ASIA, SOUTHEAST ASIA, AND SOUTH ASIA

The following are few possible reasons on why very few studies are conducted in the developing countries. The reasons include English language barrier, lack of scientific writing skill, lack of technical expertise in the economic evaluation area, and lack of skills among pharmacy practitioners to conduct research and to write scientific papers. Some of the other reasons are lack of reliable national data, community or hospital pharmacy setup not a priority on the national health agenda, missing or lack of pharmacoeconomics content in the pharmacy curriculum, and lack of demand for any such studies.

RECOMMENDATIONS

The role of health or pharmaceutical economists in pharmacy research is to plan for a rigorous study design to evaluate the pharmacy interventions, i.e., clinical (e.g., counseling, medication therapy management, self-care, chronic disease management) and nonclinical (e.g., administrative and distributive function, policy, medication supply management). They should also aim to initiate and optimize pharmacoeconomics data collection during the implementation of the intervention so that the economic evaluation findings can be presented to the different stakeholders. More studies are required to fill the existing gap and to explore whether decision-makers have the ability to interpret and utilize pharmacoeconomic evidence. Here are some additional recommendations [2,8,112,114]:

1. Training students at both undergraduate and graduate levels in the field of health technology assessment in the universities could play a major role in advancing this field in developing countries.
2. Training local academics and recruiting academics specialized in economic evaluation to fill up the position in the colleges.
3. Organizing continuous professional development programs for practicing pharmacists.
4. Encouraging collaborative research between practitioners and academicians.
5. Getting technical expertise from within or outside the country.
6. Ensuring enough quality resources and materials related to economic evaluation in the university and the country.
7. Organizing meetings, workshops, seminars, and conferences related to pharmacoeconomics and economic evaluation.
8. Mentoring program between the experts and the future researchers.
9. Providing small grants by Ministries of Health to encourage conducting economic evaluation and pharmacoeconomics studies.
10. Getting pharmacy practitioners actively involved in patient care and disease management and not just focusing on distributive function.
11. Make patient's medical record accessible to pharmacists.
12. Strengthening pharmacy and health systems so that community and hospital pharmacy can play an important part in health care system. Then perhaps conducting pharmacy-based economic evaluation is fruitful.

WHAT THIS CHAPTER ADDS?

- Evidence shows that there is lack of economic studies related to pharmacy interventions and publications in the studied regions. There is a general lack of studies in middle-income countries with additionally very few from low-income countries.

- Even though there are studies related to economic evaluation, very few are related to pharmacy services and conducted in the community pharmacy setting.
- Studies were conducted in both sectors, i.e., public and private, but more of in the public sector; more in hospital setting versus others.
- Studies which have been conducted either through simple cost analysis or cost-effectiveness method showed positive pharmacy contribution.
- In low-income countries, the focus is rather on major issues of pharmacy such as medicines accessibility, affordability, and availability, and not on minor aspects such as services of pharmacists, particularly on clinical aspects.

CONCLUSIONS

The review of literature for this 25-year period shows that the full economic evaluation or pharmacoeconomic studies in the studied regions/continents are very few, and this area is far behind as compared to western developed countries. Even though we could see the number of rigorous studies increased lately, however the proportion is too low or none in some countries. These results provide a basis for identifying opportunities for growth and development, as well as for international collaboration, to advance the profession of pharmacy, and to ensure that the patients in the developing world receive the care that they deserve. Until and unless the researchers in the countries incorporate rigorous study designs, we will not be able to provide good quality evidence to support policymaking and practice improvement. In nutshell, pharmacoeconomics could become an important tool to optimize access, cost, and quality of care to the populations of these nations, and more work is needed in this area.

ACKNOWLEDGMENT

This chapter has benefited from helpful support by Mi Seong Kwon and Ho Jin Oh.

REFERENCES

[1] Management Sciences for Health. Managing access to medicines and health technologies. Part 1: Policy and economic issues—economic for pharmaceutical management. Virginia: Management Sciences for Health, Inc; 2012.

[2] Balkrishnan R, Chang J, Patel I, Yang F, Merajver SD. Global comparative healthcare effectiveness research: evaluating sustainable programmes in low & middle resource settings. Indian J Med Res 2013;137(3):494−501.

[3] Lewin S, Lavis JN, Oxman AD, et al. Supporting the delivery of cost-effective interventions in primary health-care systems in low-income and middle-income countries: an overview of systematic reviews. Lancet 2008;372:928−39.

[4] International Pharmaceutical Federation (FIP). FIP global pharmacy workforce report, http://www.fip.org/files/members; 2012 [accessed 22.12.14].

[5] Lu H, Eriksson T, Wiffen P. Evidence based pharmacy for developing countries. Eur J Hosp Pharm 2015;22:66–72. Available from: http://dx.doi.org/10.1136/ejhpharm-2015-000643.

[6] Cornia GA. Globalization and health: results and options. Bull World Health Organ 2001;79:834–41.

[7] Collins T. Globalization, global health, and access to healthcare. Int J Health Plann Manage 2003;18(2):97–104.

[8] Doloresco F, Vermeulen LC. Global survey of hospital pharmacy practice. Am J Health Syst Pharm 2009;66(Suppl 3):S13–19.

[9] Ryś P, Władysiuk M, Skrzekowska-Baran I, Małecki MT. Review articles, systematic reviews and meta-analyses: which can be trusted? Pol Arch Med Wewn 2009;119 (3):148–56.

[10] The World Bank. How we classify countries. The World Bank Group: Washington, DC, http://data.worldbank.org/about/country-classifications; 2015 [accessed 15.08.15].

[11] Perez A, Doloresco F, Hoffman JM, Meek PD, Touchette DR, Vermeulen LC, et al. ACCP: economic evaluations of clinical pharmacy services: 2001–2005. Pharmacotherapy 2009;29 (1):128.

[12] Prado MA, Lima MP, Gomes Ida R, Bergsten-Mendes G. The implementation of a surgical antibiotic prophylaxis program: the pivotal contribution of the hospital pharmacy. Am J Infect Control 2002 Feb;30(1):49–56.

[13] Magedanz L, Silliprandi EM, dos Santos RP. Impact of the pharmacist on a multidisciplinary team in an antimicrobial stewardship program: a quasi-experimental study. Int J Clin Pharm 2012 Apr;34(2):290–4. Available from: http://dx.doi.org/10.1007/s11096-012-9621-7.

[14] Carnevale RC, de Godoi Rezende Costa Molino C, Visacri MB, Mazzola PG, Moriel P. Cost analysis of pharmaceutical care provided to HIV-infected patients: an ambispective controlled study. Daru 2015 Feb 10;23:13. Available from: http://dx.doi.org/10.1186/s40199-014-0074-5.

[15] Marin MLM, Chaves CE, Zanini AC, Faintuch J, Faintuch D, Cipriano SL. Cost of drugs manufactured by the University Hospital—role of the Central Pharmacy. Rev Hosp Clín Fac Med S Paulo 2001;56(2):41–6.

[16] Rosselli D, Rueda JD, Silva MD, Salcedo J. Economic evaluation of four drug administration systems in intensive care units in Colombia. Value Health Reg Issues 2014;5C:20–4.

[17] Obreli-Neto PR, Marusic S, Guidoni CM, Baldoni Ade O, Renovato RD, Pilger D, et al. Economic evaluation of a pharmaceutical care program for elderly diabetic and hypertensive patients in primary health care: a 36-month randomized controlled clinical trial. J Manag Care Spec Pharm 2015 Jan;21(1):66–75.

[18] de Sá Borges AP, Guidoni CM, de Freitas O, Pereira LRL. Economic evaluation of outpatients with type 2 diabetes mellitus assisted by a pharmaceutical care service. Arq Bras Endocrinol Metab 2011;55(9):686–91.

[19] Bantar C, Sartori B, Vesco E, Heft C, Saúl M, Salamone F, et al. A hospitalwide intervention program to optimize the quality of antibiotic use: impact on prescribing practice, antibiotic consumption, cost savings, and bacterial resistance. Clin Infect Dis 2003 Jul 15;37 (2):180–6.

[20] Adams EJ, Garcia PJ, Garnett GP, Edmunds WJ, Holmes KK. The cost-effectiveness of syndromic management in pharmacies in Lima, Peru. Sex Transm Dis 2003 May;30 (5):379−87.

[21] Queiroz R, Grinbaum RS, Galvão LL, Tavares FG, Bergsten-Mendes G. Antibiotic prophylaxis in orthopedic surgeries: the results of an implemented protocol. Braz J Infect Dis 2005 Aug;9(4):283−7.

[22] Rosen S, Long L, Sanne I. The outcomes and outpatient costs of different models of anti-retroviral treatment delivery in South Africa. Trop Med Int Health 2008 Aug;13 (8):1005−15. Available from: http://dx.doi.org/10.1111/j.1365-3156.2008.02114.x.

[23] Babigumira JB, Castelnuovo B, Stergachis A, Kiragga A, Shaefer P, Lamorde M, et al. Cost effectiveness of a pharmacy-only refill program in a large urban HIV/AIDS clinic in Uganda. PLoS One 2011 Mar 28;6(3):e18193. Available from: http://dx.doi.org/10.1371/journal.pone.0018193.

[24] Foster N, McIntyre D. Economic evaluation of task-shifting approaches to the dispensing of anti-retroviral therapy. Hum Resour Health 2012;10:32.

[25] Dreyer AC, Serfontein JHP, Van Der Meer HL, Wagner S. Cost savings effected by community pharmacists' interventions in the supply of medicines in the republic of South Africa. J Res Pharmaceut Econ 1998;9:1−20.

[26] Leiva A, Shaw M, Paine K, Manneh K, McAdam K, Mayaud P. Int J STD AIDS 2001;12 (7):444−52. Available from: http://dx.doi.org/10.1258/0956462011923471.

[27] Lubinga SJ, Jenny AM, Larsen-Cooper E, Crawford J, Matemba C, Stergachis A, et al. Impact of pharmacy worker training and deployment on access to essential medicines and health outcomes in Malawi: protocol for a cluster quasi-experimental evaluation. Implement Sci 2014 Oct 11;9:156. Available from: http://dx.doi.org/10.1186/s13012-014-0156-2.

[28] Strother RM, Rao KV, Gregory KM, Jakait B, Busakhala N, Schellhase E, et al. The oncology pharmacy in cancer care delivery in a resource-constrained setting in western Kenya. J Oncol Pharm Pract 2012 Dec;18(4):406−16. Available from: http://dx.doi.org/10.1177/1078155211434852.

[29] Thuray H, Samai O, Fofana P, Sengeh P. Establishing a cost recovery system for drugs, Bo, Sierra Leone. The Bo PMM Team. Int J Gynaecol Obstet 1997 Nov;59(Suppl 2): S141−7.

[30] Oshikoya KA, Oreagba I, Adeyemi O. Sources of drug information and their influence on the prescribing behaviour of doctors in a teaching hospital in Ibadan, Nigeria. Pan Afr Med J 2011;9:13.

[31] Gaziano T, Cho S, Sy S, Pandya A, Levitt NS, Steyn K. Increasing prescription length could cut cardiovascular disease burden and produce savings in South Africa. Health Aff (Millwood) 2015 Sep 1;34(9):1578−85. Available from: http://dx.doi.org/10.1377/hlthaff.2015.0351.

[32] Boyles TH, Whitelaw A, Bamford C, Moodley M, Bonorchis K, Morris V, et al. Antibiotic stewardship ward rounds and a dedicated prescription chart reduce antibiotic consumption and pharmacy costs without affecting inpatient mortality or re-admission rates. PLoS One 2013 Dec 9;8(12):e79747. Available from: http://dx.doi.org/10.1371/journal.pone.0079747.

[33] Muller AD, Jaspan HB, Myer L, Hunter AL, Harling G, Bekker LG, et al. Standard measures are inadequate to monitor pediatric adherence in a resource-limited setting. AIDS Behav 2011 Feb;15(2):422−31. Available from: http://dx.doi.org/10.1007/s10461-010-9825-6.

[34] Pillans PI, Conry I, Gie BE. Drug cost containment at a large teaching hospital. Pharmacoeconomics 1992 May;1(5):377−82.

[35] Aljbouri TM, Alkhawaldeh MS, Abu-Rumman AE, Hasan TA, Khattar HM, Abu-Oliem AS. Impact of clinical pharmacist on cost of drug therapy in the ICU. Saudi Pharm J 2013 Oct;21(4):371−4. Available from: http://dx.doi.org/10.1016/j.jsps.2012.12.004.

[36] Khalili H, Karimzadeh I, Mirzabeigi P, Dashti-Khavidaki S. Evaluation of clinical pharmacist's interventions in an infectious diseases ward and impact on patient's direct medication cost. Eur J Intern Med 2013 Apr;24(3):227−33. Available from: http://dx.doi.org/10.1016/j.ejim.2012.11.014.

[37] Gharekhani A, Kanani N, Khalili H, Dashti-Khavidaki S. Frequency, types, and direct related costs of medication errors in an academic nephrology ward in Iran. Ren Fail 2014 Sep;36(8):1268−72. Available from: http://dx.doi.org/10.3109/0886022X.2014.934650.

[38] Nasser SC, Nassif JG, Mahfouz F. Cost reduction associated with restriction policy on dispensing intravenous esomeprazole in Lebanon. Pharm World Sci 2010 Dec;32(6):707−10. Available from: http://dx.doi.org/10.1007/s11096-010-9451-4.

[39] Saddique AA. Development of clinical pharmacy services at King Khalid University Hospital and its impact on the quality of healthcare provided. Saudi Pharm J 2012 Jul;20 (3):273−7. Available from: http://dx.doi.org/10.1016/j.jsps.2012.05.001.

[40] Mousavi M, Dashti-Khavidaki S, Khalili H, Farshchi A, Gatmiri M. Impact of clinical pharmacy services on stress ulcer prophylaxis prescribing and related cost in patients with renal insufficiency. Int J Pharm Pract 2013 Aug;21(4):263−9. Available from: http://dx.doi.org/10.1111/ijpp.12005.

[41] Dashti-Khavidaki S, Khalili H, Hamishekar H, Shahverdi S. Clinical pharmacy services in an Iranian teaching hospital: a descriptive study. Pharm World Sci 2009 Dec;31 (6):696−700. Available from: http://dx.doi.org/10.1007/s11096-009-9336-6.

[42] Sabry N, Dawoud D, Alansary A, Hounsome N, Baines D. Evaluation of a protocol-based intervention to promote timely switching from intravenous to oral paracetamol for postoperative pain management: an interrupted time series analysis. J Eval Clin Pract 2015 Oct 22. Available from: http://dx.doi.org/10.1111/jep.12463.

[43] Al-Siyabi K, Al-Riyami K. Value and types of medicines returned by patients to Sultan Qaboos University Hospital Pharmacy, Oman. Sultan Qaboos Univ Med J 2007 Aug;7 (2):109−15.

[44] Amer MR, Akhras NS, Mahmood WA, Al-Jazairi AS. Antimicrobial stewardship program implementation in a medical intensive care unit at a tertiary care hospital in Saudi Arabia. Ann Saudi Med 2013 Nov−Dec;33(6):547−54. Available from: http://dx.doi.org/10.5144/0256-4947.2013.547.

[45] Nurgat ZA, Al-Jazairi AS, Abu-Shraie N, Al-Jedai A. Documenting clinical pharmacist intervention before and after the introduction of a web-based tool. Int J Clin Pharm 2011 Apr;33(2):200−7. Available from: http://dx.doi.org/10.1007/s11096-010-9466-x.

[46] Al-Ghamdi MS. Empirical treatment of uncomplicated urinary tract infection by community pharmacist in the Eastern province of Saudi Arabia. Saudi Med J 2001 Dec;22 (12):1105−8.

[47] Bozat E, Korubuk G, Onar P, Abbasoglu O. Cost analysis of premixed multichamber bags versus compounded parenteral nutrition: breakeven point. Hosp Pharm 2014 Feb;49 (2):170−6. Available from: http://dx.doi.org/10.1310/hpj4902-170.

[48] Altunsoy A, Aypak C, Azap A, Ergönül Ö, Balık I. The impact of a nationwide antibiotic restriction program on antibiotic usage and resistance against nosocomial pathogens in Turkey. Int J Med Sci 2011;8(4):339−44.

[49] Ozkurt Z, Erol S, Kadanali A, Ertek M, Ozden K, Tasyaran MA. Changes in antibiotic use, cost and consumption after an antibiotic restriction policy applied by infectious disease specialists. Jpn J Infect Dis 2005 Dec;58(6):338−43.

[50] El Hajj MS, Kheir N, Al Mulla AM, Al-Badriyeh D, Al Kaddour A, Mahfoud ZR, et al. Assessing the effectiveness of a pharmacist delivered smoking cessation program in the State of Qatar: study protocol for a randomized controlled trial. Trials 2015;16:65. Available from: http://dx.doi.org/10.1186/s13063-015-0570-z.

[51] Nunan M, Duke T. Effectiveness of pharmacy interventions in improving availability of essential medicines at the primary healthcare level. Trop Med Int Health 2011;16:647−58.

[52] Rotta I, Salgado TM, Silva ML, Correr CJ, Fernandez-Llimos F. Effectiveness of clinical pharmacy services: an overview of systematic reviews (2000−2010). Int J Clin Pharm 2015;37:687−97.

[53] Faden L, Vialle-Valentin C, Ross-Degnan D, Wagner A. Active pharmaceutical management strategies of health insurance systems to improve cost-effective use of medicines in low-and middle-income countries: a systematic review of current evidence. Health Policy 2011;100(2-3):134−43. Available from: http://dx.doi.org/10.1016/j.healthpol.2010.10.020 Epub 2010 Dec 24.

[54] Mori AT, Robberstad B. Pharmacoeconomics and its implication on priority-setting for essential medicines in Tanzania: a systematic review. BMC Med Inform Decis Mak 2012;27(12):110. Available from: http://dx.doi.org/10.1186/1472-6947-12-110.

[55] Pande S, Hiller Janet E, Nkansah N, Bero L. The effect of pharmacist-provided non-dispensing services on patient outcomes, health service utilisation and costs in low- and middle-income countries. Cochrane Database Syst Rev 2013;(2):CD010398.

[56] Babigumira JB, Stergachis A, Choi HL, Dodoo A, Nwokike J, Garrison Jr. LP. A framework for assessing the economic value of pharmacovigilance in low- and middle-income countries. Drug Saf 2014;37(3):127−34. Available from: http://dx.doi.org/10.1007/s40264-014-0143-1.

[57] Long E, Hu M, Tong R, Qin Y. Cost analysis of pharmaceutical service in hospital: a case study in a tertiary hospital in Sichuan, China. Value Health 2014;17(7):A792.

[58] Onda M, Kasuga M, Fujii S, Nanaumi Y, Imai H. Examining the effect of pharmacists' visits to homebound patients on the elimination of unused drugs—a report from a health and labour sciences study. Value Health 2014;17(3):A16.

[59] Alabid AH, Ibrahim MIM, Hassali MA. Dispensing practices of general practitioners and community pharmacists in Malaysia—a pilot study. J Pharm Pract Res 2013;43(3):187−9.

[60] Tachi T, Teramachi H, Asano S, Tanaka K, Fukuta M, Osawa T, et al. Impact of levofloxacin dose adjustments by dispensing pharmacists on adverse reactions and costs in the treatment of elderly patients. Pharmazie 2013;68(12):977−82.

[61] Miyawaki K, Miwa Y, Tomono K, Kurokawa N. The impact of antimicrobial stewardship by infection control team in a Japanese Teaching Hospital. Yakugaku Zasshi 2010;130 (8):1105−11.

[62] Imaura M, Kohata Y, Kobayashi K, Takahashi H, Yokoyama H, Akase T, et al. Effect of pharmacists' intervention on the antibiotic therapy for the methicillin-resistant *Staphylococcus aureus* (MRSA) infectious diseases in the intensive care unit. Yakugaku Zasshi 2011;131(4):563−70.

[63] Shikamura Y, Oyama A, Takahashi J, Akagi Y, Negishi K, Ijyuin K, et al. Medical economics research on awareness of community pharmacists about raising pharmaceutical questions regarding prescriptions issued by physicians. Yakugaku Zasshi 2012;132(6):753−61.

[64] Shi TL, Jiang L, Sun YC, Wu YQ, Huang Q. Roles of clinical pharmacists in prophylactic use of antibiotics during perioperative period in department of general surgery. Chin J New Drugs 2012;21(7):814−18.

[65] Gurumurthy P, Ramesh M. Impact of clinical pharmacist intervention on cost of drug therapy in intensive care units of a tertiary care teaching hospital. J Am Pharm Assoc 2011;51 (2):291−2.

[66] Li SC. An overview of community pharmacist interventions: assessing cost-effectiveness and patients' willingness to pay. Dis Manage Health Outcomes 2003;11(2):95−110.

[67] Jiang SP, Zheng X, Li X, Lu XY. Effectiveness of pharmaceutical care in an intensive care unit from China. A pre- and post-intervention study. Saudi Med J 2012;33(7):756−62.

[68] Jiang SP, Zhu ZY, Ma KF, Zheng X, Lu XY. Impact of pharmacist antimicrobial dosing adjustments in septic patients on continuous renal replacement therapy in an intensive care unit. Scand J Infect Dis 2013;45(12):891−9.

[69] Jiang SP, Zhu ZY, Wu XL, Lu XY, Zhang XG, Wu BH. Effectiveness of pharmacist dosing adjustment for critically ill patients receiving continuous renal replacement therapy: a comparative study. Ther Clin Risk Manage 2014;10(1):405−12.

[70] Shen J, Sun Q, Zhou X, Wei Y, Qi Y, Zhu J, et al. Pharmacist interventions on antibiotic use in inpatients with respiratory tract infections in a Chinese hospital. Int J Clin Pharm 2011;33(6):929−33.

[71] Xin C, Ge X, Yang X, Lin M, Jiang C, Xia Z. The impact of pharmaceutical care on improving outcomes in patients with type 2 diabetes mellitus from China: a pre- and post-intervention study. Int J Clin Pharm 2014;36(5):963−8.

[72] Zhang C, Zhang L, Huang L, Luo R, Wen J. Clinical pharmacists on medical care of pediatric inpatients: a single-center randomized controlled trial. PLoS One 2012;7(1):e30856.

[73] Zhang HX, Li X, Huo HQ, Liang P, Zhang JP, Ge WH. Pharmacist interventions for prophylactic antibiotic use in urological inpatients undergoing clean or clean-contaminated operations in a Chinese hospital. PLoS One 2014;9(2):e88971.

[74] Zhou Y, Ma LY, Zhao X, Tian SH, Sun LY, Cui YM. Impact of pharmacist intervention on antibiotic use and prophylactic antibiotic use in urology clean operations. J Clin Pharm Ther 2015;40(4):404−8.

[75] Chung JS, Lee KK, Tomlinson B, Lee VW. Clinical and economic impact of clinical pharmacy service on hyperlipidemic management in Hong Kong. J Cardiovasc Pharmacol Ther 2011;16(1):43−52.

[76] Ko GT, Yeung CY, Leung WY, Chan KW, Chung CH, Fung LM, et al. Cost implication of team-based structured versus usual care for type 2 diabetic patients with chronic renal disease. Hong Kong Med J 2011;17(Suppl 6):9−12. Available from: http://onlinelibrary. wiley.com/o/cochrane/clcentral/articles/108/CN-00920108/frame.html.

[77] Iihara H, Ishihara M, Matsuura K, Kurahashi S, Takahashi T, Kawaguchi Y, et al. Pharmacists contribute to the improved efficiency of medical practices in the outpatient cancer chemotherapy clinic. J Eval Clin Pract 2012;18(4):753−60.

[78] Ise Y, Onda M, Miura Y, Shimazaki M, Kawada K, Hagiwara K, et al. Contributions of pharmacists through the promotion of proper drug use. Yakugaku Zasshi 2007;127 (6):1021−5.

[79]   Yagi Y, Okazaki M, Higaki H, Nakai M, Hirata A, Miyamura M. Outcome evaluation of an intervention to improve the effective and safe use of meropenem. Int J Clin Pharm 2014;36(3):648—56.

[80]   Ahn S, Kim E, Kim S, La H. The cost-effectiveness evaluation for the pharmacist's therapeutic intervention in type-2 diabetes patients. J Korean Soc Health Syst Pharm 2011;28 (4):317—26.

[81]   Cho E, Yoo J, Lee E, Kim J, Sohn K, Choi K, et al. The effect of anticoagulation service on patient satisfaction and hospital profit. J Korean Soc Health Syst Pharm 1999;16 (2):214—24.

[82]   Han, JM. Effect of pharmacist interventions on optimizing patient-specific chemotherapy in high volume setting. Thesis. 2014.

[83]   Lee JH RJ, Suh YW, Lee JH, Lee ES, Lee BK, Kim KI. Assessment of medications for geriatric inpatients based on revised inappropriate medication criteria and cost avoidance by intervention of pharmacists. J Korean Soc Health Syst Pharm 2014;31(1): 629—37.

[84]   Mo YH, Rhee J, Lee EK. Effects of nutrition support team services on outcomes in ICU patients. Yakugaku Zasshi 2011;131(12):1827—33.

[85]   Park JA, Kim JH, Sohn YM, Lee YS, Lee YM. The cost effectiveness analysis of clinical pharmacokinetic consultation service by pharmacists for vancomycin. Journal of Korean Society of Health-System Pharmacists (JKSHP) 2012;29(2):107—20.

[86]   Park TKYH, Jung Y, Lee J, Lee E. The comparison analysis of the prevention of adverse drug events through order interventions by designated-pharmacists. J Korean Soc Health Syst Pharm 2014;31(1):638—43.

[87]   Sohn H, Shin H. Economic value of pharmaceutical care for the elderly patients in community pharmacies. Yakhak Hoeji 2007;51(5):327—35.

[88]   Chan AL, Hsieh HJ, Lin SJ. Pharmacist intervention in activated protein C therapy for severe sepsis: influence on health and economic outcomes. Int J Clin Pharmacol Ther 2009;47(4):229—35.

[89]   Chan ALF, Wang HY. Pharmacoeconomic assessment of clinical pharmacist interventions for patients with moderate to severe asthma in outpatient clinics: experience in Taiwan. Clin Drug Investig 2004;24(10):603—9.

[90]   Lee KL, Peng YL, Chou JL, Lee KT, Chung HM, Lee E. Economic evaluation of therapeutic drug monitoring services in renal transplant recipients treated with cyclosporine. Transplant Proc 2000;32(7):1801—6.

[91]   Lin YS, Lin IF, Yen YF, Lin PC, Shiu YC, Hu HY, et al. Impact of an antimicrobial stewardship program with multidisciplinary cooperation in a community public teaching hospital in Taiwan. Am J Infect Control 2013;41(11):1069—72.

[92]   Lu TH, Lee YY, Tsai SC, Chien HY, Chang JC, Tseng JH, et al. The outcome of clinical pharmacists' interventions in a Taiwanese hospital on pharmacoeconomics and cost saving. J Exp Clin Med (Taiwan) 2014;6(4):139—42.

[93]   Yen YH, Chen HY, Leu WJ, Lin YM, Shen WC, Cheng KJ. Clinical and economic impact of a pharmacist-managed i.v.-to-p.o. conversion service for levofloxacin in Taiwan. Int J Clin Pharmacol Ther 2012;50(2):136—41.

[94]   Lucca JM, Ramesh M, Narahari GM, Minaz N. Impact of clinical pharmacist interventions on the cost of drug therapy in intensive care units of a tertiary care teaching hospital. J Pharmacol Pharmacother 2012;3(3):242—7.

[95] Nasution A, Syed Sulaiman SA, Shafie AA. Cost-effectiveness of clinical pharmacy education on infection management among patients with chronic kidney disease in an Indonesian hospital. Value Health Reg Issues 2013;2(1):43−7.

[96] Hassan Y, Al-Ramahi RJ, Aziz NA, Ghazali R. Impact of a renal drug dosing service on dose adjustment in hospitalized patients with chronic kidney disease. Ann Pharmacother 2009;43(10):1598−605.

[97] Jing YS, Lai PSM, Siew SC, Siew PC. The impact of pharmacist intervention on the use of activated vitamin D in a tertiary referral hospital in Malaysia. Int J Pharm Pract 2009;17(5):305−11.

[98] Ping CC, Bahari MB, Hassali MA. A pilot study on generic medicine substitution practices among community pharmacists in the State of Penang, Malaysia. Pharmacoepidemiol Drug Saf 2008;17(1):82−9.

[99] Zahari Z. Non-standard drugs requests reviews: role of pharmacist at research and drug information unit (RDIU), hospital universiti sains Malaysia (HUSM). Asian J Pharmaceut Clin Res 2011;4(Suppl 2):37−9.

[100] Zaidi STR, Hassan Y, Postma MJ, Ng SH. Impact of pharmacist recommendations on the cost of drug therapy in ICU patients at a Malaysian hospital. Pharm World Sci 2003;25(6):299−302.

[101] Lim WS, Low HN, Chan SP, Chen HN, Ding YY, Tan TL. Impact of a pharmacist consult clinic on a hospital-based geriatric outpatient clinic in Singapore. Ann Acad Med Singapore 2004;33(2):220−7.

[102] Ratanajamit C, Kaewpibal P, Setthawacharavanich S, Faroongsarng D. Effect of pharmacist participation in the health care team on therapeutic drug monitoring utilization for antiepileptic drugs. J Med Assoc Thailand 2009;92(11):1500−7.

[103] Saokaew S, Maphanta S, Thangsomboon P. Impact of pharmacist's interventions on cost of drug therapy in intensive care unit. Pharm Pract 2009;7(2):81−7.

[104] Saokaew S, Permsuwan U, Chaiyakunapruk N, Nathisuwan S, Sukonthasarn A, Jeanpeerapong N. Cost-effectiveness of pharmacist-participated warfarin therapy management in Thailand. Thromb Res 2013;132(4):437−43.

[105] Sookaneknun P, Saramunee K, Rattarom R, Kongsri S, Senanok R, Pinitkit P, et al. Economic analysis of the diabetes and hypertension screening collaboration between community pharmacies and a Thai government primary care unit. Prim Care Diabetes 2010;4(3):155−64.

[106] Tasila J, Permsuwan U. Cost-benefit analysis of an intensive adverse product reactions monitoring program of inpatients in Thailand. Southeast Asian J Trop Med Public Health 2006;37(4):812−19.

[107] Thavorn K, Chaiyakunapruk N. A cost-effectiveness analysis of a community pharmacist-based smoking cessation programme in Thailand. Tob Control 2008;17 (3):177−82.

[108] Laing R. Health and pharmacy systems in developing countries. Paper presented Hosbjor, Norway. April 9, 2001.

[109] Schumock GT, et al. Economic evaluations of clinical pharmacy services—1988−1995. Pharmacotherapy 1996;16(6):1188−208.

[110] Schumock GT, et al. Evidence of the economic benefit of clinical pharmacy services: 1996−2000. Pharmacotherapy 2003;23(1):113−32.

[111]   Touchette DR, et al. Economic evaluations of clinical pharmacy services: 2006–2010. Pharmacotherapy 2014;34(8):771–93. Available from: http://dx.doi.org/ 10.1002/phar.1414.

[112]   Singer ME. Cost-effectiveness analysis developing nations left behind. Pharmacoeconomics 2008;26(5):359–61.

[113]   Villa LA, Skrepnek GH. Pharmacoeconomics and developing nations. Pharm Policy Law 2012;14(1):17–25.

[114]   Babar ZUD, et al. Is there a role for pharmacoeconomics in developing countries? Pharmacoeconomics 2010; Available from: http://dx.doi.org/10.2165/11584890-000000000-00000.

[115]   Whyte P, Hall C. The role of health technology assessment in medicine pricing and reimbursement. WHO/HAI Project on Medicine Prices and Availability. June 2013.

[116]   Briggs CJ, Garner P. Strategies for integrating primary health services in middle and low-income countries at the point of delivery (Review). Cochrane Library 2006, Issue 2. Published by John Wiley & Sons, Ltd.

[117]   Ayoub N. Point of care pharmacy service in oncology unit—clinical and economical outcomes. J Oncol Pharm Pract 2010;16(2):12–13.

[118]   Ayoub N. Impact of pharmacist interventions on 5HT3 antagonist prescribing and overall management of chemotherapy induced nausea and vomiting (CINV). J Oncol Pharm Pract 2012;18:3–4.

[119]   Chen CC, Lu TH, Liu YC, Chien SY, Chao MD, Leu WJ. Impact of pharmacist-led antimicrobial stewardship using a computerized system with prospective audit and feedback approach in a university hospital. Pharmacotherapy 2011;31(10):340e.

[120]   Chia HS, Ho J, Lim BDL. Pharmacist reviews and outcomes in nursing homes in Singapore. Ann Acad Med Singapore 2013;42(9):S78.

[121]   Chu LL, Lin HC, Huang HY, Chan AL. Outcome of pharmacist intervention in education of patients on duplicate prescribing hypnotic-sedatives. Value Health 2010;13(7):A560.

[122]   Dziehan M, Cheat WY, Thiruvanackan KAL, Azmiah N, Hui CB, Sariam N, et al. A prospective multicentre study of pharmacist initiated programme of 'Medication Therapy Management' (MTM) in government primary health clinic in the state of Selangor. Pharm World Sci 2009;31(4):498.

[123]   Heng SH, Gunn AKB, Liew HS. Effect of pharmacist interventions on cost of drug therapy in surgical wards. Med J Malaysia 2010;65:40.

[124]   Hsiao CL, Lin YM, Chang YT, Chen CC, Tsai CS, Liu HP. The financial impacts of pharmacist intervention in inpatient department of a local hospital in Taiwan. Value Health 2012;15(4):A24.

[125]   Kuo CN, Lee PY. Economical analysis of pharmacy intervention in the intensive care units in a medical center in Taiwan. Pharmacotherapy 2013;33(10):e227.

[126]   Li BK, Chee KS. Pharmacist-run medication management clinic in community wellness centre—a one-year review. Ann Acad Med Singapore 2010;39(11):S7.

[127]   Lim SH, Chen LL, Tee FMH, Ngan AMO, Kong MC. Evaluation of the economic impact of specialist outpatient clinic pharmacy interventions in a tertiary institution, Singapore. Value Health 2014;17(7):A790.

[128]   Lin CC, Tsai SC, Leu WJ, Lin YM. Impact of pharmacist intervention on the utilization of teriparatide in osteoporosis. Value Health 2012;15(4):A205.

[129] Lin HW, Lin CH, Chang CK, Yu IW, Lin CC, Li TC, et al. Economic, clinical and humanistic outcomes of a collaborative pharmacist-physician medication therapy management service for polypharmacy elderly. Value Health 2012;15(4):A24.

[130] Lin PT, Tai CL. The impact of clinical pharmacist on the medicine expenditure in the surgical intensive care unit. Pharmacoepidemiol Drug Saf 2014;23:475.

[131] Lin WC, Lee HC, Lin WL, Tai SH, Yeh FY, Chang HHJ. The positive impact of pharmacist on appropriateness of ambulatory prescriptions in medical center. Pharmacoepidemiol Drug Saf 2014;23:495.

[132] Lin YM, Tsai SC, Shiau YF, Leu WJ, Liu HP. The financial impact of medication reconciliation to reduce drug-related problems. Value Health 2010;13(3):A90.

[133] Lindenau R, McEvoy A. Evaluation of a pharmacist-implemented professional continuous glucose monitoring service at a primary care office. J Am Pharm Assoc 2015;55(2):e205.

[134] Liu KQL, Lu HP, Gong JR, Wong ICK, Chan EWY. Feasibility of pharmacist-participated anticoagulation management service (PAMS) in a regional hospital in Shanghai: a pilot study. Drug Saf 2014;37(10):878.

[135] Loganadan NK, Lim KY, Nur NM, Ariffin F. Cost-effectiveness of pharmacist managed medication therapy adherence clinic (MTAC) on type 2 diabetes patients in a Tertiary Hospital in Malaysia. Pharmacotherapy 2012;32(10):e270.

[136] Long E, Hu M, Tong R, Liu J. Pharmacoeconomics evaluation of clinical pharmacy service for diabetic inpatients. Value Health 2014;17(7):A744.

[137] Long E, Hu M, Tong R, Liu J, Zhang Z. Study on willingness to pay for the clinical pharmacy service for diabetes outpatients. Value Health 2014;17(3):A142.

[138] Low SF. The economic impact of nursing home medication reviews by pharmacists. Ann Acad Med Singapore 2011;40(11):S48.

[139] Ong KY, Chng SGJ, Chen LL, Cheen HHM, Lim SH, Lim PS, et al. Evaluation of a multidisciplinary home-based medication review program for elderly Singaporeans. Value Health 2014;17(7):A791.

[140] Pitakthum S. Evaluation of the impact of inpatient clinical pharmacy services on the quality and cost of pharmacotherapy in internal medicine wards. Value Health 2010;13 (7):A418.

[141] Sawatpanit A. Evaluation of octreotide cost after pharmaceutical care implementation at surgical ward. Value Health 2010;13(7):A532.

[142] Shiao-Feng H. Pharmaceutical care patients of chronic diseases with polypharmacy and cost saving. Value Health 2014;17(7):A763.

[143] Su HC, Chen CH, Chan AL. Cost of pharmaceutical care in patients with metabolic syndromes caused by atypical antipsychotics. Value Health 2010;13(3):A120.

[144] Su HC, Chen CH, Lin CA, Juang SY, Liang TC, Chan AL. Drug cost reduction in long-term care patients with chronic disease. Value Health 2010;13(7):A545.

[145] Su HC, Shen HC, Hu MH, Lin SC, Wang HY. To evaluate the effectiveness and cost of pharmaceutical care volunteer set up by Tainan city government involved in the hospital attached home care patients. Value Health 2012;15(7):A620.

[146] Suzuki S, Tahara M, Kobayashi T, Yajima Y, Sugiyama J, Ishiki H, et al. Pharmacist interventions lowers total cost of supportive medicines in head and neck induction cancer chemotherapy study: pilot study. Ann Oncol 2011;22:ix56.

[147] Tan CY, Lee JC, Lim HY, Lim CY. A prospective analysis of the medication review service at the Tan Tock Seng Hospital outpatient pharmacy from November 2008 to December 2009. Ann Acad Med Singapore 2010;39(11):S257.

[148]   Tan PS. Pharmacoeconomic evaluation of a pharmacist-managed diabetes clinic. Value Health 2011;14(3):A97.

[149]   Thanimalai S, Shafie AA, Ahmad Hassali MA, Sinnadurai J. Assessing the cost effectiveness of an anticoagulation clinic in comparison with the usual medical clinic in Kuala Lumpur Hospital. Value Health 2014;17(7):A487.

[150]   Tsai JD, Jseng JH, Chen CC. The impact of pharmacist-led antimicrobial stewardship in intensive care units in a regional hospital in Taiwan. Value Health 2012;15(7):A666.

[151]   Tsai YJ, Leu WJ, Lin YM, Lu TH. Pharmacist's involvement in a multidisciplinary ischemic stroke team in and its associated cost avoidance. Value Health 2012;15(7): A632.

[152]   Uaviseswong T, Chaikledkaew U, Tragulpiankit P. Cost-benefit analysis of pharmacist interventions related to determine preventable adverse drug reactions for hospitalized patients in Thailand. Drug Saf 2011;34(10):936–7.

[153]   Unahalekhaka A. Impact of collaborative quality improvement project on incidence and mortality of ventilator-associated pneumonia in 18 hospitals in Thailand. Am J Infect Control 2013;41(6):S105–6.

Chapter 4

Economic Evaluation and Its Types

D.M. Dawoud[1] and D.L. Baines[2]

[1]Cairo University, Cairo, Egypt, [2]Coventry University, Coventry, United Kingdom

Chapter Outline

INTRODUCTION

Economic evaluation is now a widely used technique. In this chapter, we introduce the basics of the approach and discuss how it may be employed in practice. We discuss the various forms of economic evaluation available, which include cost-minimization analysis (CMA), cost-effectiveness analysis (CEA), cost−benefit analysis (CBA), and cost−utility analysis (CUA). The aim of this chapter is to explain the basic building blocks of these forms of economic evaluation. To achieve this aim, we will pursue the following learning objectives:

1. What is economics and how does it guide how health economists work?
2. What costs should be measured, given a study's chosen perspective?

3. Should health be measured in terms of intermediate or final outcomes?
4. How should outcomes be measured and valued in economic evaluation studies?
5. What are the differences between the different methods of economic evaluation?
6. What is incremental analysis and how should uncertainty be represented?

To begin, let us examine how economists think when undertaking their work.

THE LOGIC OF HEALTH ECONOMICS AND ECONOMIC EVALUATION

Health economists are concerned with analyzing choices about the best use of scarce healthcare resources. Their work is underpinned by the concept of the "health production function" (Fig. 4.1).

As the health production function shows, healthcare interventions may be judged in terms of the costs of their inputs and the value of their outcomes. Health economists evaluate the relative efficiency of competing treatments by comparing their inputs to their outcomes.

Setting the Scene

Before we explain how health economists undertake an economic evaluation, it is useful to ask the question: What is economics? One popular definition states:

Economics is the science which studies human behaviour as a relationship between ends and scarce means which have alternative uses.

Robbins, p. 16 [1]

In this definition, the main elements of economic analysis are included:

1. *Scientific methods*: Economics is based upon the scientific approach of identifying a testable hypothesis, gathering the relevant data, and performing statistical analysis.
2. *Decision-making*: Economics is an aid to decision-making. Economists do not make decisions themselves. They just provide the supporting evidence so decisions may be made.
3. *Alternatives*: Decision-makers must choose between available options. Part of the job of the economist is to identify and to outline the feasible alternatives.

FIGURE 4.1 The health production function.

4. *Efficiency*: Economists must define what is meant by efficiency in a given context and support decision-makers trying to make optimal choices about resource use.
5. *Scarcity*: Resources available to improve patient health are always limited. They should be used in ways that improve efficiency.

ECONOMIC EVALUATION

Economic evaluation generates evidence to guide choices about the allocation of scarce resources. Formally, "economic evaluation" may be defined as:

> *The comparative analysis of alternative courses of action in terms of both their costs and consequences.*
>
> Drummond et al., p. 4 [2]

This definition suggests that a full economic evaluation of healthcare programs must:

- evaluate at least two alternatives, including all relevant options such as "do nothing" or "current practice/usual care,"
- assess both inputs (costs) and outputs (consequences) in terms of resource use and health gain.

When performed properly, economic evaluations provide decision-makers with structured, rigorous evidence for assessing the relative efficiency of competing healthcare interventions. However, best practice suggests that an economic evaluation is best undertaken after the following studies have been performed:

- Studies to assess whether the intervention can work (i.e., its efficacy).
- Studies to assess whether it does any harm (i.e., its safety).
- Studies to assess whether the intervention works in practice (i.e., its effectiveness).

These preliminary studies establish whether an intervention is safe and effective before the economic evaluation is executed. Once this has been established, we can consider conducting the economic evaluation. This will involve two steps: (1) measuring costs and outcomes and (2) combining both costs and outcomes to assess cost-effectiveness. In the next sections, we will cover these steps in detail.

MEASURING COSTS

Costs in economic studies are usually divided into two main types:

Direct costs: These are the costs of resources consumed during treatment. Direct costs can be incurred by social services, healthcare systems, and/or patients. They can be fixed, semi-fixed, or variable [2]. Fixed costs are those generated regardless of the numbers of patients treated. The largest components of the fixed costs are capital (e.g., buildings and equipment) and overheads (e.g., lighting, heating, and cleaning). Variable costs are those costs that vary with activity. These include any form of intervention or consumables expended during patient care (for instance, drugs, blood products, investigations, and physician time). Finally, semi-fixed costs are those that tend to increase in response to large changes in an activity. Staff costs can be an example of semi-fixed costs (unless they vary directly with activity, when they should be considered as variable costs).

Indirect costs: The biggest component of these costs relates to loss of production due to time off-work which results from illness or its treatment. It is usually referred to as "productivity costs." The importance of productivity costs is largely dependent on the disease area being considered. When considering diseases affecting working-age groups, indirect costs would be considered an important cost component. Examples include low back pain, asthma, depression, and migraine. Indirect costs are considered less important in diseases of the older age groups because the costs of not working are less. There are two major approaches to valuing indirect costs: (1) the human capital approach and (2) the friction method [3]. The differences between the estimates obtained from the two approaches are more substantial in case of long-term illness or early retirement than in the case of short periods of absence from work. The decision regarding which categories of costs to include in an evaluation depends upon the perspective of the evaluation.

Perspective

When performing an economic evaluation, the perspective taken affects how costs are measured. In formal terms, the "perspective" of an evaluation may be defined as the "view point from which the economic analysis is conducted" [2]. If the viewpoint of the analysis changes, the cost categories included in the analysis should alter. For instance, costs from the perspective of the individual paying privately for care is likely to differ from those from the perspective of the healthcare commissioner paying for care for the whole local population. In standard economic evaluations, the following perspectives are usually considered:

- Societal perspective: where all costs are included.
- Healthcare perspective: includes only the costs of healthcare services.
- Patient perspective: only the costs of services paid for privately by the patient are included.

As this list suggests, the perspective taken should determine how costs are measured. As well as the standard ones listed above, other valid perspectives could include "provider," "pharmacy," or "insurance" perspective. Again, these alternatives require measuring costs in different ways and are likely to result in different estimates of resource use. In most economic evaluations of healthcare programs, only direct costs are considered. The indirect loss to society due to reduced participation in the workforce is usually ignored. The following types of direct costs are usually included in an evaluation:

1. *Health sector costs*: these include resources expended in overheads, staffing, and treatment. For example, pharmacist time, drugs, hospital stay, surgeries, primary care visits, facilities, and administration.
2. *Costs in other sectors*: these include non-healthcare resources. For example, resources expended by social services, criminal justice, and voluntary sector.
3. *Costs to patient/family members*: resources paid for by individuals and their families. For example, travel, child care, out-of-pocket expenses, and carers' time.

The resources consumed in each of these categories are usually identified, measured, and valued. This process involves, first, stating what resources should be included. For instance, doctor and nurse time. Second, measuring patient consumption of units of these different resource types. For instance, the number of hours of a senior doctor's time engaged. Then, the units of resource consumed should be multiplied by weights that reflect national prices for these resources. For instance, an hour of senior doctor time may cost £120 at national pay rates (even though some providers may pay more or less depending upon local market conditions). Costs derived in this manner may not be the same individual commissioners pay for the identified services. Indeed, health economists view costs as *price weighted resource units* rather than *actual spends in actual markets*.

Opportunity Cost

According to many health economists, the resources consumed during patient care should be valued at their "opportunity cost" [4]. The opportunity cost of choosing one alternative over another is the benefits scarified by not pursuing the next best alternative. For instance, the cost of providing a drug utilization review for one patient should be judged in terms of the health gain sacrificed by other patients who, as a result, cannot have their medicine regimes examined. In other words, the resources used for one purpose cannot be used for another. In a health context, examples of "opportunity cost" are many. For example, opting to fund more surgeries eliminates the resources available for preventative interventions. The opportunity cost of funding one heart bypass operation could be the benefits lost from (for example) providing 100 vaccinations for Measles, Mumps, and Rubella. In this example, unvaccinated children pay for the bypass operation in terms of their lost health.

Time Horizon

When capturing the costs and benefits of an intervention, economic evaluations must account for differences in resource use and health gain over time. For instance, some interventions may have an instant, profound effect, which soon tails off. Others may have a smaller impact that lasts for longer. Therefore, economic evaluators must decide how long the costs and the outcomes of an intervention should be tracked? In other words, they must choose the "time horizon," which is defined as the "length of time over which costs and consequences are assessed." As a guiding principle, the time horizon of an evaluation should be long enough to capture significant differences in costs and consequences between the interventions being compared. If the chosen time horizon does not reflect the observed pattern of costs and consequences, then the results of an economic evaluation are likely to be unreliable. Therefore, choosing the correct time horizon is vital to a study's success. If the length of a trial is too short and fails to capture the full costs and the full benefits of an intervention, health economists call this situation "censoring" because important data has been suppressed by poor study design.

Discounting

Because resources have different values now compared to the future, the costs and benefits should be "discounted." Resources and outcomes that accrue beyond the first year should be discounted to their "net present value." Making future costs and consequences reflect their current value in this way ensures that studies reflect "positive time preference." This refers to our preference as individuals to consume benefits now but pay for them later [4]. In most studies, the "discount rate" is usually set between 0% and 6%. In the United Kingdom, for instance, the chosen discount rate is often 3.5%, which is based upon Treasury guidelines. Studies that fail to discount both costs and benefits will be seen as failing to meet the required standards for economic analysis.

MEASURING OUTCOMES

The outcomes used in economic evaluations should ideally reflect final health outcomes rather than intermediate clinical markers. This is in contrast to clinical practice, where the focus is usually on measuring intermediate physiological indicators. It is usually straightforward to decide on a final outcome measure for acute conditions, as interventions are usually curative (e.g., the use of antibiotics to cure respiratory tract infections). For chronic conditions, the use of intermediate indicators is more prevalent. If intermediate markers are used, this should be on the basis that they are surrogates for final outcomes. For example, the level of glycated hemoglobin (HbA1c) is a diabetes outcome that has a validated link to overall health and quality of life. Importantly, the choice of an outcome defines the type of the economic evaluation that may be employed. Therefore, we will describe the different outcomes that can be used in economic evaluations because the choice of outcomes measured will determine the type of studies performed.

Physiological Measures and Clinical Events

Physiological measures are disease-specific outcome measures. Physiological measures such as cholesterol levels, blood pressure (BP), and bone density are widely used in clinical practice. The link between such measures and clinical events has been widely accepted in the clinical community. For example, high BP is known to be a risk factor for stroke. The availability of such data allows intermediate outcomes to be reliably used in economic evaluations of interventions designed to prevent undesirable clinical events. Fig. 4.2 illustrates this concept.

Risk functions estimate the risk of clinical events as a function of the level of the physiological measure; controlling for other epidemiological factors such as age, gender, race, etc. This allows an economic evaluation to be undertaken to assess the cost-effectiveness of using the intervention to reduce the risk of an unwanted event. However, the ultimate aim is not only to avoid these events but to avoid their "consequences" in terms of disability or death. Therefore, intermediate outcomes do not capture the final outcome—i.e., health—that patients wish to improve or maintain. Therefore, generic measures of health such as survival or quality of life (QoL) are usually preferred.

Survival

Survival data are usually collected in randomized controlled trials (RCTs). They are normally expressed as the proportion of patients alive at the end of

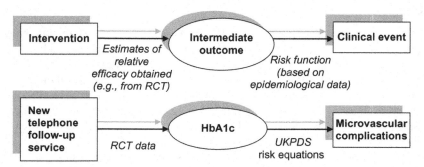

FIGURE 4.2 Linking intermediate to final outcomes. *UKPDS*,UK Prospective Diabetes Study; *RCTs*, randomized clinical trials.

a trial, the number of deaths averted, or (more commonly) the number of life years saved (LYS). As clinical trials may only last for a short period of time, extrapolating beyond the trial period might be needed to assess longer term outcomes.

Quality of Life

When evaluating interventions aimed at reducing the burden of chronic diseases, the primary objective may not be improving survival but rather improving patient functioning in terms of mental state and physical abilities. Therefore, outcome measures must be able to capture improvements across these dimensions. Within health economics, QoL measures have been developed that can complete this task of capturing health-related quality of life (HRQoL). Such measures usually follow the World Health Organization (WHO) definition of "health" being a "combination of physical, mental and social wellbeing, not merely the absence of disease" [5].

Measures of HRQoL can either be generic or disease specific [6]. Disease-specific measures focus on dimensions of the patient QoL related to a particular condition. For example, the Beck Depression Inventory (BDI) and the Multiple Sclerosis Quality of Life Inventory (MSQLI). These measures have the advantage of being more sensitive to the impact of particular diseases. However, they cannot be used for decision-making regarding the allocation of resources across more than one condition. For instance, the BDI cannot be used to compare outcomes measured with, for instance, the MSQLI. In comparison, generic measures of HRQoL do not focus on particular diseases but rather on the general dimensions of health such as depression, pain, mobility, etc. These measures are less sensitive to changes in patient disease status. Commonly used versions of this class of instruments include the Short Form-36, the Nottingham Health Profile, the Sickness Impact Profile, and the General Wellbeing Scale.

Utility

Utility is another generic measure that can be used to compare outcomes across different patient groups and disease areas. It may be defined as the "value a person places on a particular health state or health outcome" [6]. This valuation will differ from one person to another. Therefore, individuals can value different health states based on their own preferences. Usually, the utility scale ranges from 0 (the value attached to being dead) to 1 (the value attached to being in full health). Utility values can also be negative, when a health state is valued as being worse than death.

In economic evaluations, utility data are usually collected using "off-the-shelf" questionnaires that have: (1) a descriptive system that outlines the various health states and (2) an accompanying "tariff" with utility values attached to each health state. An example of a preference-based, prescored generic measure is the Euroqol-5D. This is one of the most widely used of such measures (see http://www.euroqol.org/).

As well as off-the-shelf valuation systems, it is possible to elicit health state preferences directly using a direct valuation technique deigned to elicit preferences. Two stages are involved in the process of direct elicitation: (1) describing the health state to the individual, then (2) eliciting their preference for being in this particular health state. The simplest method of eliciting preferences and measuring values is through the use of a rating scale such as the Visual Analogue Scale (VAS). As Fig. 4.3 illustrates, participants in a study can be asked to indicate where on the VAS their current health state (or a health state described to them) should be recorded.

Although informative, the values obtained using VAS are not utilities because they do not involve making a choice, between alternatives. In economic evaluation studies, the preferred methods for measuring utilities are the Standard Gamble (SG) or the Time Trade-Off (TTO) methods [2].

The SG method is the one preferred by health economists because it is based on making choices and taking risks. The method involves offering respondents two alternatives:

1. The first alternative has two possible outcomes which are: (1) living in full health (with probability p) or (2) immediate death (with probability $1-p$).
2. The second alternative has one certain outcome of living in the health state you are valuing, "h," as a chronic condition, for the remaining years of life.

The interviewer varies the probability p until the respondent is indifferent between the two alternatives. At this point, the utility attached to the chronic health state, h, is considered to be equivalent to p. This is calculated by assigning a utility value of 0 to death and 1 to being in full health. At the point of indifference, the utility of the first alternative ($1^*p + 0^*[1 - p] = p$) is equivalent to the utility of the second alternative (utility of health state "h"). Fig. 4.4 illustrates a classic SG.

In the TTO method, the respondent is offered two alternatives:

1. Alternative 1 is full health for time "X" (where $X < t$) followed by death.
2. Alternative 2 is to remain in health state "h" for time t (life expectancy the condition of interest) followed by death.

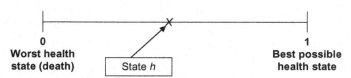

FIGURE 4.3 Example of VAS.

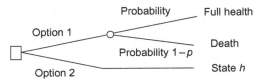

FIGURE 4.4   SG method.

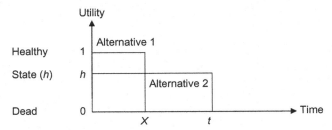

FIGURE 4.5   TTO method.

In this approach, X is varied until the respondent is indifferent between the two alternatives. At the indifference point, the utility of state "h" is given by X/t. At the point of indifference, the following holds:

$$\text{Utility of full health } (1)^*X = \text{Utility of state } h^*t$$

Therefore,

$$\text{Utility of state } h = X/t$$

Fig. 4.5 illustrates the TTO method.

Quality-Adjusted Survival

Given the importance of both survival and QoL, the use of an outcome measure that encompasses both is preferable. The quality-adjusted life year (QALY) is a generic outcome measure that captures both length of life (i.e., survival) and QoL (expressed in terms of utilities). For example, 1 year lived in full health is equal to $1^*1 = 1$ QALY. In contrast, 1 year lived with 0.5 utility is $1^*0.5 = 0.5$ QALY.

The QALY is a preferred measure for many healthcare decision-makers because it can be used for comparisons across different diseases. Alternative measures include the healthy years equivalent (HYE) and the disability-adjusted life year (DALY). These alternative measures are often used outside economic evaluation studies. For instance, DALYs have been used in international comparisons by the WHO to estimate the burden of disease [7].

Monetary Outcomes

It is also possible to express the outcomes of interventions in terms of individual or society willingness to pay for specific outcomes. Two possible approaches to valuing health outcomes in money terms are [8]:

- *The human capital approach*: where earnings are used as a measure of health benefit. For example, if one intervention allows an individual to remain in work for a greater number of years than another, the difference in earnings is used to estimate the money value of the differential health gain.
- *The willingness to pay approach*: an individual's willingness to pay for a particular amount of health gain is used to approximate its monetary value. This technique is also called Contingent Valuation. It seeks to elicit how much an individual would be willing to pay to avoid an illness or particular side effects, or to receive a specific set of health benefits.

COMBINING COSTS AND OUTCOMES USING INCREMENTAL ANALYSIS

Economic evaluation is not concerned with the absolute values of costs and outcomes. For instance, knowing that a single intervention A has a cost of £12,000 and a gain of 0.5 QALYs does not help decision-makers because this information includes no comparison. Therefore, most economic evaluations compare the cost-effectiveness of an intervention with one (or more) alternative(s). To do so, an incremental cost-effectiveness ratio (ICER) is calculated. As Eq. (4.1) shows, the mean cost (C_i) and mean effect (E_i) for each intervention is calculated and compared as follows:

$$\text{ICER} = \frac{C_B - C_A}{E_B - E_A} \tag{4.1}$$

The ICER values are usually presented graphically on a cost-effectiveness plane (Fig. 4.6), where the "anchor point" is provided by the costs and effects for intervention A. In this diagram, effects are presented on the X-axis and costs on the Y-axis. Hence, any intervention that appears higher than A will have higher costs. Similarly, any intervention that appears below will be cheaper. On the effects side, any intervention that exists to the right of A will have higher benefits. Any intervention to the left will produce lower benefits. The slope of the line connecting interventions A and B is equal to the ICER of B versus A.

The results of the comparison of B versus A can appear in any of the four quadrants. In the South East quadrant, the new intervention (B) is more effective and less costly than the comparator (A) and is said to be "dominant." Therefore, cost-effectiveness is automatically demonstrated. In the North West quadrant, the new intervention is more costly and less

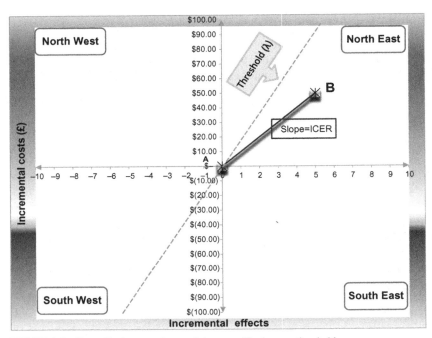

FIGURE 4.6 Cost-effectiveness plane and the cost-effectiveness threshold.

effective, so is "dominated" by the comparator (A). Hence, the intervention is not cost-effective. In the North East and South West quadrants, the new intervention is either more effective but more costly or less effective and less costly. In both cases, further consideration will be required to assess whether the gain in outcomes is worth the extra cost. This requires setting a willingness-to-pay or cost-effectiveness threshold (denoted by λ) for the decision-maker.

Although the ICER is a popular analytical tool, the use of a ratio in analyzing cost-effectiveness data can be problematic. In particular, ratios can be unstable at extreme values. Also, the ICER formula is often unable to differentiate between identical coordinates with positive and negatives values such as $(-1, -2)$ compared to $(1, 2)$. Stinnett and Mullahy [9] examined the problems of the ICER and proposed an alternative measure based upon average net health benefits (NHBs).

$$\text{NHB}_A = E_A - C_A/\lambda \qquad (4.2)$$

As Eq. (4.2) shows, the average NHB of intervention A may be calculated by taking the difference between average effects and average costs for intervention A, and using the threshold (λ) as a weighting that converts costs into effects. This approach solves the problems associated with the ICER. Using the

NHB approach, two interventions may be compared. The incremental NHB (INHB) of intervention B versus intervention A is:

$$\text{INHB}_{\text{BA}} = (E_B - E_A) - [(C_B - C_A)/\lambda] \tag{4.3}$$

As this formula suggests, incremental cost-effectiveness can be calculated in terms of NHBs. The first part of the equation ($E_B - E_A$) represents the difference in health benefits produced by the two interventions. The second part ($C_B - C_A$)/λ represents the health gain that could have been produced if incremental costs were converted into health gain at the rate given by lambda (λ). Therefore, the total formula gives the incremental net health gain produced by the comparative technologies and may be used in healthcare decision-making. Similarly, Net Monetary Benefit (NMB) can be calculated and compared between interventions, by calculating incremental NMB.

DECISION RULES

Economic evaluations are performed to provide information for decision-makers. By themselves, health economists do not make choices about the allocation of scarce resources. Consequently, the analyst must know what "decision rule" will be employed by decision-makers in making resource allocation decisions. For instance, choosing interventions that maximize clinical effectiveness is a possible decision rule. The decision rule usually chosen by health economists is dominance in terms of incremental cost-effectiveness. In other words, any intervention that has a "dominant" or superior ICER relative to its competitors should be chosen. In all forms of economic analysis, information is constructed to support the use of a specific decision rule.

For instance, the ICER may be used as a decision rule to establish dominance. To support the analysis, societal values may be included in the form of a value for the cost-effectiveness threshold. In absence of clear dominance, societal cost-effectiveness thresholds create a decision rule which stipulates that any intervention with an ICER below the threshold value should be funded. In contrast, any intervention with an ICER above the required threshold should not be adopted for use. In other words, any intervention with incremental costs and effects lying to the right of the threshold illustrated in Fig. 4.6 should be adopted.

Assessing Uncertainty

Although the ICER, NHBs and other tools have been developed to aid decision-makers, they are based on average or mean values of costs and effects. While incremental differences in average cost-effectiveness are important, point estimates of economic values fail to take account of any uncertainty surrounding the results. As most studies are sampling unknown

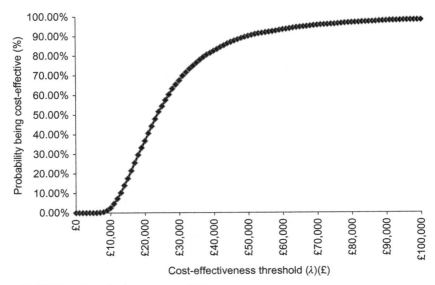

FIGURE 4.7   Cost-effectiveness acceptability curve.

population data, the mean value sampled could vary in future sampling. Therefore, there is "uncertainty" in the cost-effectiveness estimates that studies produce. In response, confidence intervals (CIs) could be fitted around the mean values of ICER and NHB calculations. As fitting CIs can be problematic, many health economists use the cost-effectiveness acceptability curve (CEAC) to represent uncertainty in the joint distribution of costs and benefits [10]. The CEAC is constructed by plotting the proportion of cost and effect pairs that are cost-effective for a given range of "λ" (Fig. 4.7). The construction process starts by calculating this proportion when the slope is zero (i.e., equivalent to the X-axis). Then the process is continuously repeated for increasing values of "λ".

In health economic analysis, the CEAC indicates the probability that an intervention is cost-effective compared with its alternative, given the observed cost and effects, under different values of "λ." The CEAC presents the probability that an intervention is cost-effective, given different degrees of uncertainty. The decision to adopt a technology should not be based solely upon the CEAC. The results of the main analysis using ICERs or NHBs should be the main driver of adoption decisions. Using the CEAC as the means of deciding whether to recommend a treatment or not is a common mistake and should be avoided. The CEAC can only represent uncertainty, the diagram cannot tell decision-makers which technology to adopt. Choices about adoption must be based upon the point estimates of analysis such as an incremental NHB calculation.

TYPES OF ECONOMIC EVALUATIONS

In all types of economic evaluation, costs are measured in the same way. So, the type of evaluation performed is largely determined by the type of outcomes that studies wish to capture. The following are the main types of economic evaluation, with a comparison of the outcomes they measure:

- CMA: where outcomes are assumed to be equal.
- CEA: where outcomes are measured as natural/physical units.
- CUA: where outcomes are measured using a generic measure such as the QALY.
- CBA: where benefits are expressed in monetary terms.

Below, we introduce these main types of economic evaluations and give examples of their use in evaluating pharmacy/pharmacist-delivered services.

Cost-Minimization Analysis

The use of CMA requires evidence that the interventions compared are identical in terms of outcomes. If this is the case, then only costs are compared. The term "comparative cost analysis" is sometimes used to describe this type of analysis. The assumption of equivalence in outcomes is a very strong one to make, given that comparators are unlikely to be completely identical in their effects. An example of a CMA study is comparing the cost of administering the same medication in different settings. For example, home administration of antibiotics for cystic fibrosis compared with inpatient treatment. Another example is the comparison of a proprietary drug with its generic equivalent. To be valid, CMA requires outcomes to be 100% equivalent in such studies. However, it is easy to see how home administration could produce different health outcomes than inpatient treatment. Similarly, generics may not be clinically equivalent to their reference standards. In such instances, CMA is a partial rather than a full economic evaluation. In response, many health technology assessment agencies across the world are reluctant to accept economic evaluations of this type as evidence of value for money [11]. Box 4.1 includes some examples of studies that used CMA to evaluate pharmacy and pharmacist services.

Cost-Effectiveness Analysis

In a CEA, outcomes are measured using natural units (e.g., number of symptom free days, strokes avoided, and life years gained). Intermediate outcomes can also be used (reduction in BP (mmHg) or reduction in blood glucose levels), if they can be linked to health outcomes. A single outcome measure is used in cost-effectiveness studies. If more than one outcome is considered, the evaluation is considered to be a cost-consequences analysis (CCA). Using CEA, it is not possible to compare different clinical areas that do not have the same primary outcome. CEA does not allow studies to

BOX 4.1 Examples of CMA

Armour et al. [12] compared the costs of a pharmacy-based central intravenous additive service (CIVAS) with those of traditional ward-based preparation of intravenous doses for a pediatric population. The analysis involved comparing the costs of labor, disposables, and diluents as well as the costs avoided as a result of using part-vials in CIVAS.

Data were collected for 20 CIVAS sessions (501 doses) and 26 ward-based sessions (30 doses). The results showed that the pharmacy-based CIVAS was cost saving ($p < 0.001$). Sensitivity analysis was conducted to test the robustness of the results to assumptions relating to the skill-mix. This showed that the cost saving was maintained over a full range of skill mixes.

Scott et al. [13] conducted a CMA alongside multicenter RCT of a community pharmacy medication management service (MEDMAN) in the United Kingdom with 12-month follow-up. The sample size was 1480 (980 intervention and 500 control). The intervention involved initial consultation at study start, with further consultations based on pharmacist-determined need. Significant differences were not found in any of the clinical outcomes including appropriate medications as defined by the National Service Framework and self-reported medication compliance. This was given as the rationale for using a CMA rather than a CEA, although the point estimate showed improvement in QoL. Comparing costs only showed that total cost for intervention subjects was higher, controlling for baseline differences ($p = 0.001$).

Perraudin et al. [14] compared home-based subcutaneous immunoglobulin (SCIg) therapy to hospital-based intravenous infusions (IVIg) with support from a multidisciplinary team including a pharmacist from a societal perspective in Switzerland. The study follow-up was 3 years. The program provided long-term support from self-administration training to the responsible use of therapy (proper adherence, optimal efficacy, and safety). The authors report that over the short term, additional costs from purchasing equipment and the drug therapy management program were offset by avoiding hospital costs.

combine more than one measure of outcome. For example, impact on quantity and quality of life cannot be considered at the same time (Box 4.2).

Cost–Utility Analysis

In CUA, outcomes are assessed using generic measures such as the QALYs. CUA is sometimes considered a special type of CEA, and some researchers use the terms interchangeably. CUA has two main advantages over other forms of economic evaluation. First, it uses measures that combine length and quality-of-life. Second, the use of a standardized, generic measure enables economic comparisons across different disease areas with very different clinical outcomes. Consequently, decision-makers, such as the UK's NICE, prefer this method because it facilitates choices about budget allocation across the whole spectrum of disease areas (Box 4.3).

BOX 4.2 Examples of CEA and CCA

Polgreen et al. [15] reported the results of a CEA conducted alongside a clinical trial (The Collaboration Among Pharmacist and Physicians to Improve Blood Pressure Now trial). The aim was to assess the cost-effectiveness of physician–pharmacist collaboration to improve hypertension control. The outcomes in the trial were the reduction in systolic and diastolic BP and proportion of patients with controlled BP. The costs included were those of medications and pharmacist and physician time. The results were reported in terms of the cost per unit reduction in BP. These showed that the collaborative intervention achieved better control of BP (average systolic BP was 6.1 mmHg lower (±3.5), diastolic was 2.9 mmHg lower (±1.9)) but had higher costs (a difference of $202.93). This means that the cost to lower BP by 1 mmHg was $33.27 for systolic BP and $69.98 for diastolic BP. The authors concluded that this collaborative service was cost-effective.

Elliot et al. [16] conducted a CEA alongside a RCT of a community pharmacy-based service, for patients prescribed new medication, compared to usual care. Patients were aged 75 years or older or suffering from stroke, cardiovascular disease, asthma, diabetes or rheumatoid arthritis, and on four or more medications. The intervention consisted of two community pharmacists trained using the self-regulatory model theory delivered intervention consisting of a telephone call to the patient 2 weeks after recruitment to enquire about how they were getting on with their medication using a semi-structured interview format. The main outcome measure was patient adherence to medication. The authors reported improvement in adherence to newly prescribed medication in the intervention group (89% vs 81%) in addition to cost saving compared to usual care (£188 vs £283 vs mean total costs per patient).

Desborough et al. [17] conducted a CCA of the Norfolk Medicines Support Service which was an adherence focused, pharmacist-led medication review service provided by community pharmacists. Patients 65 years or older and registered with a GP in Norfolk, residing in their own home, were referred to the service by anyone in their care that identified they were having difficulties managing their medication. The main health outcomes assessed in the study were HRQoL and adherence. Service provision, prescribing, and secondary care costs were considered. The results showed that the intervention reduced emergency hospital admissions and increased medication adherence but no significant change in HRQoL was observed. The costs of providing this medication review service were offset by the reduction in emergency hospital admissions and savings in medication cost, with a saving in the mean total cost per patient of £307 (95% CI: £1296–£655).

Lalonde et al. [18] conducted a CCA to evaluate pharmacist follow-up of patients receiving anticoagulants compared to normal physician follow-up. The outcomes assessed included quality of international normalized ratio (INR) control, incidence of complications, HRQoL, use of healthcare services. The study was a RCT. The results showed that pharmacist-managed patients have seen their family physician less often (95% CI −3.1 to −0.1 visits per year). Number of INR tests, incidence of complications, and HRQoL were similar in both groups. The incremental cost of the follow-up service was estimated at CAN$123.80 per patient year.

BOX 4.3 Examples of CUA

Sullivan et al. [19] evaluated the lifetime costs and benefits of managing warfarin therapy to prevent strokes in elderly patients with atrial fibrillation. They compared usual care versus anticoagulation management services, where dedicated anticoagulation professionals monitor and oversee patients. The analysis was conducted from a societal perspective. Health outcomes were measured in terms of QALYs gained. Utility values were based on a large national survey. Costs were expressed in US$ and included drugs (such as warfarin and aspirin), INR monitoring, lab and imaging investigations, clinic visits, and resource use associated with major bleeding and treatment of primary events. The results were improved effectiveness by a mean of 0.057 QALYs and reduced costs by a mean of US$2100 saving (2004 values) compared with usual care. The study suggests that anticoagulation clinic management was dominant (i.e., more effective and less costly) compared to usual care.

The RESPECT trial team [20] conducted a CUA to evaluate the provision of medication reviews in community pharmacists. The intervention was provided by pharmacists who received training that covered the theory and practice of pharmaceutical care, practical exercises in collaborating with the GPs. Training took place just before the start of each 12 months period. Forty-five practices and 62 community pharmacists participated in the study. The primary outcome assessed in this evaluation was QALYs-gained. The results showed the intervention to be more costly (incremental cost: £192; 95% CI: −£150 to £579) and more effective (incremental QALYs: 0.019; 95% CI: −0.023 to 0.102) with an ICER of £10,000 per QALY gained. Thus, the intervention was considered to be cost-effective, where the ICER is less than the UK NICE cost-effectiveness threshold of £20,000 to £30,000 per QALY-gained.

Wallerstedt et al. [21] conducted a CUA alongside a RCT to assess the cost-effectiveness of a clinical pharmacist service at two internal medicine wards at a university hospital in Sweden. The intervention was a composite in-hospital clinical pharmacist service (medication reviews, drug treatment discussion with the patient at discharge, and a medication report). The main health outcome in the economic evaluation was the number of QALYs gained. The results showed that although the intervention patients gained an additional 0.0035 QALYs on average, with an incremental cost of €1622 per patient, the intervention was not considered to be cost-effective as this resulted in an ICER of €463,371 per adjusted QALY gained. The probabilistic uncertainty analysis revealed that, at a willingness-to-pay threshold of €50,000/QALY, the probability that the intervention was cost-effective was approximately 20%.

Cost−Benefit Analysis

In CBA, outcomes are valued in monetary terms, where money values are attached to the health states resulting from the interventions being compared. To be considered a CBA, formal assessment of willingness to pay for the outcomes should be undertaken using recognized elicitation methods.

Formal methods for eliciting preferences may measure either stated or revealed preferences [22]. These methods include conjoint analysis using Discrete Choice Experiments. CBA is useful for the allocation of resources on the macro-level (e.g., allocating funding across healthcare programs) because it gives a net return on investment that can be compared across all programs. In CBA, a societal perspective is used for costing. However, CBA is rarely used in healthcare evaluations due to the lack of acceptability of assigning monetary value to health outcomes and the majority of the studies that claim to be a CBA are in reality not considered to be so.

SUMMARY

In this chapter, we introduced the theoretical basis of economic evaluation. We introduced the building blocks required for conducting economic evaluation studies, namely: measuring costs and outcomes. We also explained how decision rules may be used in judging cost-effectiveness and how decision-makers may use them to reach decisions regarding the adoption of new interventions. Finally, we discussed the different types of economic evaluations and gave examples of their use in the evaluation of pharmacy services.

REFERENCES

[1]   Robbins L. An essay on the nature and significance of economic science. London: Macmillan; 1932.

[2]   Drummond M, Sculpher M, Claxton K, Stoddart G, Torrance G. Methods for the economic evaluation of health care programmes. 4th ed. Oxford: Oxford University Press; 2015.

[3]   Bala MV, Mauskopf JA, Wood LL. Willingness to pay as measure of health benefits. Pharmacoeconomics 1999;15(1):9−18.

[4]   Folland S, Goodman AC, Stano M. The economics of health care. Oxford: Maxwell MacMillan International; 1993.

[5]   The World Health Organization. Preamble to the Constitution of the World Health Organization as adopted by the international health conference. New York: 1946; signed on 22 July 1946 by the representatives of 61 States (Official Records of the World Health Organization, no. 2, p. 100) and entered into force on 7 April 1948.

[6]   Brazier J, Ratcliffe J, Tsuchiya A. Measuring and valuing health benefits for economic evaluation. Oxford, New York: Oxford University Press; 2007.

[7]   GBD 2013 DALYs and HALE Collaborators. Global, regional, and national disability-adjusted life years (DALYs) for 306 diseases and injuries and healthy life expectancy (HALE) for 188 countries, 1990−2013: quantifying the epidemiological transition. Lancet 2015;386(1009):2145−91.

[8]   Olsen JA, Smith RD. Theory versus practice: a review of "willingness-to-pay" in health and health care. Health Econ 2001;10:39−52.

[9]   Stinnett A, Mullahy J. Net health benefits a new framework for the analysis of uncertainty in cost-effectiveness analysis. Med Decis Making 1998;18(2):S68−80.

[10] Barton G, Briggs A, Fenwick E. Optimal cost-effectiveness decisions: the role of the cost-effectiveness acceptability curve (CEAC), the cost-effectiveness acceptability frontier (CEAF), and the expected value of perfection information (EVPI). Value Health 2008;11(5):886−97.

[11] Briggs AH, O'Brien BJ. The death of cost-minimization analysis?. Health Econ 2001;10(2):179−84.

[12] Armour D, Cairns C, Costello I, Riley S, Davies E. The economics of a pharmacy-based central intravenous additive service for paediatric patients. Pharmacoeconomics 1996;10(4):386−94.

[13] Scott A, Tinelli M, Bond C, Community Pharmacy Medicines Management Evaluation Team. . Costs of a community pharmacist-led medicines management service for patients with coronary heart disease in England: healthcare system and patient perspectives. Pharmacoeconomics 2007;25(5):397−411.

[14] Perraudin C, Bourdin A, Spertini F, Berger J, Bugnon O. Switching patients to home-based subcutaneous immunoglobulin: an economic evaluation of an interprofessional drug therapy management program. J Clin Immunol 2016;36(5):502−10.

[15] Polgreen L, Han J, Carter B, Ardery G, Coffey C, Chrischilles E, et al. Cost-effectiveness of a physician-pharmacist collaboration intervention to improve blood pressure control. Hypertension 2015;66(6):1145−51.

[16] Elliott RA, Barber N, Clifford S, Horne R, Hartley E. The cost effectiveness of a telephone-based pharmacy advisory service to improve adherence to newly prescribed medicines. Pharm World Sci 2008;30(1):17−23.

[17] Desborough JA, Sach T, Bhattacharya D, Holland RC, Wright DJ. A cost-consequences analysis of an adherence focused pharmacist-led medication review service. Int J Pharm Pract 2012;20(1):41−9.

[18] Lalonde L, Martineau J, Blais N, et al. Is long-term pharmacist-managed anticoagulation service efficient? A pragmatic randomized controlled trial. Am Heart J 2008;156:148−54.

[19] Sullivan P, Arant T, Ellis S, Ulrich H. The cost effectiveness of anticoagulation management services for patients with atrial fibrillation and at high risk of stroke in the US. Pharmacoeconomics 2006;24(10):1021−33.

[20] RESPECT Trial Team. Cost-effectiveness of shared pharmaceutical care for older patients: RESPECT trial findings. Br J Gen Pract 2010;60(570):e20−7.

[21] Wallerstedt SM, Bladh L, Ramsberg J. A cost-effectiveness analysis of an in-hospital clinical pharmacist service. BMJ Open 2012;2:e000329.

[22] Morris S, Devlin N, Parkin D. Economic analysis in health care. Chichester, Hoboken, NJ: John Wiley & Sons; 2007.

FURTHER READING

Briggs A, Gray A. The distribution of health care costs and their statistical analysis for economic evaluation. J Health Serv Res Policy 1998;3(4):233−45.

Luce BR, Elixhauser A. Estimating costs in economic evaluation of medical technologies. Int J Technol Assess Health Care 1990;6:57−75.

Weinstein MC. Principles of cost-effective resource allocation in health care organisations. Int J Technol Assess Health Care 1990;6:93−103.

Coyle D., Tolley K. Discounting of health benefits in the pharmacoeconomic analysis of drug therapies. An issue for debate? Pharmacoeconomics 1992 Aug;2(2):153−62.

Van Hout BA. Discounting costs and effects: a reconsideration. Health Econ 1998;7:581−94.

Euroqol Group. Euroqol: a new facility for the measurement of health related quality of life. Health Policy 1991;16:199–208.

Green C, Brazier J, Deverill M. Valuing health-related quality of life. A review of health state valuation techniques. Pharmacoeconomics 2000;17:151–65.

Torrence GW. Measurement of health state utilities for economic appraisal: a review. J Health Econ 1986;5:1–30.

Elliott R, Payne K. Essentials of economic evaluation in healthcare. London: Pharmaceutical Press; 2005.

Catwright N. Nature's capacities and their measurement. Oxford: Clarendon; 1994.

Raiffa H. Decision analysis: introductory lectures on choices under uncertainty. Reading, MA: McGraw-Hill Inc; 1968.

Caro J, Briggs A, Siebert U, Kuntz K, ISPOR-SMDM Modeling Good Research Practices Task Force. Modeling good research practices—overview: a report of the ISPOR-SMDM Modeling Good Research Practices Task Force-1. Value Health. 2012;15(6):796–803.

Claxton K, Sculpher M. Using value of information analysis to prioritise health research: some lessons from recent UK experience. Pharmacoeconomics 2006;24(11):1055–68.

The National Institute for Health and Care Excellence. Developing NICE guidelines: the manual. 2014. Available at: http://www.nice.org.uk/article/PMG20/chapter/1%20Introduction%20and%20overview [last accessed 28.11.15].

Gold M, Siegel J, Russel L, Weinstein M. Cost-effectiveness in health and medicine. New York: Oxford University Press; 1996.

Briggs A, Sculpher MJ, Claxton K. Decision modelling for health economic evaluation. Oxford: Oxford University Press; 2011.

Culyer AJ. The dictionary of health economics. 3rd ed. Cheltenham: Edward Elgar; 2014.

Karamouz M, Szidarovszky F, Zahraie B. Water resources systems analysis. CRC Press; 2003.

Rascati K. Essentials of pharmacoeconomics. 2nd ed. Philadelphia: Lippincott Williams and Wilkins; 2013.

World Health Organization. Report of WHOQOL Focus Group Work. Geneva: WHO (MNH/PSF/93.4); 1993a.

Chapter 5

Design Principles for Economic Evaluations in Pharmacy

J.A. Whitty
University of East Anglia, Norwich, United Kingdom

Chapter Outline

INTRODUCTION

The aim of this chapter is to discuss some key considerations and concepts that are important to the design of an economic evaluation used to address a decision problem. While the key considerations apply to all economic evaluations in health, there are many texts published on the methods for economic evaluation that cover the concepts of this chapter in depth. Therefore, our intention is not to create another generic economic evaluation text; the interested reader is referred for example to Drummond et al. [1,2] or Gold et al. [3]. Instead, this chapter aims to draw particular attention to how these key concepts might be relevant in the context of the evaluation of pharmacy services and the impact they may have on design of a pharmacy services evaluation. Throughout the chapter, key concepts related to economic evaluation are highlighted in boxes.

THE ECONOMIC DECISION PROBLEM

Imagine the following scenario. You are a Director of the Pharmacy Department of a large tertiary referral hospital. Your hospital manager is able to allocate additional funding to your department for the next financial year, if you can make a business case for the value that this would add to your service and for patient care. You discuss this opportunity with your lead clinical pharmacist, who would like to introduce a clinical pharmacist-led anticoagulation outpatient service. How would you decide whether an anticoagulation outpatient service is the best use of the additional funding? How would you go about valuing such a service, to make a case for access to the funding to implement such a service? And how would you evaluate the service after implementation, to see if it achieved value for the money invested in it?

This scenario highlights an economic decision problem, because it starts from a position that we have finite resources and unlimited possible uses for those finite resources (see Box 5.1 for a definition of an economic problem). We only have a certain amount of additional funding, yet we have multiple potential uses for the additional funds—even within clinical pharmacy services alone. For example, should the funds be allocated to introduce the proposed new anticoagulant outpatient service? Or should they be used to provide a pharmacist-led asthma outpatient service? Or should they be used to expand the existing clinical pharmacy ward service to additional wards? Or to include a second visit to each ward currently provided with a service? Or to provide a clinical pharmacy service at weekends? And so on for many more potential uses of these limited funds.

In this scenario, you would first need to consider the costs of implementing the new service, and the benefits achieved by the service, and compare these to the costs and benefits of the current model of care that would be replaced by the new service (often termed "usual care" in evaluations). You would then need to consider whether any additional cost of implementing the new service was worth spending in order to achieve any additional benefit the new service may provide. This would indicate the comparative value for money, or cost-effectiveness, of implementing the new pharmacist-led service compared to the existing anticoagulant service.

To address the question in the scenario above, you would then need to compare the cost-effectiveness of the pharmacist-led outpatient service alongside the comparative value for money provided by every other possible use for the additional funds. This is to decide which would provide the best value for money. You may in fact be able to implement more than one service, until your additional funds are expended. From an economic point of view, you

---

BOX 5.1 Key Concept: Economic Problem

The *economic problem* is one of scarcity and choice: How do we make the best use of limited, or scarce, resources? The resources available to satisfy needs and wants are finite and insufficient to satisfy the unlimited needs and wants of society.

would implement the services in order of the value for money they provide starting with the best value for money, until your budget has been exhausted. In a nutshell, this is what you are trying to achieve with economic evaluation—the best outcome for each additional resource (in this case dollar) input. We will return to this scenario during this chapter to illustrate some of the key principles of economic evaluation in the context of pharmacy services.

As with any research study, an economic evaluation should start by closely defining the decision problem. Economic evaluations are designed to compare the costs and benefits of two (or more) options. Thus, they tell us about the value for money, or cost-effectiveness, of implementing different, mutually exclusive alternatives. In pharmacy, the alternatives in question could for example be different interventions (pharmaceuticals, dosage regimens, dosage forms, etc.), different strategies (e.g., combining a pharmaceutical within a holistic lifestyle program), or different services (e.g., a new model of clinical pharmacy service).

Chapter 8, Economic Evaluation of Pharmacy Services in Portugal and Chapter 9, Economic Evaluation of Pharmacist Managed Warfarin Therapy: A Review of Studies provide some examples of previously published economic evaluations in the pharmacy context. Some examples of the research questions related to pharmacy services that have previously been addressed by economic evaluations are provided in Box 5.2 (Refs. [4−17]). These research questions are ultimately designed to inform a decision problem of whether to implement a particular pharmacy service or not.

With any decision problem related to assessing the cost-effectiveness of an alternative, it is necessary to define the context for the decision. This can be done using existing frameworks that might be used for clinical evaluation, and extending them also to consider costs. One example of a pneumonic used to formulate an answerable question in evidence-based medicine is the PICO (Population, Intervention, Comparator, Outcome—see Box 5.3). This is recommended by the Cochrane collaboration to frame a clinical question for their systematic reviews [18]. The PICO can be used for economic evaluations as well. To illustrate this, a possible PICO for the anticoagulant outpatient service scenario is presented in Box 5.3. Considering the PICO is important, as the findings of the economic evaluation only apply to the context for which the evidence is based; the findings may not be generalizable to a wider population. Thus, defining the PICO is an important aspect of defining the decision problem.

POPULATION

It is important in a decision problem to specify the population or patients who are of interest for the evaluation. It cannot be assumed that the findings from an economic evaluation can be translated to another population or setting [19,20]. When considering clinical outcomes, they are not necessarily

BOX 5.2 Example Research Questions Addressed by Economic Evaluations of Pharmacy Services

Wright et al. [4]	Is a community pharmacy-based COPD disease support service cost-effective in delivering QALY gain compared to no service?
Carnevale et al. [5]	Is a pharmaceutical care service for patients with HIV cost-effective in improving clinical outcomes compared to usual care?
Elliott et al. [6]	Is a pharmacist-led information technology intervention for reducing rates of clinically important errors in medicines management in general practices cost-effective compared to simple feedback?
Hendrie et al. [7]	Is a pharmacist-led diabetes management education program for reducing glycemic episodes in type II diabetes cost-effective compared to standard care?
Bojke et al. [8]	Is shared pharmaceutical care for older people cost-effective in delivering QALY gain compared to usual care?
Khdour et al. [9]	Is a pharmacy-led education and self-management program for patients with COPD cost-effective in delivering QALY gain compared to usual care?
Rubio-Valera et al. [10]	Is a community pharmacist intervention cost-effective in delivering QALY gain in depressed patients initiating treatment with antidepressants in primary care, compared to usual care?
Perraudin et al. [11]	Is a community pharmacist-led sleep apnea screening program cost-effective in delivering QALY gain in patients who are at risk of moderate to severe obstructive sleep apnea syndrome, compared to screening with no community pharmacist involvement or no screening?
Jodar-Sanchez et al. [12]	Is a medication review with follow-up service for older adults with polypharmacy in Spanish community pharmacies cost-effective in delivering QALY gain, compared to usual medication dispensing?
Adibe et al. [13]	Is a pharmaceutical care intervention in Nigerian patients for the management of type II diabetes cost-effective, compared to usual care?
Obreli-Neto et al. [14]	Is a pharmaceutical care program for early diabetic and hypertensive patients in primary care cost-effective in delivering QALYs, compared to usual care?
Borges et al. [15]	What are the costs of delivering a pharmaceutical care service to assist outpatients with type II diabetes, as compared to standard care? (no joint evaluation of effectiveness: therefore, partial evaluation only)
Claus et al. [16]	What are the assumed cost savings associated with the identification and implementation of pharmacist interventions? (implicitly assumes a hypothetical comparator of no intervention and no evaluation of effectiveness: therefore, partial evaluation only)
Bauld et al. [17]	Is a smoking cessation service in Glasgow consisting of group-support cost-effective, compared to an alternative service consisting of one-to-one pharmacist counseling?

COPD, chronic obstructive pulmonary disease; QALY, quality-adjusted life year.

BOX 5.3 An Indicative PICO for the hypothetical Pharmacist-Led Anticoagulant Service Scenario

Question: What is the cost-effectiveness of implementing a new pharmacist-led anticoagulant outpatient service compared to the existing anticoagulant service (usual care)?

Population	Who are the relevant patients?	Adults ≥ 18 years, under the care of the specific tertiary teaching hospital medical teams and prescribed warfarin for the management of atrial fibrillation or venous thromboembolism
Intervention	What is the management strategy, diagnostic test, or exposure you are interested in?	Attendance at an outpatient clinic with telephone follow-up and referral where required to the treating medical team, led by a pharmacist with postgraduate training in clinical pharmacy
Comparator	What is the alternative management strategy or control?	Usual care, i.e., attendance at an outpatient clinic led by the medical team, with general practitioner follow-up when required
Outcome	What are the relevant consequences of the intervention?	Number of bleeds Time spent in therapeutic range QALYs Cost to the health care system Cost-effectiveness, expressed as incremental cost per QALY gained

---

generalizable to other population groups. Economic outcomes can also be problematic. The resources used to deliver a pharmacy service or its comparator and consequently their costs may differ between different settings. For example, implementation of a pharmacy outpatient clinic may have quite different costs as well as benefits in a small rural hospital than in a large tertiary hospital, or in a tertiary hospital in one health jurisdiction as compared to another, even if you are aiming to treat the same patient group.

INTERVENTION

Interventions that might be assessed in economic evaluations in the context of pharmacy services are numerous and include for example pharmacist-led

> **BOX 5.4 Key Concept: Marginal Analysis**
> An assessment of the additional costs and benefits that result from a one unit change in service provision [3].

disease support, self-management or pharmaceutical care services, screening or smoking cessation programs, or pharmacy interventions to reduce adverse drug events (see Box 5.2).

COMPARATOR

Economic evaluations ask the question of value for money *at the margin* (Box 5.4). That is, economic evaluations assess the consequences of a change in scale in provision of a service. They assess the costs and benefits from a one unit *change* in service provision. It is important to always compare the costs and benefits of a "new state of the world" (intervention) to the costs and benefits of the "existing state of the world" (comparator). This is also important to evaluate the *change* in costs and benefits at the margin (e.g., the additional number of dollars and units of outcome associated with one additional unit of service provision). In the anticoagulant outpatient service example, this would mean comparing the additional cost and benefit of managing one additional patient via the new service to that of managing one additional patient via the existing service.

OUTCOME (THE MAXIMAND)

In the anticoagulant outpatient service scenario above, we stated that the aim of an economic evaluation is to provide evidence allowing us to achieve the best outcome for each additional resource input that is available. This begs the question—what is the "best outcome"? That is, what are we trying to maximize? This is where there are some diverging opinions and different "schools of thought." In economics more widely (i.e., in sectors outside health), conventional economic theory suggests we are trying to maximize "utility," which is an abstract concept but can be thought of as some overall sense of satisfaction or welfare. This theoretical approach is termed "welfare economics." However, the values implicit in welfare economics are not shared by all decision-makers, and many consider the social goal of the health sector is to maximize health as an output, rather than utility [3]. While health is one factor likely to affect utility, it is not the only factor (e.g., income is also likely to affect utility). A theoretical approach in which society values health as a merit good which should be available to people, regardless of their willingness or ability to pay for it, is often termed "extra-welfarism" [3]. Thus, the outcome measured in health economic evaluation is often a measure or surrogate for a health outcome. This is discussed further in the section, Choosing an Evaluation Approach later in this chapter. In considering the introduction of a new pharmacy service, we are usually trying to achieve either:

1. an improved health outcome for more dollars invested; where the additional dollar investment is considered to be worthwhile given the additional outcome achieved; or
2. an improved or equal health outcome for less dollars invested; or
3. a lower health outcome for less dollars invested; where the dollars saved are considered worthwhile given the health outcome forgone.

The majority of economic questions in health, including pharmacy services, are likely to fall into the first two of these categories. The latter category is less commonly faced in practice; although, considering disinvesting is a service might fall in the third category.

Whether achievement of a benefit is considered worthwhile depends on the "opportunity cost" of achieving that benefit. Opportunity cost is an important concept in health economics (Box 5.5). The opportunity cost of choosing one alternative over another is the health benefit forgone because the next best alternative was not selected [3]. In the anticoagulant outpatient service example (Box 5.3), the opportunity cost of choosing the new pharmacist-led service is the value of the benefits lost from not choosing the existing service.

PARTIAL VERSUS FULL ECONOMIC EVALUATION

The question that is being asked in the evaluation can have several levels or steps, often addressed sequentially when undertaking an evaluation. The first is to ask which of the alternatives is least costly. However, this gives an indication only of the inputs required to deliver each alternative. It tells us nothing about the outputs or benefits achieved by each alternative. This is therefore called a *partial* economic analysis. The second step might be to ask which of the alternatives is most effective, according to the measure of outcome that is of interest. This is also called a *partial* economic analysis, as at this point costs and benefits have only be considered individually. The next steps apply to a *full* economic analysis, in which both the costs and

---

BOX 5.5 Key Concept: Opportunity Cost

The value of the benefits lost because the next best alternative was not selected; that is, the benefits forgone as a consequence of choosing one alternative over another.

benefits of different alternatives are compared jointly. The third step is to consider for each alternative whether it is cost-effective compared to the comparator or referent. This involves jointly considering the comparative costs and benefits of the intervention, often using an incremental cost-effectiveness ratio (ICER). An acceptable level of "cost-effectiveness" must be defined according to a decision rule (for more details regarding ICERs and decision rules, see chapters: Chapter 4, Economic Evaluation and its Types; Chapter 6, Steps in Conducting an Economic Evaluation). Finally, in the case of an evaluation in which more than two alternatives are considered, it is necessary to ask which of the alternatives is the *most* cost-effective.

CHOOSING AN EVALUATION APPROACH

There are a number of different evaluation types. They all measure the inputs for delivering an intervention and comparator in terms of cost (dollar value). They differ in terms of how they measure and present the outcome, and the decision rule that is applied based on the findings (Box 5.6).

Chapter 4, Economic Evaluation and its Types describes the decision rules; it also elaborates the types of economic evaluation described in Box 5.6. However, for the purpose of this current chapter it is important to note that the measurement of outcome has implications for the design of the study and the conclusions that can be drawn from the economic evaluation. Therefore, choosing the right type of evaluation is crucial to address the decision problem.

CA makes no assumption at all about the comparative outcome achieved by an intervention. Therefore, it can only tell us which alternative costs the least. But without knowledge of which alternative gives the greatest benefit, it is unable to inform a decision about the cost-effectiveness of the interventions. Hence, it is termed a partial (and not full) economic evaluation. CMA makes a conclusion regarding cost-effectiveness under the assumption that the extent to which the relevant outcome is achieved is the same for each alternative, which can be a strong assumption and should be backed by evidence. CEA can only compare interventions whose outcomes can be measured in the same units. CUA is currently considered the "gold standard" for economic evaluation in most circumstances in the health context. The unit of outcome used in CUA is normally the QALY, which is a preference-based measure combining quality of life and survival. Therefore, it can be used to compare any intervention in health that improves survival and/or quality of life and whose outcome can therefore be converted to this metric. CBA requires outcomes to be converted to a monetary value, which is ethically and pragmatically challenging (see chapters: Chapter 4, Economic Evaluation and its Types; Chapter 6, Steps in Conducting an Economic Evaluation for further discussion of CBA). Therefore, CBA is seldom applied in health economics at this time; although, there is much research in this area that might expand the usefulness of CBA in the future. CCA has

BOX 5.6 Type of Economic Evaluation, Associated Outcome Measure, Implication for Design of the Economic Evaluation, and Usual Decision Rule

Type	Outcome Measure	Implication for Design	Decision Rule
Cost analysis (CA)	Outcomes not considered	Compares costs only; therefore cannot be used to make any conclusion regarding cost-effectiveness	Unable to infer cost-effectiveness (partial evaluation)
Cost-minimization analysis (CMA)	Outcomes assumed to be the same	Makes a conclusion regarding cost-effectiveness under the assumption that the relevant outcome is achieved is the same for each alternative	The least costly intervention is the most cost-effective (given equivalent outcome)
Cost-effectiveness analysis (CEA)	Units of effectiveness, often clinical or surrogate outcomes, e.g., unit reduction in blood pressure, stroke avoided, additional responder	Can only be used to compare the cost-effectiveness of interventions whose outcome can be measured in the same metric	ICER; a judgment is needed as regards whether the ICER is of acceptable cost-effectiveness
Cost–utility analysis (CUA)	QALYs	Patient relevant outcome (survival and quality of life combined), weighted for the preference of the public for being in different health states. Can be used to compare the cost-effectiveness of interventions whose outcome can be measured in a combined index of survival and quality of life	ICER; a judgment is needed as regards whether the ICER is of acceptable cost-effectiveness
Cost–benefit analysis (CBA)	Monetary value ($)	Can incorporate health and non-health benefits. Requires the conversion of a health outcome into a monetary value. If achieved, can be used to compare health and non-health interventions	Net monetary benefit (NMB). If NMB > $0 then intervention is cost-effective
Cost-consequences analysis (CCA)	Outcomes specified in disaggregated form (as an array of outcomes)	Can incorporate health and non-health benefits; benefits are listed transparently. Does not require the conversion of a health outcome into a monetary value. However, requires decision-maker to make a judgment regarding the relative value of the disaggregated outcomes	Costs and benefits are not usually combined into a single indicator. Requires judgment regarding the relative weight to be placed on different outcomes.

not often been used in health contexts. However, it may be of particular use for the evaluation of a pharmacy service, where some of the outcomes of relevance (such as reduction of risk for a heterogeneous group of adverse medication—related events associated with clinical pharmacy interventions) may be difficult to convert into either a QALY or monetary value.

In the anticoagulant outpatient service example (Box 5.3), a CA could be undertaken using just the "cost" outcome, but this would not fully inform decision-makers about the value of the service. Preferably, a CUA (using both the cost and the QALY outcomes) or CEA (using both the cost and the bleeds avoided outcome) would be undertaken. This would indicate the incremental cost per additional QALY gained or per bleed avoided respectively. If we had good quality evidence that the health outcomes were the same for both the new and existing services, then a CMA could be performed; although, some researchers argue that a CEA or CUA are preferable to a CMA in nearly all circumstances [21].

WHICH COSTS ARE RELEVANT?

The relevant costs are determined by the perspective of the evaluation. The study perspective indicates from whose view point the economic evaluation is undertaken. For example, a national health service perspective would measure and include all costs associated with the intervention or its comparator that are accrued to the health system. For the evaluation of a pharmacy service, this might include, for example the cost of medicines, pharmacist time, appointments with a health care practitioner, the costs of tests and monitoring, the costs of emergency department and hospital admissions, and so on. An individual hospital perspective would only consider those accruing to that individual hospital. This distinction can become important in the evaluation of a pharmacy service, if pharmaceuticals or other resources are funded through a system external to the institution where the pharmacy service is provided. A broader societal perspective would include costs to society such as those associated with lost productivity, as well as costs accruing to the patient themselves or the health system.

TRIAL-BASED VERSUS MODELED EVALUATION

Economic evaluations are often described as being either "trial-based" or "model-based." Trial-based evaluations are undertaken alongside a clinical trial. Data on resource use is collected and then costed alongside the clinical data. This then allows an evaluation of the comparative costs of the different interventions and of their cost-effectiveness, as well as their comparative clinical efficacy. However, evaluations undertaken alongside a trial are necessarily limited to the comparator, outcomes, and time horizon for the data collected by the trial. Economic evaluation is undertaken to inform a decision to implement or subsidize an intervention in practice and requires a focus on "real world" effectiveness rather than "efficacy" in a research setting. The decision problem may require consideration of a different question than that asked by a trial, extrapolation of findings to a different population or often to a longer time frame. It may also require assumptions to be made regarding the translation of short-term surrogate clinical outcomes into longer term outcomes (such as survival and quality of life) that are more meaningful to patients. Thus, modeled evaluations are frequently undertaken to achieve this.

If an evaluation has a time horizon greater than a year, then discounting of costs and benefits needs to be considered, in order to account for time preference [1]. This is more likely to occur in a modeled evaluation, but can also occur in a trial-based evaluation. Discounting is discussed in Chapter 4, Economic Evaluation and its Types, and Chapter 6, Steps in Conducting an Economic Evaluation.

THE IMPORTANCE OF BEST PRACTICE GUIDELINES

Finally, while this chapter has briefly outlined a few of the key considerations for design of economic evaluations, there are a growing series of guidelines and checklists available that provide detailed recommendations around evaluation methods. These should be considered when designing or reporting an economic evaluation. Key guidance documents are developed by professional and research organizations, such as the International Society for Pharmacoeconomics and Outcomes Research (ISPOR). ISPOR task forces constitute eminent researchers and practitioners in the field and have developed and published a range of Good Practice guidance for economic evaluation methods. Their guidance is available via the ISPOR website http://www. ispor.org/workpaper/practices_index.asp. The Consolidated Health Economic Evaluation Reporting Standards statement has also been developed and adopted by a number of international health journals [22].

CONCLUSIONS

Careful design is crucial for the development of a high quality and useful economic evaluation study. Good design starts with the definition of a clear decision problem and context. Different types of evaluations differ in terms of the outcome that is measured; therefore, the selection of a relevant outcome is important for design and has an impact on the conclusions that can be inferred from the evaluation. The relevant perspective will indicate the costs that must be considered; while, the available data on population, outcomes, and time horizon may suggest that a modeled evaluation is required to extrapolate trial data to reflect real life costs and effectiveness. There are many guidelines which outline the methods of economic evaluation, and these should be consulted when designing an economic evaluation of a pharmacy service.

REFERENCES

[1] Drummond MF, Sculpher MJ, Torrance GW, O'Brien B, Stoddart GL. Methods for the economic evaluation of health care programmes. 3rd ed. New York: Oxford University Press; 2005.

[2] Drummond M, McGuire A, editors. Economic evaluation in health care: merging theory with practice. Oxford: Oxford University Press; 2001.

[3] Gold MR, Siegel JE, Russell LB, Weinstein MC, editors. Cost-effectiveness in health and medicine. New York: Oxford University Press; 1996.

[4] Wright D, Twigg M, Barton G, Thornley T, Kerr C. An evaluation of a multi-site community pharmacy−based chronic obstructive pulmonary disease support service. Int J Pharm Pract 2015;23(1):36−43.

[5] Carnevale RC, Molino CD, Visacri MB, Mazzola PG, Moriel P. Cost analysis of pharmaceutical care provided to HIV-infected patients: an ambispective controlled study. Daru 2015;23(1):13.

[6] Elliott RA, Putman KD, Franklin M, Annemans L, Verhaeghe N, Eden M, et al. Cost effectiveness of a pharmacist-led information technology intervention for reducing rates of clinically important errors in medicines management in general practices (PINCER). Pharmacoeconomics 2014;32(6):573−90.

[7] Hendrie D, Miller TR, Woodman RJ, Hoti K, Hughes J. Cost-effectiveness of reducing glycaemic episodes through community pharmacy management of patients with type 2 diabetes mellitus. J Prim Prev 2014;35(6):439−49.

[8] Bojke C, Philips Z, Sculpher M, Campion P, Chrystyn H, Coulton S, et al. Cost-effectiveness of shared pharmaceutical care for older patients: RESPECT trial findings. Br J Gen Pract 2010;60(570):e20−7.

[9] Khdour MR, Agus AM, Kidney JC, Smyth BM, Elnay JC, Crealey GE. Cost-utility analysis of a pharmacy-led self-management programme for patients with COPD. Int J Clin Pharm 2011;33(4):665−73.

[10] Rubio-Valera M, Bosmans J, Fernández A, Peñarrubia-María M, March M, Travé P, et al. Cost-effectiveness of a community pharmacist intervention in patients with depression: a randomized controlled trial (PRODEFAR Study). PLoS One 2013;8(8):e70588.

[11] Perraudin C, Le Vaillant M, Pelletier-Fleury N. Cost-effectiveness of a community pharmacist-led sleep apnea screening program—a Markov model. PLoS One 2013;8(6): e63894.

[12] Jódar-Sánchez F, Malet-Larrea A, Martín JJ, García-Mochón L, del Amo MP, Martínez-Martínez F, et al. Cost-utility analysis of a medication review with follow-up service for older adults with polypharmacy in community pharmacies in Spain: the conSIGUE program. Pharmacoeconomics 2015;33(6):599−610.

[13] Adibe MO, Aguwa CN, Ukwe CV. Cost-utility analysis of pharmaceutical care intervention versus usual care in management of Nigerian patients with type 2 diabetes. Value Health Reg Issues 2013;2(2):189−98.

[14] Obreli-Neto PR, Marusic S, Guidoni CM, de Oliveira Baldoni A, Renovato RD, Pilger D, et al. Economic evaluation of a pharmaceutical care program for elderly diabetic and hypertensive patients in primary health care: a 36-month randomized controlled clinical trial. J Manag Care Pharm 2015;21(1):66−75.

[15] Borges AP, Guidoni CM, Freitas OD, Pereira LR. Economic evaluation of outpatients with type 2 diabetes mellitus assisted by a pharmaceutical care service. Arq Bras Endocrinol Metabol 2011;55(9):686−91.

[16] Claus BO, Vandeputte FM, Robays H. Epidemiology and cost analysis of pharmacist interventions at Ghent University Hospital. Int J Clin Pharm 2012;34(5):773−8.

[17] Bauld L, Boyd KA, Briggs AH, Chesterman J, Ferguson J, Judge K, et al. One-year outcomes and a cost-effectiveness analysis for smokers accessing group-based and pharmacy-led cessation services. Nicotine Tob Res 2011;13(2):135−45.

[18] Higgins J, Green S, editors. Cochrane handbook for systematic reviews of interventions version 5.1.0 [updated March 2011]. The Cochrane Collaboration. 2011.

[19] Manca A, Willan AR. 'Lost in translation': accounting for between-country differences in the analysis of multinational cost-effectiveness data. Pharmacoeconomics 2006;24(11): 1101−19.

[20] Drummond M, Barbieri M, Cook J, Glick HA, Lis J, Malik F, et al. Transferability of economic evaluations across jurisdictions: ISPOR Good Research Practices Task Force report. Value Health 2009;12(4):409−18.

[21] Dakin H, Wordsworth S. Cost-minimisation analysis versus cost-effectiveness analysis, revisited. Health Econ 2013;22(1):22−34.

[22] Husereau D, Drummond M, Petrou S, Carswell C, Moher D, Greenberg D, et al. Consolidated Health Economic Evaluation Reporting Standards (CHEERS)—explanation and elaboration: a report of the ISPOR Health Economic Evaluation Publication Guidelines Good Reporting Practices Task Force. Value Health 2013;16(2):231−50.

Chapter 6

Steps in Conducting an Economic Evaluation

A.A. Shafie[1], G.N. Chua[1] and Y.V. Yong[2]

[1]*Universiti Sains Malaysia, Penang, Malaysia*, [2]*Ministry of Health Malaysia, Selangor, Malaysia*

Chapter Outline

INTRODUCTION

A local hospital management team is evaluating a new innovative pharmacy service that requires six full-time equivalent (FTE) pharmacists and two FTE pharmacy technicians. The service is initiated to improve adherence among diabetes patients in the hospital. The team is under tremendous pressure from the ministry to justify the service due to the recent budgetary cut to the hospital. The situation is challenging for them.

However, they are not alone in this situation. Health policy and decision-makers throughout the globe face similar challenges—Should clinicians check the blood pressure of each adult who walks into their offices? Should individuals be encouraged to request annual check-ups? Should a new, expensive drug be listed in the formulary? Should a proposed health promotion program be approved? Should a Medication Therapy Adherence Service be initiated in the hospital?

Economic Evaluation of Pharmacy Services.
© 2017 Elsevier Inc. All rights reserved.

Traditionally, decision-making in health care relies on strict univariate comparison of price or efficacy alone. For example, drug with the lowest price or highest efficacy would usually be chosen. However, such narrow comparison would miss out accounting for the total cost of a treatment. Let us say for example a new drug (Drug B) is compared to Drug A (Table 6.1). An efficacy-based decision-maker would choose Drug B over A on the basis that the Drug B would provide longer survival. This is common among clinician who looks to maximize the clinical efficacy of their treatment. However, such decision would ignore that Drug B is more expensive than A. Price-based decision-maker would choose Drug A as the cheaper option. This is a common decision rule adopted by many healthcare reimbursements and funding agencies. However, deciding on price alone meaning, ignoring the higher cost of treating adverse drug reaction (ADR) associated with Drug A. As a result, the decision to remain with Drug A because of price alone could cost the hospital a higher cost in the long run. However, if we look at the whole scenario, there is further challenge that though the Drug B is more effective, it is also more expensive.

It is an established fact that our resources are insufficient (or scarce) to accommodate all the choices that we have made. In an ideal world, we would like to provide the best treatment to everyone. However, in reality, there are only limited health care resources at our disposal. In Malaysia, for example, there is only 1.82 hospital bed per 1000 Malaysian, 1 pharmacist per 4000 Malaysian, and 1 anesthesiologist to 42,000 Malaysian [1]—in short, our scarce resources forced us to make a choice. The issue has become more critical particularly with the increasing cost of healthcare, changing clinical practice, aging population, and with the severe shortage of healthcare human resources. In this context, many countries are now striving to utilize their resources efficiently in order to produce the maximum output. Although we can make a choice arbitrarily or randomly, it is always better to choose rationally.

TABLE 6.1 Comparison of Drug A and B

	Drug A	Drug B
Benefit		
Survival	7 years	10 years
Cost		
Drug price (unit cost)	USD 10	USD 20
Drug price	USD 3650	USD 7300
ADR treatment	USD 2000	USD 50
Total	USD 5660	USD 7370

Economics evolved very much on rational decision-making. Its subfield, pharmacoeconomics can be defined as the study of how to choose pharmaceutical product/service in the healthcare system, with or without the use of money to employ scarce productive resources that would have alternative uses, and produce health now or in the future among various people and groups in the society [2]. The example in Table 6.1 clearly demonstrates the importance of considering both cost and consequences in evaluating choices. Economics offers a tool called economic evaluation that could compare the costs and consequences of alternatives and ensure an efficient choice that could maximize benefit while using minimal cost. As such, it has become an increasingly attractive tool to many healthcare payers and policy makers who seek to contain the escalating health care costs, while ensuring quality access to health care.

Many countries now require economic evaluation evidence either as part of their drug reimbursement or as registration process on top of traditional requirement of safety and efficacy evidence. This additional layer of regulation or so-called "the fourth hurdle" is now mandatory in many European and some Asian countries. No such evidence is required for pharmacy services but many decision-makers have found that it is useful given the similar budgetary constraint that they face. As such, knowledge in economic evaluation is essential for modern pharmacy practice.

ECONOMIC EVALUATION OF PHARMACY SERVICES

Two key features of economic evaluation are that they have to compare both cost and consequences of at least two alternatives (Table 6.2). If, for example a study only evaluates the cost of managing a disease—it is only classified as cost description study. This is true for all burdens of disease studies that usually only described the cost associated with managing a disease, without joint comparison of cost and consequences of alternatives. A number of studies fall under this category, as they only described the cost of cervical cancer, tuberculosis, or diabetes mellitus [3−5]. Similarly, if a study only evaluates the consequences of disease/treatment, it can only be considered as outcome description study. There are various examples of such studies. For example, Liau et al. [6] described health-related quality of life (HRQoL) among employees in a public institution in Malaysia, Chiew et al. [7] described HRQoL among methadone users, and Kocarnik et al. [8] evaluated pharmacy service impact on diabetes adherence.

Economics offers three[1] evaluation tools that can be used separately or altogether, i.e., cost−benefit analysis (CBA), cost-effectiveness analysis (CEA), and cost−utility analysis (CUA) [9,10]. All three used costs in

---

1. Previous text usually described four economic evaluation tools by including cost-minimization analysis (CMA). However, due to the need for joint consideration of cost and consequences, CMA is no longer considered as full economic evaluation.

TABLE 6.2 Distinguishing Features of Economic Evaluation

Is there comparison of two or more alternatives?	Are both cost (inputs) and consequences (output) of the alternatives examined?			
		NO		**YES**
		Examine only consequences	Examines only costs	
	NO	*Not Economic Evaluation*		*Not Economic Evaluation*
		Outcome description	Cost description	Cost–outcome description
		Not Economic Evaluation		*True Economic Evaluation*
	YES	Efficacy or effectiveness evaluation	Cost analysis	CEA
				CUA
				CBA

Source: Adapted from Drummond MF, Sculpher MJ, Claxton K, Stoddart GL, Torrance GW. Methods for the economic evaluation of health care programmes. 4th ed. Oxford University Press; 2015 [9]; Schmid GP. Understanding the essentials of economic evaluation. J Acquir Immune Defic Syndr Hum Retrovirol. 1995;10(Suppl. 4):S6–13 [11].

TABLE 6.3 Simplified Difference Between CEA, CUA, and CBA

Method	Cost Unit	Benefit Unit
CBA	Monetary	Monetary
CEA	Monetary	Natural
CUA	Monetary	Preference, quality-adjusted life year (QALY)

monetary terms. The main distinctions between them are that their consequences are treated differently.

Whereas CEA uses the measured health consequences in natural terms, CUA uses the valued health consequences in term of preference and CBA values it in term of money (Table 6.3). For example, in a study that evaluate treatment choice for treating diabetes, CEA could use reduction in blood sugar as a consequence, while CUA would look at how much the reduction is preferred and CBA would assess how much it is valued in monetary terms. Most of economic evaluation studies in health care applied CEA in their research. One example is Ref. [12] which analyzes the cost-effectiveness therapeutic drug monitoring service among children diagnosed with structural-metabolic epilepsy.

In the above paragraphs, we have briefly discussed the feature and types of economic evaluation. Here we are presenting steps in conducting an economic evaluation.

STEPS IN CONDUCTING AN ECONOMIC EVALUATION

The basic tasks when conducting an economic evaluation study are to *identify*, *measure*, *value*, and to *compare* the cost and consequences of the alternatives being considered. In order to understand how these tasks are accomplished, one need to be familiar with some of its important elements that will be briefly discussed in this chapter.

Here are the steps to conduct an economic evaluation of a pharmacy service:

1. Establishing the research question
2. Planning the study design
3. Identifying, measuring, and valuing cost and consequences
4. Analyzing the cost and consequences.

Establishing the Research Question

As in any scientific enquiry, an answerable economic question should be first defined. The question should clearly identify the *alternatives being compared* and the *perspective* from which the comparison is to be made.

Comparator

The comparator should be comprehensively described. The comparator is the program/treatment/action/service that we wish to compare to the current/standard treatment. It can even be an action of doing nothing. Whereas describing pharmaceutical product in an economic evaluation is straightforward in a sense that the dosing regimen is detailed, descriptions of pharmacy service are often inadequate, and the standard alternative of usual care (UC) service is often taken for granted. This could reduce generalizability of the results given that most of the services are delivered within the local context. Hence, it is important for researcher to provide sufficient structural and contextual details of the service.

Analysis that does not have comparator is considered as partial evaluation (Table 6.2). A large body of literature that deals with burden of illness, or cost of illness such as Ref. [5], only describe cost without any comparison and as such falls under partial evaluation.

Perspectives

Perspective is the subject/entities that incur the cost/benefit. If we focus on costs, then the perspective determines the subjects that sustain the costs.

TABLE 6.4 How Perspective Affects Identification of Costs

Cost Elements	Perspectives			
	Societal	Public	Private	Provider
Health service costs	All	Covered expenses	Covered expenses	Expenses of provided services
Productivity costs	Included	Excluded	Excluded	None
Informal cares	Included	Excluded	Excluded	Excluded
Transportation	All	If any paid	If any paid	Excluded
Other non-health service costs	All	If any paid	If any paid	Excluded

Source: From Luce B, Manning W, Siegel JE, Lipscomb J. Estimating costs in cost-effectiveness analysis. In: Gold MF, Siegel JE, Russell LB, Weinstein MC, eds. Cost effectiveness in health and medicine. New York: Oxford University Press; 1996:176–213 [13].

Commonly taken perspective include societal (e.g., UK societal), provider (e.g., National Health Service (NHS) Trust Hospital), and payer (e.g., insurance company). The broadest would be societal perspective while the narrowest would be the provider perspective. Perspective would determine the resources and consequences evaluated (Table 6.4). As such, study that takes NHS Trust Hospital perspective (provider) would exclude the travel cost of the patient to the ambulatory clinic, whereas study done from the UK's societal perspective would include it.

The most relevant perspective should be considered. Most guidelines from public sector Health Technology Assessment Agency recommended that the analysis should be undertaken from either a provider or funder perspective.

Planning the Study Design

Similar to any scientific investigation, economic research problem requires thorough planning for the overall research design that could integrate the different elements of economic evaluation in a coherent and logical way. This usually constitutes the blueprint for the identification, measurement, and analysis of the data. Generally, an economic evaluation is designed either alongside trial (EAT), whereby cost and outcome are collected together, or as a simulation model, whereby cost and outcome are sourced from different studies. Designing economic evaluation alongside trial, especially in a randomized controlled trial framework, is usually desirable given the lower risk of bias inherent in its design. However, EAT occasionally suffers from short study time horizon, measurement of intermediate outcome only, and limited comparators under study. Hence, many researchers have incorporated modeling in their study either as a standalone modeling study or an extension of their trial that allows synthesis of evidence and simulation of outcome beyond the original trial.

Identifying, Measuring, and Valuing Costs and Consequences

Economists argued that the real costs to society are resources utilized by the patients, in terms of their opportunity costs (economic costs), and the benefits that could have been obtained from the next best use of these resources.

In other terms, costs are all resources which have alternative uses. Resources on the other hand are those that contribute to the production of the output. As such, money is not a resource because until it is converted into a resource, it contributes nothing to production.

Costs

Resources consumed by a program/treatment/service are considered to comprise of four components:

1. *Health care sector* consist of items such as drugs, equipment, hospitalization, physician visits, etc. However, please note that this include the cost for providing initial program/treatment/service and its continuing care. For example, the cost of kidney transplant should not be limited to the surgery cost alone but should also include the costs of immunosuppressive drugs and costs of treating an infection from the procedure.
2. Resources consumption in *other sectors* depends on the nature of the program/treatment/service, e.g., program for elderly need to include costs of treatment at nursing homes.
   a. The *patient and family resources* could consist of out-of-pocket expenses in travelling to hospital, various co-payments, and expenditure at home (e.g., adapting a room to accommodate a home dialysis machine). One of the most important patient and family resources consumed in treatment is time, e.g., time of the patient seeking and receiving care, or time of family members in providing informal nursing support at home.

In each component, their quantities (q) would be measured and the total cost calculated by multiplying the quantities with the relevant prices (p) would be evaluated.

Consequences

The consequences of program/treatment/service can be a change in health state, or/and saving from treatment. As benefit forgone is the opportunity cost for the pursued program, the saving from treatment would be incorporated in the costs part of the analysis as the difference in cost with the other program. Its identification, measurement, and valuation then would be similar to what has been discussed above.

Health State Change

Changes in health state are health outcomes of a treatment or program.

The changes in health state can be measured in its physical/natural form, e.g., clinical parameters (blood pressure), quality of life, or length of life. Outcomes should be measured using valid tools/instruments. Tools for clinical outcome measurement are usually less contentious. However, tools/instruments that are used to measure subjective outcomes like quality of life need to have their validity and reliability.

Outcomes that are measured in short time horizon is called intermediate outcome while those that are measured in lifetime is called final outcome. The intermediate outcome is usually measured as clinical parameters that should have evidence of strong correlation with the final outcome. Intermediate outcome is easier to design and execute. Another advantage is that health units are common and natural outcomes are routinely measured in clinical and practical setting, hence these parameters are familiar for practitioners. As such, economic evaluation that used this measure (CEA) is the most common type of economic evaluation found in health care.

The final outcome is usually measured as length of life. However, critics have argued that improvement in clinical or survival alone does not necessarily make an alternative preferred choice in rational decision-making. There are many diseases (e.g., cancer) where patient expressed discontent with the high toxicity level of their treatment, even though it is highly efficacious. As such, an outcome that adjusts for quality of life is proposed with the most widely used is called QALYs. QALY is preferable for the following conditions [9]:

- When HRQoL is *the/an* important outcome.
- When the program affects both morbidity and mortality and common unit of outcome is needed.
- When the programs compared have a wide range of different kinds of outcomes and a common unit of output is needed for comparison.
- When a program is compared to others that have already been evaluated using CUA.
- When dealing with a limited budget situation. Limited budget situation requires selection of programs/service that need be eliminated/or reduced in order to free up funding for the new program/services. When the objective is to allocate limited resources optimally by considering all alternatives and using constrained optimization to maximize the health gain achieved.

In addition, health state change in natural unit is narrow and can only be used in CEA to compare with the treatment/program/service that has similar objectives. For example, measuring only reduction of blood pressure for a new pharmacy service for hypertensive patients can only be compared to other service that has similar objective (and measured outcome). The comparison will provide the answer to the question of what is the best way to achieve the objective of reducing blood pressure. This is a question of *technical efficiency*. However, what if the treatment/program has multiple clinical outcomes, e.g., the drug could lower blood pressure, cholesterol, and blood glucose? Such a narrow measure might also restrict the analysis to answer only within the given objective, not challenging the objective. This is perhaps a question of *allocative efficiency*. Decisions on the expansion of the budget require consideration of the opportunity cost that is likely to fall outside the health care sector.

Valuation of Outcomes

Changes in health state can be valued as preference directly by standard gamble, time trade-off, or rating scale. It can also be valued indirectly by applying societal preference (utility) to changes in health states as measured by multi-attribute utility instruments such as the EuroQol-5 dimensions (EQ-5D), HUI3, or the QWB scale. As utilities may be influenced by local cultural factors, preferences obtained directly from the target and local populations are preferred. Where local preferences are not available, preferences from populations with greatest similarity to the local population should be employed. Any instrument used should be assessed for their validity and reliability in the local context.

The preference of that quality of life will be adjusted with the measured length of life. This could be used to calculate QALYs. Assuming that the quality of life is constant, QALY can simply be calculated as multiplication of length of life with quality of life. Therefore, if patient who received pharmacy service A could live 3 years longer, with 0.5 quality of life, his QALY would be 1.5 (3 years ×0.5 QoL). This means that even though he lives for 3 years, it only equates to 1.5 of years in perfect healthy life.

Beside valuation by preference, changes in health state can also be valued in monetary term using either human capital approach, or contingent valuation, or revealed preference, or discrete choice experiment.

Health outcomes in natural form and measured as intermediate/final outcome can only be used in CEA. However, only final outcome valued by utility can be analyzed using CUA while outcomes that are valued as monetary term can only be analyzed by using CBA.

Analyzing the Costs and Consequences

Economics offers three evaluation tools that can be used separately or altogether, i.e., CBA, CEA, and CUA, all are used in a systematic way to address an economic problem.

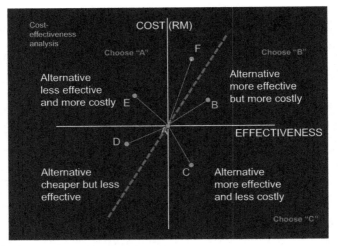

FIGURE 6.1   Cost-effectiveness plane.

The goal of economic evaluation analysis is to obtain efficiency based on the arithmetic mean of cost and benefit of the compared alternatives.

As economic evaluation is a comparative study, and a comparator could be either:

- more expensive, and less effective—dominated,
- cheaper, but less effective,
- cheaper, and more effective—dominant,
- more expensive, but more effective.

This could be illustrated in a cost-effectiveness plane as shown in Fig. 6.1.

The plane can further be divided into cost-effectiveness grid that could assist in interpreting the analysis (Fig. 6.2).

If comparison falls in:

- Red (Dark gray in print versions)-shaded cells (B, C, F): New alternative WOULD NOT be considered cost effective.
- Light gray-shaded cells (D, G, H): New alternative considered cost effective.
- If comparison shows similar effectiveness and similar cost (cell E), other factors may be considered.
- Cells A or I: more information is needed (e.g., how much extra cost per unit outcome as determined by ICER).

Incremental Cost-Effectiveness Ratio

Frequently, one alternative is BOTH more costly AND more effective (cells A or I). If so, then there is no answer to the cost-effectiveness question.

Cost effectiveness	Lower cost	Same cost	Higher cost
Lower effectiveness	A Conduct ICER	B	C Dominated
Same effectiveness	D	E Arbitrary	F
Higher effectiveness	G Dominant	H	I Conduct ICER

FIGURE 6.2   Cost-effectiveness grid.

All we can do is show how much extra it costs to gain an extra unit of outcome.

This is called the incremental cost-effectiveness ratio (ICER), which is the additional costs that one service or treatment imposes over another, compared with the additional effects, benefits, or utilities it delivers

$$\text{ICER} = \frac{\text{Cost A} - \text{Cost B}}{\text{Effectiveness A} - \text{Effectiveness B}} \tag{6.1}$$

The calculated ICER then would be compared with external criteria. It is usually done in the form of threshold that would determine if it is cost-effective or otherwise. This is usually represented as dotted line in the cost-effectiveness plane (Fig. 6.1). If the alternative is between B versus A, B would be more cost-effective as it is below the threshold. Whereas if it is between F and A, F would not be considered as cost-effective as it is above the threshold.

Net Monetary Benefit

The above are true for CEA and CUA. However, in CBA, as both cost and benefit are in the same unit (monetary terms), no external criterion is needed. The comparison can simply be made as the difference between benefit and cost, e.g., in a net monetary benefit (NMB) framework.

$$\text{NMB} = \text{Benefit} - \text{Cost}$$

If NMB is >0, then the alternative is more cost-effective.

Adjustment for Future Value—Discounting

Discounting is used in economic evaluation based on the rationale that we value cost and outcome differently according to when they occur—money received today is worth more than money received a year later. This reflects the preference for having resources now rather than later. As such, the timing of costs and benefits of a particular intervention determines an investment's attractiveness. In order to allow for differential timing of costs and benefits between programs, all future costs and benefits should be stated in terms of their present value.

Discounting is applied to calculate the present value of future costs and benefits if the time horizon of the project extends beyond 1 year. The present value is calculated by dividing the future cost (or benefit) with a function of the discount rate and the number of years over which the cost or benefit is accrued:

$$PV = (FV)/(1+r)^a \tag{6.2}$$

where,

PV = present value at time zero (the base year),
r = discount rate,
a = time (year),
FV = amount of benefit or cost in year a.

The discount rate varies between countries and typically ranges from 3% to 5%. Regardless of the rate employed, sensitivity analysis (SA) should be undertaken by changing the discount rate to examine its impact on the study results.

Sensitivity Analysis

Although economic data is widely used to guide and inform studies in healthcare, there is still need to acknowledge and address the uncertainties that lie within this data. There are several reasons why uncertainties in data can occur. This could be due to variability in sample data, variation in method of analysis across studies, as well as the need to generalize and extrapolate study results. In order to determine the effect of data uncertainty or the effect of assumptions made on our study conclusions, SA is employed. It is a technique that involves mathematical manipulation of key variables/ parameters across a range of plausible values to examine the robustness of the economic evaluation results and conclusions.

SA is divided into deterministic and probabilistic. Under deterministic SA, the most common form being simple SA (one-way, two-way, threshold, or extreme SA) where one or more key parameters are varied across certain values. For example, if a particular pharmacy service A is found to be cost-effective compared to pharmacy service B at current effectiveness of 10%, will it remain cost-effective if the effectiveness of pharmacy service A decreases or if the effectiveness of pharmacy service B increases?

An alternative to simple SA technique is the probabilistic SA where instead of assigning a single value to each parameter, a distribution is assigned to all key parameters. One value for each parameter will then be randomly selected and simulated. This process is iterated many times (e.g., 10,000 times) to examine the variation in the economic evaluation results.

Regardless of the type of SA employed, ultimately, if the study results do not substantially vary during SA, then the study result is described as being insensitive to that parameter and thus, it further strengthens the conclusion. Without SA, the robustness and reliability of an economic evaluation cannot be confirmed.

CASE STUDIES

Pharmacist's role has shifted to patient focused services for and it includes patient/medication counseling and medication-dependent disease management for patients with chronic diseases [14].

It capitalizes on the pharmacist expertise in medicine, the availability and accessibility of pharmacy service, and the fees being reimbursed by the funders. In both hospital (institution) and community pharmacy settings, the enhanced pharmacy services have proven to increase the effectiveness of pharmacological treatments by improving adherence to medicines, resolving drug-related problems, and optimizing pharmaceutical care [15–18]. It is worth noting that the success of this service very much depends on the volume of investment in manpower, equipment, consumables, and educational material. Hence, economic evaluation of these services is essential to determine the service's value to the overall improvement in health. To date, there are a number of economic evaluations on pharmacy services that have been conducted either alongside a trial or in a modeling framework [19,20]. This chapter will discuss examples of such evaluations according to their design and setting.

Institutional Setting

Pharmacist practicing in an institution (e.g., hospital) benefits from the vast availability of resources such as space and access to other healthcare professionals. Institution is the main place for patients to be clinically diagnosed and to follow-up. Most of the time, patients who are in need of an institution healthcare service are those who require specialist/consultant care. Being one of the major healthcare professionals in the institutional healthcare team, pharmacists play an important role as part of a holistic patient care. There are many types of services that a pharmacy department can offer at an institution level, such as ward pharmacy services, inpatient services, outpatient services, and therapeutic drug monitoring services. Nevertheless, the resources could be scarce with the increasing number of patients and the type of pharmacy services offered. In this context conducting an economic evaluation of a service can be very useful.

Here are the few examples in which economic evaluation is being undertaken:

Alongside Trial [21]

Background

Drug-related problems can contribute toward irrational use of drugs and inefficient healthcare resources utilization. One possible way to reduce these problems is through enhanced clinical pharmacist services. This study was conducted to evaluate the cost-effectiveness of an in-hospital clinical pharmacist service versus normal care, from a healthcare provider perspective on elderly patients.

Resources

The resources used for the intervention, inpatient and outpatient care, and reimbursed drugs were measured by using activity-based costing method and by using regional database.

Effectiveness

The effectiveness measure used in this study was QALY. This was evaluated by administering EQ-5D questionnaires during baseline and at 6-month follow-up.

Discounting

Discounting on the costs and effectiveness is not required as the study time horizon was less than 1 year.

Incremental Analysis

The incremental cost was €1622 and the incremental QALY was 0.0035. Overall, the ICER of the clinical pharmacist service was €463,371 per QALY gained, when compared with the UC (Fig. 6.3).

Sensitivity Analysis

The probabilistic SA results showed that the inpatient clinical pharmacist service was more cost-effective than the UC by only 20%, at the threshold of €50,000 per QALY gained. The ICER was €178,137 per QALY gained in the subgroup of patients alive at 6-month follow-up, and the clinical

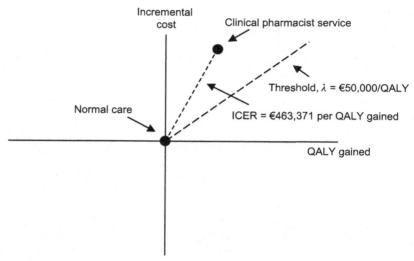

FIGURE 6.3 A cost-effectiveness plane of inpatient clinical pharmacist service versus normal care.

pharmacist service was found to be dominant in the subgroup of patients who were dead at 6-month follow-up.

Modeling Framework [22]

Background

Asthma is a chronic respiratory disease that needs long-term management to maintain good control of the disease. Respiratory Medication Therapy Adherence Clinic (RMTAC) is a pharmacist-led nonpharmacological asthma management clinic which was run adjunct to the usual physician care. This study aimed to evaluate the cost-effectiveness of RMTAC and UC versus UC alone, from the healthcare provider perspective.

Resources

The resources considered in this study were healthcare-related (including drugs, pharmacists' time, clinic visits, and hospitalizations). These were measured using the activity-based costing method and by using patient records. The unit costs of these were obtained from the healthcare provider sources.

Effectiveness

1. QALY—utilities were measured using standard gamble method on asthma patients.
2. Hospitalization averted.

Discounting

Both costs and outcomes were discounted at a 3% rate annually.

Incremental Analysis

This economic evaluation was analyzed in a lifetime horizon Markov cohort model with a cycle length of 1 month. The transition probabilities from asthma control to exacerbation states and the costs incurred were obtained from primary and secondary data sources. The costs and outcomes (both QALY gained and hospitalization averted) of RMTAC were more than that of UC. The ICERs were RM227.95 per QALY gained and RM587.35 per hospitalization averted (Fig. 6.4).

Sensitivity Analysis

At the willingness-to-pay (WTP) threshold of RM29,000 per an additional QALY gained, RMTAC was found to be more cost-effective at 99% and 63% of the time. This was for QALY gained and for hospitalization averted outcomes respectively. The base-case results were also found to be robust when a subgroup and scenario analysis was conducted.

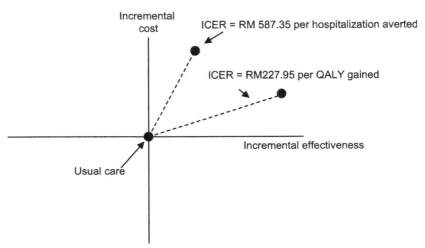

FIGURE 6.4 A cost-effectiveness plane of "RMTAC and UC versus UC" from healthcare perspective.

Community Pharmacy Setting

Community pharmacists (CPs) work closely with other healthcare professionals especially the General Practitioners (GPs), in order to provide better and coherent healthcare services to the patients. A common pharmacy service that a community pharmacy usually offers is the disease management services for patients with chronic diseases such as diabetes and asthma. Here is an example.

Alongside Trial [23]

Background

Depression is a highly prevalent disease that has high economic burden, partly due to lower rates of adherence to its treatment. CPs could help in addressing this issue. The study aimed to evaluate the cost-effectiveness of a community pharmacist intervention (CPI) in comparison with the UC among patients who were already initiated with the antidepressants in primary care. The study is conducted from a societal and healthcare perspective.

Resources

The resources consumed in this study were healthcare-related (including drugs, pharmacists' time, clinic visits) and lost productivity. These were measured from computerized pharmacy records, patient study chart, and by using client service receipt inventory. The unit cost for each of the resource was obtained from published sources of the same jurisdiction.

Effectiveness (Measured as)

1. Number of adherent patient—measured by using medication possession ratio (MPR), with a MPR less than 80% was considered as poor adherence.
2. QALY—utilities were measured by using EQ-5D, based on Spanish tariffs.
3. Remission of symptoms—measured by using the Patient Health Questionnaire 0-item depression module (PHQ-9), with scores superior to 50%.

Discounting

Discounting on the costs and effectiveness is not required as the study time horizon was less than 1 year.

Incremental Analysis

The 6-month ICER from societal and healthcare perspective for each of the outcome measure is described in Figs. 6.5 and 6.6, respectively. The CPI

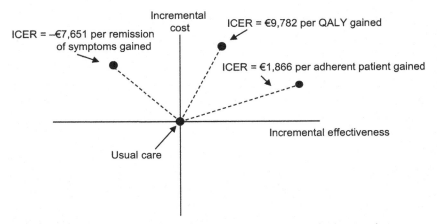

FIGURE 6.5 A cost-effectiveness plane of "CPI versus UC" from societal perspective.

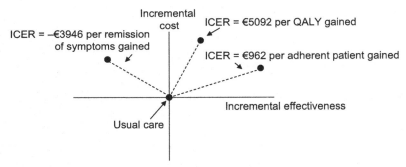

FIGURE 6.6 A cost-effectiveness plane of "CPI versus UC" from healthcare perspective.

was dominated by UC from both perspectives. This is because CPI has higher cost but lower remission.

Sensitivity Analysis

The base-case results were robust to the one-way SA. From the probabilistic SA, the results showed that if the WTP is €30,000 per extra adherent patient, remission of symptoms, or QALYs, the probability of the CPI being cost-effective was 0.71, 0.46, and 0.75, respectively (societal perspective). From a healthcare perspective, the probability of the CPI being cost-effective in terms of adherence, QALYs, and remission was of 0.71, 0.76, and 0.46, respectively.

Modeling [24]

Background

Obstructive sleep apnea syndrome (OSAS) is an under-diagnosed problem, and CPs can help in screening OSAS before patients start to develop other complications. This study was conducted to assess the cost-effectiveness of a CP-led sleep apnea screening program (in collaboration with GPs) among patients who are at risk of having moderate to severe OSAS. The study was conducted from a societal perspective. The "screening strategy with CP" was compared with different options; "screening strategy without CP" and "no screening" at all.

Resources

The resources that were considered for this model were the consultations, diagnostic tests, and treatment. These were valued against their unit costs which were obtained from the health insurance fund database and by using expert opinion. The cost of untreated OSAS patients was obtained from the estimates of two studies (one retrospective, while another one was prospective).

Effectiveness

The effectiveness measure used in this study was QALY. The utilities were obtained from two studies that used standard gamble method as a utility measurement tool.

Discounting

All costs and outcomes were discounted at 3% rate.

Incremental Analysis

This analysis was conducted in a 5 years Markov model with a 1 year cycle. From the results, it was observed that the "screening strategy with CP" had the lowest cost and highest QALYs if compared to the "screening strategy without CP" and if we use "no screening" at all. Therefore, the "screening strategy with CP" is considered as the most dominant, followed by the "screening strategy without CP" versus "no screening" (Fig. 6.7).

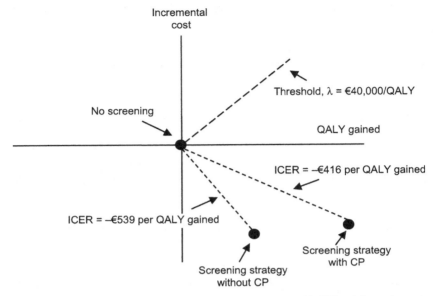

FIGURE 6.7   A cost-effectiveness plane of "screening strategy with CP" and "screening strategy without CP" versus "no screening."

Sensitivity Analysis

The probabilistic SA results showed that the "screening strategy without CP" was found to be dominant over "no screening" for half of the time during simulations, while it was cost-effective at other times. Similar results were obtained while comparing "screening strategy with CP" versus "screening strategy without CP." The one-way SA results showed that the base-case results were robust, even when different screening rates were utilized.

CONCLUSIONS

This chapter presented the basic steps in conducting economic evaluation that stemmed from the basic task of identifying, measuring, and comparing cost and consequences of different alternatives. There are various approaches to undertake the tasks in an economic evaluation. This is reflected in the four case studies that illustrated how pharmacy service can be evaluated based on their setting and design. The choice of approach would further depend on many interrelated factors including data availability, accessibility, feasibility, and the required accuracy.

Data on cost and consequences are normally available to be collected alongside any conducted studies and trials. However, when this data cannot be collected researchers would then opt for local data outside the trial that is readily available. However, the researchers have to be able to justify their choice of using other data sources. Some of the questions are, for example with different population characteristics produce the same outcome.

This is particularly true for complex innovative pharmacy service that requires accurate estimation of multiple resources in different cost center.

Nevertheless, the method chosen to measure and value the cost and consequences has to be weighed against the extra cost and manpower (among others) that would incur. If these could not be afforded by the researchers, then the method may not feasible after all.

Economic evaluation of pharmacy service would allow decision-makers to maximize the benefit obtainable from the use of limited resources to offer a new pharmacy service. Careful consideration to undertake the different tasks of conducting economic evaluation is required to increase its validity for decision-making.

GLOSSARY OF TERMS

Cost—benefit analysis a comparative analysis of alternative interventions where consequences are valued in monetary terms.

Cost-effectiveness analysis a comparative analysis of alternative interventions where consequences are valued in common natural units (e.g., reduction of blood pressure; life years saved).

Cost—utility analysis a comparative analysis of alternative interventions where consequences are valued in utility-weighted life years (e.g., QALY).

Discounting conversion of future cost and benefit to its present value at a predetermined rate, typically 3—5%.

Multi-attribute utility instruments instruments measuring quality of life across several dimensions (attributes) such as physical, mental, and social well-being.

Opportunity cost cost of the next best alternative that is forgone when a decision is made to adopt a particular intervention.

Quality-adjusted life year the function of preference of a particular quality of life (utility) and the number of years spent in that state.

Reliability the extent to which a particular instrument that is used to measure an outcome is capable of reproducing the same results across repeated measurements.

Sensitivity analysis a technique to examine the robustness of the economic evaluation results by mathematically manipulating of key variables/parameters across a range of plausible values.

Utility the measure of preference for a particular health state or benefit.

Validity the degree of an instrument logically and accurately measuring what it intends to measure.

TEST YOUR KNOWLEDGE

1. A CEA measures health outcomes in physical units.	
☐ True	☐ False
2. A CEA would be useful for an organization to determine the return on investment from a health program.	
☐ True	☐ False
3. For a CEA to be useful in comparing two different programs, common health outcomes must be employed.	
☐ True	☐ False
4. In CBA, outcomes can be measured either in natural or monetary units.	
☐ True	☐ False
5. In CUA, result is expressed as cost per quality-adjusted life years gained	
☐ True	☐ False
Answers: 1. True, 2. False, 3. True, 4. False, 5. True.	

REFERENCES

[1] Ministry of Health Malaysia. National healthcare establishments & workforce statistics 2008–2009. Kuala Lumpur; 2011.

[2] Samuelson PA, Nordhaus WD. Economics. 17th ed. New York: McGraw-Hill; 2000.

[3] Aljunid S, Zafar A, Saperi S, Amrizal M. Burden of disease associated with cervical cancer in Malaysia and potential costs and consequences of HPV vaccination. Asian Pac J Cancer Prev 2010;11(6):1551–9.

[4] Elamin E, Ibrahim M, Sulaiman S, Muttalif A. Cost of illness of tuberculosis in Penang, Malaysia. Pharm World Sci 2008;30(3):281–6.

[5] Ibrahim WN, Aljunid S, Ismail A. Cost of type 2 diabetes mellitus in selected developing countries. Malays J Public Health Med 2010;10(2):68–71.

[6] Liau SY, Shafie AA, Ibrahim MIM, et al. Stages of change and health-related quality of life among employees of an institution. Health Expect 2013;16(2):199–210.

[7] Chiew GP, Shafie AA, Hassali MA, Awaisu A, Cheah WK. Pharmacist-run methadone clinic in a Malaysian public health center: evaluating patient satisfaction and quality of life outcomes. Value Health 2010;13(7):A556.

[8] Kocarnik BM, Liu C-F, Wong ES, et al. Does the presence of a pharmacist in primary care clinics improve diabetes medication adherence? BMC Health Serv Res 2012;12(1): 1–9.

[9] Drummond MF, Sculpher MJ, Claxton K, Stoddart GL, Torrance GW. Methods for the economic evaluation of health care programmes. 4th ed. Oxford University Press; 2015.

[10] Briggs AH, O'Brien BJ. The death of cost-minimization analysis? Health Econ 2001; 10(2):179–84.

[11] Schmid GP. Understanding the essentials of economic evaluation. J Acquir Immune Defic Syndr Hum Retrovirol. 1995;10(Suppl 4):S6–13.

[12] Salih MRM, Bahari MB, Shafie AA, et al. Cost-effectiveness analysis for the use of serum antiepileptic drug level monitoring in children diagnosed with structural-metabolic epilepsy. Epilepsy Res 2012;104(1-2):151−7.

[13] Luce B, Manning W, Siegel JE, Lipscomb J. Estimating costs in cost-effectiveness analysis. In: Gold MF, Siegel JE, Russell LB, Weinstein MC, editors. Cost effectiveness in health and medicine. New York: Oxford University Press; 1996. p. 176−213.

[14] Cooksey JA, Knapp KK, Walton SM, Cultice JM. Challenges to the pharmacist profession from escalating pharmaceutical demand. Health Aff 2002;21(5):182−8.

[15] Al-Jumah KA, Qureshi NA. Impact of pharmacist interventions on patients' adherence to antidepressants and patient-reported outcomes: a systematic review. Patient Prefer Adherence 2012;6:87−100.

[16] Nkansah N, Mostovetsky O, Yu C, et al. Effect of outpatient pharmacists' non-dispensing roles on patient outcomes and prescribing patterns. Cochrane Database Syst Rev 2010;(7): CD000336.

[17] Omran D, Guirguis LM, Simpson SH. Systematic review of pharmacist interventions to improve adherence to oral antidiabetic medications in people with type 2 diabetes. Can J Diabetes 2012;36(5):292−9.

[18] Pande S, Hiller JE, Nkansah N, Bero L. The effect of pharmacist-provided non-dispensing services on patient outcomes, health service utilisation and costs in low- and middle-income countries. Cochrane Database Syst Rev 2013;(2):Cd010398.

[19] Altowaijri A, Phillips CJ, Fitzsimmons D. A systematic review of the clinical and economic effectiveness of clinical pharmacist intervention in secondary prevention of cardiovascular disease. J Manag Care Pharm 2013;19(5):408−16.

[20] Yong YV, Shafie AA. Economic evaluation of enhanced asthma management: a systematic review. Pharm Pract 2014;12(4):493.

[21] Wallerstedt SM, Bladh L, Ramsberg J. A cost-effectiveness analysis of an in-hospital clinical pharmacist service. BMJ Open 2012;2(1):e000329.

[22] Yong YV. Economic Evaluation of Respiratory Medication Therapy Adherence Clinic (RMTAC) on Asthma Patients in Malaysia. MSc [thesis]. Malaysia: Universiti Sains Malaysia; 2016.

[23] Rubio-Valera M, Bosmans J, Fernandez A, et al. Cost-effectiveness of a community pharmacist intervention in patients with depression: a randomized controlled trial (PRODEFAR Study). PLoS One 2013;8(8):e70588.

[24] Perraudin C, Le Vaillant M, Pelletier-Fleury N. Cost-effectiveness of a community pharmacist-led sleep apnea screening program—a Markov model. PLoS One 2013;8(6): e63894.

Chapter 7

Evaluation of the Community Pharmacist-led Anticoagulation Management Service (CPAMS) Pilot Program in New Zealand

J. Shaw, J. Harrison and J.E. Harrison
University of Auckland, Auckland, New Zealand

Chapter Outline

INTRODUCTION

This chapter describes the evaluation of a new model of care, namely, the community pharmacist-led anticoagulation management service (CPAMS) in New Zealand. The chapter sets out the background to the development of the service, the nature of the service, and the key findings from the evaluation, including a preliminary cost—benefit analysis.

BACKGROUND

Despite the recent introduction of new oral anticoagulants, warfarin retains an important place in the prevention and treatment of thromboembolism. Its principal indication is the prevention of ischemic stroke secondary to atrial fibrillation [1,2]. The incidence of atrial fibrillation and its sequelae is increasing worldwide and it can be supposed that the number of patients on warfarin will also increase [3]. Warfarin requires careful individual titration because the dose required varies from person to person and can alter over time, affected by factors such as changes to diet, alcohol intake, other medications, or concurrent illness. Too low a dose results in inadequate protection or treatment; too high a dose can lead to hemorrhagic complications [4,5].

Regular blood tests to monitor the rate of blood clotting (reported as the international normalized ratio or INR) and dose reviews are essential to ensure that therapy remains in range. The proportion of time in therapeutic range (TTR) is a widely used measure of the quality of anticoagulation control. International guidelines recommend maintaining a TTR of 60% or above in order to maximize the benefits of warfarin and to limit adverse events [6,7].

In New Zealand, warfarin management for patients in primary care has traditionally been provided by general practices. Patients attend their local blood collection center or general practice where a venous blood sample is taken and sent to a centralized laboratory service for testing. The result is later reviewed at the practice and dose adjustments communicated to the patient by telephone. Responsibility for coordination is sometimes delegated to a practice nurse. This model of care is often fragmented, involving multiple parties and processes, and has been demonstrated, both overseas and in New Zealand, to deliver a TTR that is typically less than 60% [8—10].

The role of pharmacists in secondary care anticoagulation management services (AMS) is well documented [11]. There are some published reports of community-based AMS involving pharmacists but these typically describe pilot or small studies. These reports indicate that potential benefits of community-based AMS involving pharmacists include improved accessibility and greater convenience for patients, improved anticoagulation control, and a reduction of the burden on general practice [12,13].

DEVELOPMENT OF THE PROJECT

Following positive results from a small trial at a single community pharmacy in 2009, the Pharmaceutical Society of New Zealand (PSNZ) was approached with the idea of a larger study. Discussions took place in early 2010 between PSNZ, Roche Diagnostics NZ, the developers of INR Online, and the University of Auckland (as evaluators).

A proposal for a Community Pharmacist-led Anticoagulation Management Service (CPAMS) pilot study was submitted to Health Workforce New Zealand (HWNZ), a government agency that promotes the development of new and extended workforce roles, scopes of practice, and models of care, in mid-2010, and was approved as an Innovation Demonstration Project. A multi-disciplinary steering group was established in September 2010, and ethics approval to proceed was granted by the New Zealand Multi-region Ethics Committee in December 2010 [14].

AIMS OF THE COMMUNITY PHARMACIST-LED ANTICOAGULATION MANAGEMENT SERVICES (CPAMS) EVALUATION

The overall aim of the CPAMS project was to investigate whether the role of community pharmacists should be extended to provide a new service to patients for the monitoring of anticoagulant (warfarin) therapy. The aim of the evaluation was to ascertain whether this innovative model of care could provide safe, effective, and cost-effective care that is acceptable to patients and other healthcare providers. The CPAMS evaluation was carried out in three parts:

1. Effectiveness and safety
2. Acceptability
3. A preliminary cost–benefit analysis

DESIGN OF CPAMS

After receipt of expressions of interest from over 100 pharmacies throughout New Zealand, 15 community pharmacies were selected to participate in the project, representing a range of urban, suburban, and rural populations and a variety of socio-demographic and ethnicity profiles. Pharmacists participating in the CPAMS service underwent a structured training and accreditation program run by PSNZ.

Patients were referred to CPAMS by their general practitioner (GP). The patient's three most recent INR results were supplied to the pharmacist and were entered into the decision support system. The authority to review results and implement dose adjustments was delegated to the pharmacist by the patient's GP. The GP retained overall responsibility for patient management but a collaborative care protocol was developed whereby the pharmacist acted autonomously, sending INR results and dose changes electronically to the patient's electronic health record and discussing management decisions with the GP where there were safety concerns.

Enrolled patients had their INR tested at the pharmacy using a point-of-care testing device (CoaguChekXS Plus, supplied by Roche Diagnostics New Zealand) and a capillary blood sample [15–17]. The results were made available immediately, and dose adjustments were made by the pharmacist with the aid of an online decision support system that incorporated a dosing algorithm (INROnline, www.inronline.net) [18]; pharmacists were able to override dosing recommendations provided by the decision support system. A record was made if the patient reported any bleeding or bruising or had been admitted to hospital since the previous test.

All patients were initially tested once a week, regardless of their previous test frequency. If patients' subsequent results were stable, the interval between tests was gradually extended to a maximum of 4 weeks. All patients were eligible for inclusion except those with antiphospholipid syndrome (INR results obtained from point-of-care testing devices can be unreliable in these patients) and those undergoing treatment for neoplasm.

Patient recruitment took place from December 2010 to January 2011. All enrolled patients were included in the program evaluation. Patients were followed up from the time of enrollment until the program evaluation ended on July 31, 2011 or until they left the service, whichever came earlier. Pharmacies were paid a fee for the initial training and set-up of the service and a fee for each patient visit to cover the cost of time and consumables [14].

EFFECTIVENESS AND SAFETY OF CPAMS

Data Extraction and Management

Data on each patient's age, gender, pharmacy and GP, indication for warfarin treatment, INR target, test results, test dates, adverse events, and hospitalizations were extracted from INR Online. Reasons for patients withdrawing from the service were obtained either from the database or directly from pharmacists. Information on hospitalization and bleeding events was extracted from INR Online. Major bleeding was defined as bleeding requiring hospitalization or blood transfusion. In the absence of a separate code for thromboembolic events, these were identified by review of the patient record.

To enable a meaningful comparison of INR control during GP-led care and pharmacist-led care, pre-pharmacy INR data was obtained from GPs to allow a paired before–after comparison. Patient consent was requested to allow collection of a further 6 months of INR results and enable the calculation of TTR under GP-led care.

Data Analysis

The TTR was calculated for each patient based on their target INR, as recorded in the decision-support system. In line with standard practice, the patient's therapeutic range was defined as the target INR $\pm$ 0.5 units. The

TTR was calculated using the linear interpolation method described by Rosendaal et al. [6].

The period analyzed was that from the first recorded pharmacy test to the last. The mean TTR, the mean time below range (TBR), and the mean time above range (TAR) were calculated at an individual-patient level prior to aggregation into appropriate groups to allow additional analysis to be performed, for example comparing the mean TTR achieved at each pharmacy. The proportions of tests with INRs more than 1.0 unit below target, INRs below 2.0, above 5.0, and INRs above 8.0 were calculated (these values being outside the British Committee for Standards in Haematology (BCSH) safety indicator thresholds [19], as were the numbers of patients with one or more tests with these values.

The frequency of testing, the interval between tests, and the difference between planned and actual test dates were calculated. A descriptive analysis of the number, incidence, and nature of adverse events and hospitalizations was undertaken. The analyses described above were repeated for the subgroup of patients for whom pre- and post-enrollment data were available.

Results

Forty-one community pharmacists were accredited to provide CPAMS. A total of 693 patients, under the care of 115 GPs from 52 practices, were enrolled in the service. A median 47 patients were enrolled at each pharmacy (range 26— 75). Some pharmacies recruited patients from a single practice; others recruited from multiple practices. The median number of patients per practice was 4 (range 1—64). Two hundred twenty-one patients gave consent to their historical community laboratory data being used for the paired comparison between GP- and pharmacist-led care.

Of the 693 patients enrolled, 106 patients left the CPAMS before the end of the follow-up period; of these 22 were excluded from analysis because they had insufficient test results (a minimum of two results was required to allow calculation of TTR). The remaining 671 patients were included in the analysis, with median duration of follow-up of 197 days (interquartile range 168—219). The patients enrolled were predominantly male (62.4%), aged over 65 (70.6%), and the great majority were receiving warfarin for prevention of ischemic stroke complicating atrial fibrillation (73.8%).

The mean TTR for the 671 patients whose results were evaluated was 78.6%, rising to 79.4% and 80.2% for patients who had been in the CPAMS for 16 weeks or 26 weeks, respectively (Table 7.1; Fig. 7.1). Of the 693 patients enrolled, 587 remained in the service at July 31, 2011. A fuller description of the results in this section is found in a paper by the authors [20].

Table 7.2 summarizes the number and proportion of INR tests outside recommended efficacy and safety thresholds for patients for whom both standard care and CPAMS data were available.

TABLE 7.1 TTR Based on Target ± 0.5 Units

	Patients Included in the Analysis	Patients with 16 Weeks or More of Tests in the CPAMS	Patients with 26 Weeks or More of Tests in the CPAMS
Number of patients	671	624	421
Mean TTR	78.6%	79.4%	80.2%
95% Confidence Interval	49.3–100%	52.6–100%	55.0–100%
Number (percent) of patients with TTR ≥60.0%	598 (89.1%)	562 (90.1%)	385 (91.4%)
Number (percent) of patients with TTR ≥70.0%	514 (76.6%)	487 (78.0%)	338 (80.3%)
Number (percent) of patients with TTR ≥80.0%	375 (55.9%)	357 (56.3%)	249 (59.1%)

All pharmacy sites achieved a mean TTR in excess of 70% (range 71.4–84.1%) well above the recommended target of 60% (Fig. 7.1).

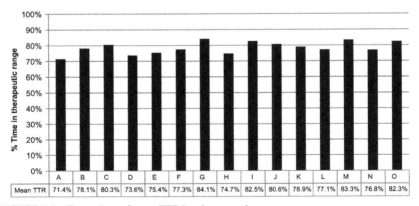

FIGURE 7.1   Comparison of mean TTR by pharmacy site.

TABLE 7.2 INRs Outside Efficacy and Safety Thresholds

Total Number of Patients	671		
Total Number of CPAMS Tests Performed up to July 31, 2011	9265		
	INR >1.0 Below Target[a]	INR Above 5.0	INR 8.0 or Above[b]
Number of test results	311	65	7
Percentage of test results	3.4%	0.7%	0.1%
Number of patients with one or more test results in band stated	152	43	5
Percentage of patients with one or more test results in band stated	22.7%	6.4%	0.8%

[a]This column may include test results from patients recently started or restarted on warfarin, whose INRs had not yet reached the therapeutic range.
[b]The measure ≥8.0, rather than >8.0 as recommended in the guidelines of the BCSH (23), was used because the CoaguChek XS device has a maximum INR reading of 8.0.

TABLE 7.3 Interval between Tests

	For Whole Period of CPAMS up to July 31, 2011	For Months 1−3 of CPAMS	For Months 4−6 of CPAMS
Number of patients	671	671	635
Mean interval between tests	14.4 days	9.7 days	16.7 days
95% Confidence Interval	4−31 days	2−22 days	4−31 days
Median interval between tests	10	8	15
Inter-quartile range	8−21	7−12	8−27

The mean interval between tests across the whole study was 14.4 days; with more frequent testing in months 1−3 (every 9.7 days) but increasing to 16.7 days in months 4−6 (Table 7.3). Compliance with appointments was excellent with 83.1% of tests occurring on or before the due date.

TABLE 7.4 Comparison of TTR During Standard Care and Under CPAMS

	Standard Care	CPAMS
Number of patients	154	154
Mean TTR	60.4%	77.5%
95% Confidence Interval	9.9–100%	51.8–100%

TABLE 7.5 Adverse Events and Hospitalizations Recorded for CPAMS Patients

Category of Adverse Event	Number	Incidence per 100 Patient Years of Follow-Up
Minor bleeding	429	125.0
Major bleeding	7	2.0
Thromboembolism	3	0.9
Category of Hospitalization	**Number**	**Incidence per 100 Patient Years of Follow-Up**
Related to warfarin treatment	10	2.9
Potentially related to warfarin treatment	8	2.3
Unrelated to warfarin treatment	174	50.7
Total[a]	192	56.0

[a]It was noted that some of the entries recorded under hospital admissions appeared to relate to outpatient appointments or visits to the emergency department, rather than inpatient stays.

Prior INR data (6 months) was obtained for 154 patients from six sites. For these patients, mean TTR for CPAMS was 77.5% and for standard care was 60.4%; whereas the mean interval between tests was similar with 12.6 days for CPAMS and 13.5 days for standard care (Table 7.4).

There were 436 episodes of bleeding or bruising recorded during the study; of these seven were categorized as major bleeds (Table 7.5). Three thromboembolic events were recorded during the study. There were 192 recorded hospitalizations during the study, of these 174 were judged to be unrelated to warfarin treatment and ten definitely related to warfarin treatment (Table 7.5).

Discussion of Effectiveness and Safety of CPAMS

In all sites, the mean TTR exceeded 70% and was well in excess of the BCSH standard of 60%. The mean TTR across the whole study was 78.6%, rising to 80.2% for patients with 26 weeks or more of tests. Using TTR as a measure of the quality of anticoagulation control, this result strongly suggests that community pharmacists, appropriately trained and accredited, can provide a high-quality service [21,22]. Other measures, such as compliance with appointments, are further evidence of the effectiveness of the service.

It is difficult to assess safety in a study like this and we cannot firmly conclude that there was a decrease in the incidence of warfarin-related adverse events for patients in the CPAMS. The incidence of adverse events in the literature is in the order of 5%; therefore, a very large sample of patients would be required to show a clinically significant difference. Furthermore, the information collected via INR Online lacked sufficient detail to verify that all events had been identified and documented. The incidence of adverse events and hospitalizations in this study were no greater than that reported in the literature [23–25].

ACCEPTABILITY OF THE SERVICE

Questionnaires

Separate questionnaires were developed for patients, accredited pharmacists, GPs, and practice nurses. The questionnaires were designed to collect opinions on:

1. the accessibility and convenience of the CPAMS for patients
2. the safety of the CPAMS
3. the impact of the CPAMS on patients' anticoagulant control
4. participants' confidence in pharmacists' ability to take on this additional role
5. the impact of the CPAMS on the workload of general practices
6. the effect of the CPAMS on the relationship between patients and pharmacists
7. the effect of the innovation service on professional relationships
8. the performance of the point-of-care testing device
9. the performance of the decision-support system
10. whether the service should be continued
11. whether the service should be made more widely available

The questionnaires comprised Likert-scaled statements (1 = strongly agree to 5 = strongly disagree). Some negatively phrased statements were included to guard against polarity bias. Additional space was provided for participants to record any other comments. Patient questionnaires were distributed via the pharmacies. Pharmacist (41), GP (115), and practice nurse (89) questionnaires were mailed directly to participants. Questionnaire responses were entered (with 10% double entry) into SPSS v20 (SPSS, Inc., Chicago, IL, USA). Results are presented as frequency distributions of responses; the "agree" and "strongly agree" and "disagree" and "strongly disagree" responses were aggregated to give an overall indication of agreement/disagreement with the statements. A fuller description is found in a paper by the authors [26].

Interviews and Site Visits

A sample of respondents was selected with the aim of canvassing a range of opinions, in particular, from participants who expressed opinions contrary to the majority. Interviews were brief; participants were asked to expand on their responses to the questionnaire and give any additional feedback on the service that they felt was important. A semi-structured interview was conducted with one or more of the accredited pharmacists at each pharmacy. The aim was to gather more detailed information about how the service had worked in practice and to identify changes that would be needed if the service were to be continued or expanded, as well as the impact on pharmacists' job satisfaction and on multidisciplinary team functioning.

Results

In presenting the results from this section of the evaluation, we have only included the summary results from the questionnaires and have aggregated the "SA + A" and "SD + D" responses for clarity. We have not presented the full range of responses nor additional written comments and interview comments, because of space constraints. Questionnaire responses were recorded from 60% of patients; 83% of pharmacists; 24% of GPs; and 29% of practice nurses. Selected patient, pharmacist, GP, and practice nurse questionnaire responses are shown in Table 7.6.

The great majority of patients found CPAMS to be convenient and accessible, preferable to the previous system, and expressed confidence in the pharmacist to perform the service. Many patients felt that it had increased their involvement with treatment. A small proportion of patients expressed a preference for GP care. Most patients wanted the service to continue but there was divided opinion on whether they would use it if they had to pay a fee.

Pharmacists were overwhelmingly positive about the service. All were pleased to play a much more patient-focused role. They felt that their relationships with both patients and other health professionals had improved and they were confident in their ability to provide a safe and effective service. They unanimously supported continuation of the service.

TABLE 7.6 Patient, Pharmacist, General Practitioner (GP), and Practice Nurse Questionnaire Responses

Questionnaire Item	Patients (n = 412)			Pharmacists (n = 34)			GPs (n = 28)			Practice Nurses (n = 22)		
	SA + A (%)	N (%)	SD + D (%)	SA + A (%)	N (%)	SD + D (%)	SA + A (%)	N (%)	SD + D (%)	SA + A (%)	N (%)	SD + D (%)
I find it more convenient to have my blood test at the pharmacy	96.9	2.2	0.9									
I would rather have a finger-prick blood test than have blood taken from my arm using a needle	98.1	1.7	0.2									
I like knowing my test result and dose immediately, rather than having to wait until later	99.3	0.5	0.2									
I find it useful to be able to discuss my warfarin treatment with the pharmacist when I go for my test	95.4	4.1	0.5									
Using the warfarin service at the pharmacy has also meant that the pharmacist has also been able to help me with other aspects of my healthcare	78.7	17.4	3.9									

(Continued)

TABLE 7.6 (Continued)

Questionnaire Item	Patients (n = 412)			Pharmacists (n = 34)			GPs (n = 28)			Practice Nurses (n = 22)		
	SA + A (%)	N (%)	SD + D (%)	SA + A (%)	N (%)	SD + D (%)	SA + A (%)	N (%)	SD + D (%)	SA + A (%)	N (%)	SD + D (%)
I would prefer to have my warfarin managed by my family doctor	7.9	31.7	60.4									
I would still want to use the warfarin service at the pharmacy even if I had to pay a fee	46.3	24.5	29.2									
I have enough information about my patients' medical history to enable me to provide them with appropriate management of their warfarin treatment				91	6	3						
I am confident that the review system I have in place with my GPs for INRs above 4.0 or below 1.5 is effective				91	6	3						

Statement						
Providing a warfarin management service has improved my relationship with the patients involved	100	0	0			
As a direct result of seeing patients for their INR testing, I have been able to help them with other aspects of their healthcare	94	3	3			
I would like to be able to continue to offer a warfarin management service to my patients	100	0	0			
I am confident that the pharmacist can manage our patients' warfarin treatment safely	89	7	4	95	5	0
As a direct result of seeing my patients for warfarin management, the pharmacist has helped them with other aspects of their healthcare	36	60	4	50	45	5

(Continued)

TABLE 7.6 (Continued)

Questionnaire Item	Patients (n = 412)			Pharmacists (n = 34)			GPs (n = 28)			Practice Nurses (n = 22)		
	SA + A (%)	N (%)	SD + D (%)	SA + A (%)	N (%)	SD + D (%)	SA + A (%)	N (%)	SD + D (%)	SA + A (%)	N (%)	SD + D (%)
Having my patients enrolled in the CPAMS has saved me time							85	4	11	95	0	5
I would like the CPAMS to continue to be available to our patients							82	14	4	100	0	0
It is more convenient for patients to have their INR blood test at the pharmacy										91	9	0
As a direct result of our warfarin patients being involved in the CPAMS, they have missed out on help I could give them										0	52	48

KEY: SA + A, Strongly Agree + Agree; N, Neither Agree Nor Disagree; SD + D, Strongly Disagree + Disagree.

While the sample sizes were small, the majority of both GPs and practice nurses expressed confidence in pharmacists' ability to offer the service and felt that there were positive benefits for both patients (convenience) and themselves (time saved). Some concerns were expressed about communication of results and possible fragmentation of services. The majority wished to see continuation of the service and wider availability.

Discussion of the Acceptability of the Service

While those involved in the CPAMS were a self-selected cohort, they were consistently positive about its benefits in terms of accessibility and convenience. They found it helpful to be able to go to the pharmacy at any time during opening hours rather than having to attend the blood collection center by a certain time.

The majority of respondents (patients, pharmacists, GPs, and practice nurses) thought that the CPAMS model of care offered greater convenience for patients. A large majority of patients reported that having their warfarin managed by the pharmacist had saved them time. Many commented that there were no long queues, unlike at the blood collection centers. They also found it convenient to find out their result and dose straightaway, removing the need to contact their GP practice later. There is considerable literature that links patient knowledge and adherence to improved anticoagulation control [27−30].

The CPAMS reduced fragmentation of care by the incorporation of sampling, testing, and dose adjustment into one consultation involving a single health professional. Results found to be out-of-range could be dealt with immediately and patients were given a printout of their dose instructions. One of the concerns expressed by some GPs and practice nurses was possible fragmentation of care; interestingly, this concern diminished as the study progressed and patients acted as advocates for the service to their GPs and practice nurses. Pharmacists were very enthusiastic about the opportunity for enhanced patient care roles and better utilization of their clinical knowledge and skills.

COST−BENEFIT ANALYSIS

Background to the Cost−Benefit Analysis

The analysis presented here was conducted using the Economic Model of Oral Anticoagulation Therapy (OAT) developed by Oblikue Consulting [31]. The model takes the perspective of the payer, in this case the government. Only direct costs accrued by the health system are included. Costs to the patient, whether direct costs (such as out-of-pocket expenses for travel), or indirect costs (such as lost earnings due to taking time off work), are not accounted for.

Costs of Providing Anticoagulation Management

Pharmacist staff costs were calculated using data on timings collected in a time and motion study conducted during the evaluation, and professional fees for an equivalent service obtained from the National Pharmacist Services Pricing Guidance at the time. Nurse and GP time spent reviewing was estimated at 10% of what was required under standard care. The cost of consumables was based on acquisition costs and depreciation over 5 years. Overhead costs that were considered essential to the delivery of CPAMS, including internal and external quality assurance programs and computer decision support, were included as a cost per test. All costs per test variables in the CPAMS arm were based on the assumption that each pharmacy had 80 patients enrolled and conducted two tests per patient per month. No allowance was made in the model for the additional staff costs incurred during the CPAMS enrollment process and initial consultation.

Comparative data on staff costs incurred under the standard model of care (including GP time, nurse time, and professional fees) were derived from a published study of warfarin management in general practice in New Zealand [32]. The cost of laboratory testing was based on a report from one District Health Board. Costs of laboratory consumables and the cost of laboratory quality control programs were assumed to be overheads included in the laboratory test fee and were not added to the model for the standard care arm. No costs for blood collection at the general practice were included. No costs for quality assurance of practice management (practice audits) were included.

The frequency of testing in the CPAMS arm was derived from an analysis of the CPAMS data; the average number of tests per month across the entire CPAMS follow-up was used (Table 7.3). The frequency of testing in the standard care arm was based on published research from New Zealand [8]; these data indicate that test frequencies in standard care and the CPAMS are broadly similar. A summary of the costs is provided in Table 7.7.

Costs of Thromboembolic and Hemorrhagic Events

New Zealand specific data on age-specific mortality rates, thromboembolic and hemorrhagic event rates and costs per event were entered into the cost-benefit model. The data were sourced from DHB hospital cost data and analysis of discharge codes reported to the National Minimum Data Set. All patients admitted to hospital were followed-up for 3 years to identify ongoing costs. The cost data included in the model are summarized in Table 7.8.

TABLE 7.7 Costs of Anticoagulation Management

Standard care	Cost in NZ$	CPAMS	Cost in NZ$
Laboratory testing[a]	**9.39**	**Point-of-care testing[b]**	**7.32**
		INR test strip	*6.12*
		Consumables (lancing device, gloves, tissue, plaster, medical waste charges)	*0.84*
		Cost of POC-INR device (based on depreciation over 5 years)	*0.36*
Quality assurance/ quality control	**–**	**Quality assurance/quality control[b]**	**0.54**
Laboratory QA/QC costs assumed included in tests fee		Coaguchek XS quality control test (monthly *plus* at change of batch)	*0.28*
Practice audit not currently required		External Quality Assurance Programme (based on Royal College of Pathologists of Australasia (RCPA) program)	*0.26*
Computer decision support system	**–**	**Computer decision support system**	**0.50**
Not routinely used		Fee for service (based on INR Online commercial pricing)	*0.50*
Professional fees	**44.85**	**Professional fees**	**29.48**
Pharmacist time	–	Pharmacist time[d] (10 min, comprising 7 min consultation and 3 min administration and follow-up)	*25.00*
GP time[c] (8.8 min @ $200/h)	*29.35*	GP time (assumed 10% of standard care)	*2.93*
Nurse time[c] (18.6 min @ $50/h)	*15.50*	Nurse time (assumed 10% of standard care)	*1.55*
Cost (per patient per visit)	**54.24**	**Cost** (per patient per visit)	**37.84**
Total cost[e] (per patient per year)	**1301.76**	**Total cost[e]** (per patient per year)	**908.16**

[a]*Based on Canterbury Laboratory Services Consultation Report.*
[b]*Based on pharmacy enrolling 80 patients and conducting two tests per month; total 1920 tests per year.*
[c]*Derived from [32] (Table 7.1).*
[d]*Derived from time and motion study.*
[e]*Based on mean test frequency of two tests per month (see text).*

TABLE 7.8 Cost and Frequency of Hospital Admissions for Thromboembolic and Hemorrhagic Events

Complication	Year 1		Subsequent Years	
	Cost (NZ$)	Proportion of Event Category	Cost (NZ$)	Proportion of Event Category
Thrombotic event				
Thrombotic stroke (ICD-10 codes: I63.0, I63.3, I63.6)	10,846.47	62	7685.55	57
Transient ischemic attack (ICD-10 codes: G45)	6186.34	28	8542.57	33
Pulmonary embolism (ICD code: I26)	10,447.98	10	8476.45	10
Hemorrhagic event				
Cerebral hemorrhage (ICD-10 codes: I60.x; I61.x; I62.x)	14,067.47	48	7611.88	28
GI Bleed (ICD-10 codes: K92)	8401.64	52	7500.74	72

Estimation of the Effect of Improved Anticoagulation Control

The size of the patient group enrolled in the project was not sufficiently large to detect small differences in adverse event rates between the CPAMS and those reported in the literature [33,34]. The TTR was therefore used as a surrogate measure of event rates. Extrapolating the mean improvement in TTR achieved in the innovation project to a reduction in event rates, based on the assumptions above, suggests that the expected thromboembolic event rate in the CPAMS group would be 1.9% (95% CI 0.5−5.1%) per year compared to an assumed rate of 4.6% (95% CI 3.0−6.5%) for standard care. Similarly, the rate of hemorrhagic complications would be expected to fall to 2.1% (95% CI 0.2−8.9%) from an assumed rate of 3.7% (95% CI 1.4−7.0%). The assumed rates for standard care were derived from a large systematic review and meta-analysis.

Prevalence of Warfarin Treatment in New Zealand

The model assumes that 46,000 patients are treated with warfarin at any given time; this figure is taken from the model for the CPAMS, submitted to HWNZ.

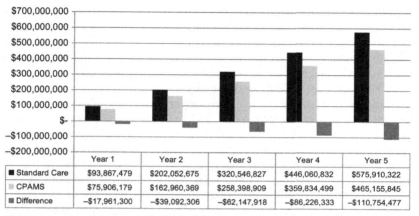

	Year 1	Year 2	Year 3	Year 4	Year 5
■ Standard Care	$93,867,479	$202,052,675	$320,546,827	$446,060,832	$575,910,322
CPAMS	$75,906,179	$162,960,369	$258,398,909	$359,834,499	$465,155,845
■ Difference	−$17,961,300	−$39,092,306	−$62,147,918	−$86,226,333	−$110,754,477

FIGURE 7.2   Cost−benefit analysis (50% of eligible patients managed under CPAMS).

Cost−Benefit Analysis

From a government-payer perspective, the cost of delivering the CPAMS is 30% lower than the cost of the standard care model (NZ$908.16 versus NZ $1301.76 per patient per year). The main cost in both models of care is the cost of staff time. The economic analysis is therefore potentially sensitive to changes in both the time spent on delivering the service and on professional pay rates.

When considering the improvement in anticoagulation control and extrapolating this to a reduction in both thromboembolic and major bleeding complications, the CPAMS model appears to offer substantial cost savings. The economic analysis is driven by the high costs of both thromboembolic, particularly stroke, and major bleeding events. In this scenario, where 50% of patients are managed under CPAMS and the remaining 50% under standard care, the predicted budget impact from a government perspective is a net reduction in anticoagulation-associated costs of approximately NZ$111M over 5 years (Fig. 7.2).

Discussion of Cost−Benefit Analysis

The evaluation did not seek to undertake an extensive health economic analysis. The project was not designed with a comparator group and the patient group was not sufficiently large to be able to detect a difference in adverse event rates.

It is important to note that the cost−benefit analysis takes the view of the payer, in this case the government. It assumes that all costs and all benefits are accrued in the same system. In reality, costs are accrued in one place and benefits elsewhere. Similarly, cost−benefit analyses are frequently criticized for promising savings that cannot be realized without, for example withdrawing funding from other services. The analysis should perhaps be viewed as describing discretionary spending. In theory, money saved on the costs of managing anticoagulation and its related complications, and by avoiding thromboembolic events, can be redirected to other areas of care.

In the project, all patients were initially tested weekly as a requirement of the transition to dosing using the decision-support system. For some patients this meant more frequent testing than under standard care; however the interval between tests gradually reverted to a more "normal" pattern. The economic model assumes that the same number of tests is performed per patient, per year for both models of care. This assumption appears to be justified both by the literature and by data collected during the study period. Irrespective of the cost−benefit analysis, a simple analysis of the cost of management indicates that the CPAMS offers a cost-effective alternative to the standard model of care.

CONCLUSION

The aim of the evaluation was to ascertain whether the CPAMS could provide safe, effective, and cost-effective care that was acceptable to patients and other healthcare providers.

Using TTR as a measure of the quality of anticoagulation control, this study strongly suggests that community pharmacists, appropriately trained and accredited, can provide a high-quality service. Other measures, such as compliance with appointments, are further evidence of the effectiveness of the service [20,26].

The study demonstrated the contribution community pharmacists can make to patient care beyond their accepted roles of medicines provision, medication counseling and treating minor ailments. The majority of both patients and primary care practitioners accepted this extended role. Pharmacists reported high levels of satisfaction with being able to put their clinical knowledge to use in direct patient care. There were some concerns, particularly with regard to ensuring that there was adequate communication between healthcare providers and wider implementation will require strong collaborative relationships.

The limitations of cost−benefit analysis in a study such as this are acknowledged. Nevertheless, using data validated in this study, the cost per patient per year is about 30% less for CPAMS than standard care. Economic modeling would further suggest that the improvements in anticoagulation control could lead to substantial cost savings through the reduction of both thromboembolic and major bleeding events.

There were both strengths and limitations in this evaluation. Amongst the strengths was the fact that the project was overseen by a multidisciplinary steering group with representation from all major players: pharmacy, general practice, industry, laboratory services, and the University as evaluators. In addition the project was supported by Health Workforce New Zealand, an organization that seeks to develop innovative healthcare delivery services. The majority of the data on safety and effectiveness of the service was captured through the INR Online decision-support database—this was both a powerful and valuable research tool and the principal vehicle for patient management. As well as investigating the clinical impact of the service, the evaluation also explored its acceptability and cost−benefit. This provided a rich and comprehensive set of evidence concerning the overall effectiveness and acceptability of the service.

The major limitation of the study was the lack of a control group and this attracted criticism at the time. In an ideal world this would have been attempted but in terms of practicalities and funding, this was simply not feasible. The study did not set out to prove that CPAMS was "better" than standard care (or any other model of care); rather that the service could be provided safely and effectively by pharmacists, at no greater cost to the public purse. Another limitation was the relatively poor response to the GP and practice nurse questionnaires. Although this was disappointing, it was not surprising as even our medical colleagues find it difficult to achieve much better. Lastly, the limitations of our cost−benefit analysis have already been acknowledged.

As a postscript to this study, CPAMS was established as a contracted community pharmacy service in New Zealand in late 2012 and, at the time of writing, about 150 of the 900 pharmacies throughout New Zealand were providing the service.

REFERENCES

[1] Gladstone DJ, Bui E, Fang J, Laupacis A, Lindsay MP, Tu JV, et al. Potentially preventable strokes in high-risk patients with atrial fibrillation who are not adequately anticoagulated. Stroke 2009;40(1):235−40.

[2] Marinigh R, Lip GYH, Fiotti N, Giansante C, Lane DA. Age as a risk factor for stroke in atrial fibrillation patients implications for thromboprophylaxis: Implications for thromboprophylaxis. J Am Coll Cardiol 2010;56(11):827−37.

[3] Ogilvie IM, Welner SA, Cowell W, Lip GYH. Characterization of the proportion of untreated and antiplatelet therapy treated patients with atrial fibrillation. Am J Cardiol 2011;108(1):151−61.

[4] Gallus AS, Baker RI, Chong BH, Ockelford PA, Street AM. Consensus guidelines for warfarin therapy. Recommendations from the Australasian Society of Thrombosis and Haemostasis. Med J Aust 2000;172(12):600−5.

[5] Hylek EM, Singer DE. Risk factors for intracranial hemorrhage in outpatients taking warfarin. Ann Intern Med 1994;120(11):897−902.

[6] Rosendaal FR, Cannegieter SC, van der Meer FJ, Briet E. A method to determine the optimal intensity of oral anticoagulant therapy. Thromb Haemost 1993;69(3):236−9.

[7] Anon. Guidelines on oral anticoagulation: third edition. Br J Haematol 1998;101(2):374−87.

[8] Young L, Ockelford P, Harper P. Audit of community-based anticoagulant monitoring in patients with thromboembolic disease: is frequent testing necessary? Intern Med J 2004;34(11):639−41.

[9] Baker WL, Cios DA, Sander SD, Coleman CI. Meta-analysis to assess the quality of warfarin control in atrial fibrillation patients in the United States. J Manage Care Pharm 2009;15(3):244−52.

[10] Garcia DA, Witt DM, Hylek E, Wittkowsky AK, Nutescu EA, Jacobson A, et al. Delivery of optimized anticoagulant therapy: consensus statement from the Anticoagulation Forum. Ann Pharmacother 2008;42(7):979−88.

[11] Saokaew S, Permsuwan U, Chaiyakunapruk N, Nathisuwan S, Sukonthasarn A. Effectiveness of pharmacist-participated warfarin therapy management: a systematic review and meta-analysis. J Thromb Haemost. 2010;8(11):2418−27.

[12] Jackson SL, Peterson GM, Bereznicki LR, Misan GM, Vial JH, et al. Improving the outcomes of anticoagulation in rural Australia: an evaluation of pharmacist-assisted monitoring of warfarin therapy. J Clin Pharm Ther 2005;30(4):345−53.

[13] Coleman B, Martin C, Barber N, Patterson D. An evaluation of the safety and acceptability of an anticoagulation clinic in a community pharmacy setting—a pilot study. Pharm J 2004;273(7328):822−4.

[14] Shaw J, Harrison J, Harrison JE. Community Pharmacist-led Anticoagulation Management Service: Final Report. Wellington, New Zealand: Health Workforce New Zealand; September, 2011.

[15] Leichsenring I, Plesch W, Unkrig V, Newhart A, Kitchen S, Kitchen DP, et al. Results of the master lot calibration of a new coagulation monitoring system for patient self testing. J Thromb Thrombolysis 2005;3(Suppl 1):P0884.

[16] Perry DJ, Fitzmaurice DA, Kitchen S, Mackie IJ, Mallett S. Point-of-care testing in haemostasis. Br J Haematol 2010;150(5):501−14.

[17] Woods K, Douketis JD, Schnurr T, Kinnon K, Powers P, Crowther MA. Patient preferences for capillary vs. venous INR determination in an anticoagulation clinic: a randomized controlled trial. Thrombosis Research 2004;114(3):161−5.

[18] Harper P, Pollock D. Improved anticoagulant control in patients using home international normalized ratio testing and decision support provided through the internet. Intern Med J 2011;41(4):332−7.

[19] Baglin TP, Cousins D, Keeling DM, Perry DJ, Watson HG. Safety indicators for inpatient and outpatient oral anticoagulant care: [corrected] Recommendations from the British Committee for Standards in Haematology and National Patient Safety Agency.[Erratum appears in Br J Haematol. 2007;136(4):681]. Br J Haematol. 2007;136(1):26−9.

[20] Harrison J, Shaw JP, Harrison JE. Anticoagulation management by community pharmacists in New Zealand: an evaluation of a collaborative model in primary care. Int J Pharm Pract 2015;23(3):173−81.

[21] Rose AJ, Hylek EM, Ozonoff A, Ash AS, Reisman JI, Berlowitz DR. Risk-adjusted percent time in therapeutic range as a quality indicator for outpatient oral anticoagulation: results of the Veterans Affairs Study to Improve Anticoagulation (VARIA). Circ Cardiovasc Qual Outcomes 2011;4(1):22−9.

[22] Shalev V, Rogowski O, Shimron O, Sheinberg B, Shapira I, Seligsohn U, et al. The interval between prothrombin time tests and the quality of oral anticoagulants treatment in patients with chronic atrial fibrillation. Thromb Res 2007;120(2):201−6.

[23] Gitter MJ, Jaeger TM, Petterson TM, Gersh BJ, Silverstein MD. Bleeding and thrombo-embolism during anticoagulant therapy: a population-based study in Rochester, Minnesota. Mayo Clinic proceedings Mayo Clinic 1995;70(8):725–33.

[24] Steffensen FH, Kristensen K, Ejlersen E, Dahlerup JF, Sorensen HT. Major haemorrhagic complications during oral anticoagulant therapy in a Danish population-based cohort. J Intern Med 1997;242(6):497–503.

[25] Connolly SJ, Pogue J, Eikelboom J, Flaker G, Commerford P, Franzosi MG, et al. Benefit of oral anticoagulant over antiplatelet therapy in atrial fibrillation depends on the quality of international normalized ratio control achieved by centers and countries as measured by time in therapeutic range. Circulation 2008;118(20):2029–37.

[26] Shaw J, Harrison J, Harrison JE. A community pharmacist-led anticoagulation manage-ment service: Attitudes towards a new collaborative model of care in New Zealand. Int J Pharm Pract 2014;22:397–406.

[27] Davis NJ, Billett HH, Cohen HW, Arnsten JH. Impact of adherence, knowledge, and qual-ity of life on anticoagulation control. Ann Pharmacother 2005;39(4):632–6.

[28] Arnsten JH, Gelfand JM, Singer DE. Determinants of compliance with anticoagulation: A case-control study. Am J Med 1997;103(1):11–17.

[29] Tang EO, Lai CS, Lee KK, Wong RS, Cheng G, Chan TY. Relationship between patients' warfarin knowledge and anticoagulation control. Ann Pharmacother 2003;37(1):34–9.

[30] Dantas GC, Thompson BV, Manson JA, Tracy CS, Upshur RE. Patients' perspectives on taking warfarin: qualitative study in family practice. BMC Fam Pract 2004;5:15.

[31] Connock M, Stevens C, Fry-Smith A, Jowett S, Fitzmaurice D, Moore D, et al. Clinical effectiveness and cost-effectiveness of different models of managing long-term oral antic-oagulation therapy: a systematic review and economic modelling. Health Technol Assess (Winchester, England) 2007;11(38):iii–iv, ix–66.

[32] Geevasinga N, Turner N, Mackie D. Therapeutic monitoring of warfarin—an audit of monitoring protocols and outcomes. N Z Fam Physician 2004;31(5):307–9.

[33] Heneghan C, Alonso-Coello P, Garcia-Alamino JM, Perera R, Meats E, Glasziou P. Self-monitoring of oral anticoagulation: a systematic review and meta-analysis. Lancet 2006; 367(9508):404–11.

[34] Wan Y, Heneghan C, Perera R, Roberts N, Hollowell J, Glasziou P, et al. Anticoagulation control and prediction of adverse events in patients with atrial fibrillation: a systematic review. Circ Cardiovasc Qual Outcomes 2008;1(2):84–91.

Chapter 8

Economic Evaluation of Pharmacy Services in Portugal

S. Costa

Center for Health Evaluation & Research (CEFAR) of the National Association of Pharmacies (ANF), Lisboa, Portugal

Chapter Outline

BRIEF OVERVIEW OF ECONOMIC EVALUATION OF PHARMACY SERVICES IN PORTUGAL

Over the last 25 years, Portuguese pharmacies have provided various patient care services, defined as complex health interventions, both in health promotion and disease prevention, as well as in disease/medication management which were often beyond, but not necessarily excluding, the medication supply role. Examples of these services include needle exchange program; flu immunization; early screening and referral (obesity, cardiovascular, diabetes, asthma, COPD, brown bag review of elderly patients on four or more medicines); methadone directly observed therapy; disease management (hypertension and/or hyperlipidemia, diabetes, asthma, and/or COPD, smoking cessation); and medication management/pharmaceutical care [1,2].

Needle exchange, methadone, and diabetes management were provided free under agreement with the Minister of Health. The other services, also provided free, were driven by the National Association of Pharmacies (ANF), an association of owners of pharmacies comprising 95% of Portuguese pharmacies. This was as a mean to push for a more active role for the pharmacies and the pharmacists.

All of these services included evaluation; however, they were limited in scope. The set of indicators collected and assessed suggested important achievements performed by pharmacies, but the design did not enable to establish effectiveness, except for the diabetes management, which demonstrated positive benefits [3]. As a result, the government agreed to remunerate pharmacies for the diabetes management program in 2003. This became the first capitated payment experience for a service in Portuguese pharmacies; however, the government decided to end it in 2010.

LITERATURE REVIEW OF ECONOMIC EVALUATION OF PHARMACY SERVICES IN PORTUGAL

To get an understanding regarding the work being undertaken with regards to evaluation of pharmacy services in Portugal, literature search was performed. The articles and literature was searched in NHS Economic Evaluation Database (NHS EED), PubMed, MEDLINEIn-Process & Other Non-Indexed Citations, MEDLINE, and EMBASE (via the OVID SP interface) up to 14 June 2016 to identify published papers describing or containing cost-effectiveness, cost−utility, cost−benefit, or cost−consequence analysis of community pharmacy services in Portugal. Studies that compared outcomes only or costs only were not included. Also descriptive cost studies were not included. This search resulted in one study which was retrieved and published in 2001. This was a multicenter, multicountry, randomized, controlled, longitudinal, clinical trial performed in seven European countries, including in Portugal. The study was related to pharmaceutical care (medication management) in elderly patients [4]. From a methodological perspective, health outcomes were not summarized and no summary benefit measure were evaluated in this study. A cost−consequences analysis was carried out looking at outcomes and direct costs plus cost-savings separately. Cost-savings seemed to be associated with the intervention in most countries, including in Portugal, although differences in total costs did not show statistical significance [4].

A second search was performed based on the author's knowledge of research studies presented at conferences or the studies which were recently completed. The Needle Exchange Program was the first public health initiative in pharmacies in Portugal and provided for free for almost 20 years. The first economic evaluation of this program was performed in 2002, 8 years after its onset. This was done when the concept of economic evaluation of pharmacy services in Europe was still very new [5]. From a methodological perspective, this economic evaluation used a Markov model adapted from the literature for 98 monthly cycles. This allowed for a dynamic transition between disease states combining three dimensions: epidemiologic (transmission and disease progression); demographic (confinement of injecting drug users in different sub-populations); behavioral (drug injecting risk). Nonparametric bootstrapping was used to estimate survival time after HIV infection, since major changes occurred in HIV drug therapy regimen during this period. Sensitivity analysis used three additional scenarios in the base case and probabilistic sensitivity analysis through Monte Carlo simulation [5].

This evaluation estimated that more than 7000 new HIV infections were averted per 10,000 injecting drug users in the first 8 years of the program. This represents at least, 400 million Euro in savings for the Portuguese National Health Service (NHS). Despite this evidence, no remuneration was provided to the pharmacies [5]. Also, between 2005 and 2014, pharmacies incurred severe remuneration losses, as a consequence of successive policies, which limited the scope to continue to provide these services for free [6–8].

A study on the economic value of Portuguese pharmacy services was performed in 2009. This was done by using a cross-sectional evaluation in pharmacies and a choice experiment method in a sample size of the population to judge consumers' willingness-to-pay [9]. A total of 38.8 million pharmacy interventions was provided for free in 2008 on a daily basis. The top three interventions represented 17.8 million interventions that costed 28.4 million Euros. The gross aggregate value was estimated at 76.5 million Euro, as valued by the population [9]. The difference between these, the net aggregate value was estimated at 48.1 million Euro. It is the monetary value of the society's welfare increment generated by these services [9]. Considering point-of-care measurement as an example, the net aggregate value was estimated at 17.7 million Euro [9]. Another study performed in 2012 evaluated the impact of policies in pharmacies included an update of the net aggregate value for point-of-care measurement, and this was in the range of 17.7 million Euro to 12.9 million Euro [6].

In 2014, the Ministry of Health and the National Association of Pharmacies (ANF) signed a Pharmacy Framework Agreement, which included for the first time, the principle of incentives for generics. It was also decided to evaluate experimental public health interventions [10]. Based on this, the Needle Exchange Program, which had been suspended in 2013, restarted at pharmacies in 2015 on an experimental basis. This was subject to payment if proven to be cost-effective [10].

At the time of submission of this chapter, the second economic evaluation of the Needle Exchange Program 2015 was finalized. From a methodological standpoint, the research consortium produced three pieces of research. This included an overview of systematic reviews aiming at synthesizing worldwide evidence on the effectiveness of needle exchange programs and also describing pharmacy needle exchange programs where sufficient information was available [11]. The second part was to conduct an economic evaluation of the program reintroduced in pharmacies in 2015 which also used a statistical model from the literature according to more recent disease epidemiology patterns for a time horizon of 5 years [12,13]. Equity impact assessment was also carried out as it used inequality Gini coefficient and Lorenz curves to compare weekly hours of needle exchange and the number of exchange sites per thousand inhabitants across the country with and without pharmacies [14,15].

Preliminary findings report that there is some evidence that needle exchange programs are likely to be effective in reducing HIV transmission and injecting risk behaviors among injection drug users. It also shows that the multicomponent programs which include other features in addition to needle exchange, including those provided in pharmacies, seem to be more beneficial despite the scarcity of quality research [11]. The economic evaluation demonstrated a 3.01€ annual net benefit per needle exchange in Pharmacies in a scenario that considers a fixed reimbursement rate to pharmacies per needle [12,13]. Finally, the impact assessment on equity demonstrated that access inequality Gini coefficient drops 63% when pharmacies were included [14,15]. These preliminary findings were presented at the Scientific Symposium of the 12th Congress of Pharmacies in April 2016, in Lisbon. The positive economic outcomes are expected to change policy regarding remuneration for pharmacies.

In 2015, another economic evaluation was performed on the social and economic value of pharmacy-based public health interventions. This research used a decision tree model to estimate the costs and benefits generated by pharmacy services. However, this excluded issues related to medicines supply. This used 25 years data on effectiveness, quality of life, and on healthcare use available from the previous descriptive research studies of these pharmacy services. This approach was supported from the literature and was further validated by a panel of experts [16,17].

Preliminary findings estimated that the economic value generated per year, measured as the difference between costs avoided and costs incurred by the society were 879.6 million Euros. The pharmacy interventions that generated nearly 54% of this benefit included: interventions to improve adherence (237.6 million Euro) and chronic disease interventions in hypertension, diabetes, hyperlipidemia, and asthma/COPD (236.9 million Euro) [16,17].

A Google Scholar search was also conducted to search published Master or PhD theses addressing the economic evaluation of pharmacy services in Portugal. One PhD thesis, published in 2015, assessed the economic impact of pharmaceutical care performed during 19 months on 39 patients, in a controlled, longitudinal trial. A within analysis on a subset of intervention patients with higher NHS direct costs reported that these patients achieved better clinical outcomes. However, the intervention was performed by a pharmacist in an NHS family health unit and this was not conducted in a community pharmacy [18].

Finally, we also requested health economists to assist in identifying ongoing research regarding economic evaluation of pharmacy services in

Portugal. However, no additional research was reported at the time of submission of this chapter.

A COLLABORATIVE CARE PILOT PROJECT BETWEEN PHARMACIES AND NHS: ECONOMIC EVALUATION ALONGSIDE A TRIAL

In late 2014, the concept of a collaborative care experiment between pharmacies and an NHS primary care family health unit began to take shape in Portugal. The intervention areas were selected by physicians themselves based on the local unmet healthcare needs that could benefit of collaboration with the pharmacies. Despite the practical nature of an intervention project, it was also decided that it should be designed as a controlled trial to meet research objectives.

The aim of the combined action-research project was to test a collaborative care model between a group of pharmacies and a local NHS family health unit in selected pharmacy-based public health intervention areas. The specific objectives were to assess the effectiveness of selected interventions; to perform an economic evaluation of selected interventions; and to assess the feasibility, process, patient and providers' satisfaction. This research study was designed as a multicenter, pragmatic controlled trial.

Pharmacies were selected according to predefined eligibility criteria.

The current status is that the Pilot Project USFarmácia is about to make its first steps as the trial is expected to start at a later stage in 2016.

Intervention areas include cardiovascular risk assessment; hypertension and/or hyperlipidemia management; uncomplicated female urinary tract infection screening and treatment; and acute pharyngitis infection screening and treatment.

There are several innovative features in this Project.

Innovative features of this project were pharmacy intervention protocol. This was pre-agreed with the physicians and included into the pharmacy dispensing software. The protocols include information on screening and point-of-care tests / monitoring. An adherence program based on mobile text messaging reminders to patients from pharmacies was also developed and included in the pharmacy dispensing software. Another important innovative feature is technology-driven communication between pharmacist and physician enabling text messaging to physicians, and scheduling of medical appointments directly from the pharmacy software on behalf of the patient. Innovation features also include regular interprofessional meetings between pharmacists, physicians, and nurses (Quality Circles).

Outcome measures include: blood pressure; lipid levels; other cardiovascular risk factors; proportion of controlled/treated patients; time-to-symptom free days; pharmacy and health resource use; quality-of-life;

patient preferences; patient reported outcomes; adherence; persistence; process indicators; patient satisfaction; and health providers' satisfaction.

Patients will be recruited in pilot pharmacies according to inclusion criteria upon written informed consent. Data will be collected alongside the trial using three data sources. These are web interface between pharmacy dispensing software and family health unit patient record software; telephone questionnaires to patients; questionnaires and focus groups for patients and providers.

The economic evaluation of the project comprises several stages of research. This includes an overview of systematic reviews of economic evaluations of pharmacy-based health interventions; review of evidence of selected interventions and economic evaluation of selected interventions using cost-effectiveness, cost−utility, and cost−benefit analysis alongside a trial.[1]

The overview was registered with the International Prospective Register of Systematic Reviews PROSPERO database on January 7, 2016. Review reference number PROSPERO 2016: CRD42016032768 (http://www.crd.york.ac.uk/PROSPERO/display_record.asp?ID=CRD42016032768).

The objective of this overview is to review the methods and issues most frequently found in systematic reviews of the economic evaluation of pharmacy services. The other objectives are to compare these methods with recommendations on the economic evaluation of public health interventions and with guidelines on economic evaluations conducted alongside clinical and pragmatic trials. The aim is also to develop a proposed system for the measurement and valuation of costs and health effects and the types of analysis feasible for the economic evaluation studies of pharmacy services. This review attempts to follow early work of Schumock [19,20] and recent contributions of Elliott [21], focusing on the community pharmacy setting. At the time of submission of this chapter, this overview is still ongoing.

Both the review of evidence and the economic evaluation are also expected to contribute to the economic evaluation methods and tools and to increase the knowledge on the effectiveness, value, and acceptability of selected pharmacy services under collaborative practice within primary care. It is also expected that this would advance the standards of care, and to raise questions about the role of complementary innovative payment models of healthcare providers, including pharmacies.

1. The economic evaluation of project USFarmáCia is the author's PhD thesis research project of Suzete Costa entitled "A Contribution for the Economic Evaluation of Pharmacy Services in a Collaborative Care Model in Portugal," currently undertaken at the National School of Public Health (ENSP), Universidade NOVA de Lisboa, Portugal, supervised by João Pereira, PhD (National School of Public Health, Universidade NOVA de Lisboa, Portugal), co-supervised by Céu Mateus, PhD (Lancaster University, Division of Health Research, Health Economics at Lancaster, UK), collaboration of Dennis K Helling, PhD (University of Colorado Skaggs School of Pharmacy and Pharmaceutical Sciences, USA).

FUTURE DEVELOPMENTS

Although the Pilot Project USFarmácia has been designed as a bottom-up experiment of a collaborative care between pharmacists and NHS providers, it has been well received by the National Association of NHS Family Health Units (comprising primary care physicians, nurses, and other health care providers) which has recently expressed interest in expanding this to other Family Health Units and to other disease areas.

Meanwhile, a second Framework Agreement between the Ministry of Health, the Ministry of Finance and ANF is expected to replace the former, with a more comprehensive framework. The newer framework is based on three principles. These are clear and transparent criteria for remunerating pharmacies for the supply of medicines ensuring patient access to medicines through a viable and sustainable network of pharmacies, efficiency incentives against agreed targets, as a contribution to the sustainability of the NHS; and community pharmacy providing health interventions that will again be subject to economic evaluation. These interventions are likely to include but not limited to antiretroviral therapy (ART) medication supply and specialized services (currently available in hospital pharmacy only); diabetes services; medication adherence and management; and flu immunization. However, some of these services are not new to pharmacies.

In fact, it is a process somewhat similar to the reimbursement of medicines and other health technologies that first need to be built on the evidence case of added therapeutic value and economic benefit.

The principles agreed seemed to have paved the way to enact legislation. The law was approved by the Government in July 2016 and it will be implemented in the forthcoming months. The law establishes the terms and conditions for the provision of public health interventions in pharmacies. Among other things, the law also includes payment terms for the Needle Exchange Program.

The new legislation and the formal signature of this Agreement— expected to take place still in 2016—will represent a major advancement in pharmacy practice policy in Portugal.

FINAL REMARKS

It is vital to summarize these recent developments into the context of a primary healthcare reform initiated in Portugal 10 years ago, which led to a reorganization of local NHS primary care family health units, some of which opted for more advanced models that embraced quality and efficiency targets and willingness to work according to a multiprofessional team approach (physicians, nurses and other NHS healthcare providers). This new multiprofessional team model, even though confined to NHS providers only, paved the way for exploring new partnerships with pharmacies. The Project USFarmácia is an excellent example of how things have begun to change and pharmacies and pharmacists are to be seen as trusted healthcare partners.

Also, the current economic pressure on the health budget is likely to pose challenge for politicians, as it will no longer be possible for them to ignore and underutilize community resources. In nutshell, all these developments bring opportunities to foster innovative, collaborative practice between pharmacies and the NHS primary care services.

PROJECT USFARMÁCIA

The promoters of the project USFarmácia are ANF and the NHS Primary Care Health Centre Group of Baixo Mondego region.

The project team USFarmácia is composed by the NHS Family Unit Leading Physician and a cross-sectorial team of: Pharmacy-Based Services Department of ANF; Center for Health Evaluation & Research (CEFAR) of ANF; Drug Information Center (CEDIME) of ANF; Information Technology and Computer Systems of ANF and of Glintt Farma.

The research team USFarmácia for effectiveness, feasibility, process and satisfaction is composed by pharmacists, epidemiologist, health economists, and statisticians of the Center for Health Evaluation & Research (CEFAR) of ANF.

ACKNOWLEDGMENTS

The author wishes to thank Maria Cary, health economist of CEFAR, for her contribution in the search for economic evaluation studies of pharmacy services in Portugal in EMBASE and MEDLINE that might have been published, in an attempt to make this description as accurate as possible.

The author also thanks Prof. Carlos Gouveia Pinto (School of Economics and Management ISEG, Technical University of Lisbon UTL), Prof. João Pereira (National School of Public Health, Universidade NOVA de Lisboa), Prof. Miguel Gouveia (Center for Applied Studies, CATÓLICA LISBON School of Business & Economics), and Prof. Pedro Pita Barros (NOVA School of Business & Economics) for assisting in identifying possible additional ongoing research in Portugal.

CONFLICT OF INTEREST STATEMENT

The author is a pharmacy owner and the Executive Director of the Centre for Health Evaluation & Research (CEFAR) employed by the National Association of Pharmacies in Portugal and is the USFarmácia Project Manager. The project USFarmácia is funded by the ANF and the NHS Primary Care Health Centre Group of Baixo Mondego region.

REFERENCES

[1] Costa S, Santos C, Silveira J. Community pharmacy services in Portugal. Ann Pharmacother. 2006;40(12):2228−34.

[2] Costa S. Os desafios da próxima década na prestação de serviços farmacêuticos em ambulatório. In: Aguiar AH, editor. Farmacêuticos 2020. Lisboa: Hollyfar; 2012. p. 185.

[3] Martins AP, Horta MR, Costa S, Miranda A, Ferreira A, Crisóstomo S, et al. Evaluating the Portuguese Pharmacy-Based Diabetes Management Program. Where do we stand now? Poster session presented at: 68th International Congress of FIP; 2008 [cited 2016 Jun 15] Aug 29−Sept 4; Basel. Available from: <http://www.fip.org/abstracts?page=abstracts&action=generatePdf&item=2551>.

[4] Bernsten C, Bjorkman I, Caramona M, Crealey G, Frokjaer B, Grundberger E, et al. Improving the well-being of elderly patients via community pharmacy-based provision of pharmaceutical care: a multicentre study in seven European countries. Drugs and Aging 2001;18(1):63−77.

[5] Félix J, Inês M, Acosta C. Relatório: Estimativa do Impacto do Programa "DIZ NÃO A UMA SERINGA EM SEGUNDA MÃO" no Risco de Infecção por VIH/SIDA na população Portuguesa de Utilizadores de Droga Injectada. Alhos Vedros: Exigo Consultores; 2002 [cited 2016 Jun 15]. Available from: <http://www.pnvihsida.dgs.pt/programatrocaseringas/relatorios/avaliacao-do-programa-diz-nao-a-uma-seringa-em-segunda-mao-2002.aspx>.

[6] Pita Barros P, Martins BD, Moura AC, Teixeira I, Costa S, Queirós S. The pharmacists' and patients' side of pMeasures in pharmaceutical markets: the effects of changing pharmacy margins. Value Health 2012;15(7):A322 [cited 2016 Jun 15] Available from: http://www.valueinhealthjournal.com/article/S1098-3015(12)02440-0/pdf

[7] Pita Barros P. "Lessons from the European Union. Case Study 2: Changes in the Health Sector under Economic Crisis and Financial Rescue: Portugal. In: Hou X, Veléni EV, Yazbeck AS, Iunes RF, Smith O, editors. Learning from Economic Downturns: How to Better Assess, Track, and Mitigate the Impact on the Health Sector. Directions in Development. Washington, DC: World Bank; 2013. p. 162. http://dx.doi.org/10.1596/978-1-4648-0060-3. License: Creative Commons Attribution CC BY 3.0

[8] Teixeira I, Guerreiro JP, Costa S. Impact of the changes in the Portuguese remuneration system. Value Health 2015;18(7):A539.

[9] Gouveia M, Machado F, Mendes Z, Costa S. Free But Valuable: The Economic Significance of Services Provided by Portuguese Pharmacies. Poster session presented at: 70th International Congress of FIP; 2010 [cited 2016 Jun 15] Aug 28−Sept 2; Lisbon. Available from: <http://fip.org/abstracts?page=abstracts&action=generatePdf&item=3649>.

[10] Portugal. Ministério da Saúde. Acordo entre o Ministério da Saúde e a Associação Nacional das Farmácias sobre a implementação de programas de Saúde Pública. Lisboa: INFARMED; 2014 [cited 2016 Jun 15]. Available from: http://www.infarmed.pt/portal/page/portal/INFARMED/MAIS_NOVIDADES/Acordo_MS_ANF_09_%2007_2014.pdf

[11] Fernandes R, Costa J, Cary M, Duarte G, Jesus G, Alarcão J, et al. Effectiveness of Needle and Syringe Programmes in People Who Inject Drugs − An Overview of Systematic Reviews. Poster session presented at: Scientific Symposium of the 12th Congress of Pharmacies; 2016 [cited 2016 Jun 15] Apr 14−16; Lisbon. Available from: http://www.anf.pt/SiteCollectionDocuments/Documentos/Effectiveness%20of%20needle%20and%20syringe%20programmes.pdf

[12] Borges M, Gouveia M, Fiorentino F, Jesus G, Cary M, Guerreiro JP, et al. Avaliação Económica do Programa de Troca de Seringas nas Farmácias Iniciado em 2015. Poster session presented at: Scientific Symposium of the 12th Congress of Pharmacies; 2016 [cited 2016 Jun 15] Apr 14−16; Lisbon. Available from: http://www.anf.pt/ SiteCollectionDocuments/Documentos/Avaliacao%20Economica%20do%20PTS.pdf

[13] Borges M., Gouveia M., Fiorentino F., Jesus G., Cary M., Guerreiro J.P., et al. Economic Evaluation of the Portuguese Needle Exchange Programme in Community Pharmacies (NEP-CP). Abstract accepted [in press] at: ISPOR 19th Annual European Congress; 2016 [cited 2016 Aug 25] October 29−November 2; Vienna.

[14] Borges M., Gouveia M., Fiorentino F., Jesus G., Guerreiro J.P., Cary M., et al. Impacto das Farmácias na Equidade no Acesso ao Programa de Troca de Seringas. Poster session presented at: Scientific Symposium of the 12th Congress of Pharmacies; 2016 [cited 2016 Jun 15] Apr 14-16; Lisbon. Available from: <http://www.anf.pt/SiteCollectionDocuments/ Documentos/Impacto%20das%20farma%CC%81cias%20na%20equidade%20no%20acesso %20ao%20PTS.pdf>.

[15] Gouveia M., Borges M., Fiorentino F., Jesus G., Guerreiro J.P., Cary M., et al. The impact of Community Pharmacies (CP) on regional equity in the access to the Portuguese Needle and Exchange Programme (NEP). Abstract accepted [in press] at: ISPOR 19th Annual European Congress; 2016 [cited 2016 Aug 25] October 29−November 2; Vienna.

[16] Félix J., Vandewalle B., Ferreira C., Ferreira D., Gomes M., Silva M., et al. Valor social e económico das intervenções em Saúde Pública dos farmacêuticos nas farmácias em Portugal. Poster session presented at: Scientific Symposium of the 12th Congress of Pharmacies; 2016 [cited 2016 Jun 15] Apr 14-16; Lisbon. Available from: <http://www. anf.pt/SiteCollectionDocuments/Documentos/Congresso%20Farma%CC%81cias%20Valor %20Social%20e%20Econo%CC%81mico.pdf>.

[17] Félix J., Vandewalle B., Ferreira C., Ferreira D., Gomes M., Silva M., et al. Social and Economic Value of Portuguese Community Pharmacies in Public Health. Abstract accepted [in press] at: ISPOR 19th Annual European Congress; 2016 [cited 2016 Aug 25] October 29−November 2; Vienna.

[18] Condinho M. Contributo para o Estudo do Impacto Económico do Acompanhamento Farmacoterapêutico [unpublished dissertation]. Coimbra: Universidade de Coimbra; 2015 [cited 2016 Jun 15]. Available from: <https://estudogeral.sib.uc.pt/handle/10316/26344>.

[19] Schumock G, Butler M. Evaluating and Justifying Clinical Pharmacy Services. Pharmacoeconomics and Outcomes: Applications for Patient Care. 2nd ed. Kansas City: American College of Clinical Pharmacy; 2003.

[20] Schumock GT. Methods to assess the economic outcomes of clinical pharmacy services. Pharmacotherapy. 2000;20(10 Pt 2):243S−52S.

[21] Elliott RA, Putman K, Davies J. A review of the methodological challenges in assessing the cost effectiveness of pharmacist interventions. PharmacoEconomics 2014;32: 1185−99.

Chapter 9

Economic Evaluation of Pharmacist-Managed Warfarin Therapy: A Review of Studies

S. Saokaew[1,2], N. Samprasit[1], P. Kulchaitanaroaj[3] and N. Chaiyakunapruk[2,4,5,6]

[1]University of Phayao, Phayao, Thailand, [2]Monash University Malaysia, Selangor, Malaysia, [3]University of Iowa, Iowa City, IA, United States, [4]Naresuan University, Phitsanulok, Thailand, [5]University of Wisconsin, Madison, WI, United States, [6]University of Queensland, Brisbane, Australia

Chapter Outline

INTRODUCTION

Warfarin is scientifically known as a 3-α-acetonyl benzyl-4-hydroxcoumarin; thus also called as Coumarin. Warfarin is a compound synthesized in 1948 and it was first used as a rodenticide [1]. Later it was approved as anticoagulation therapy in the early 1950s [2] to prevent and treat thromboembolism [3]. However, warfarin has a narrow therapeutic index (difference in a therapeutic dose and a toxic dose is small), and this can lead to warfarin interactions with food, disease, or other medicines [4]. Warfarin major side effect is bleeding which can lead to disability and a fatal hemorrhagic event. Major and fatal bleeding events occur at rates of 7.2 and 1.3 per 100 patient-years, respectively. This was observed in a meta-analysis of 33 studies [5].

Economic Evaluation of Pharmacy Services.

Pharmacists usually intervene and work toward to optimize the dose of warfarin in an anticoagulation clinic [6]. Their roles range from ordering relevant laboratory tests, maintaining target international normalized ratio (INR), adjusting warfarin dose, reviewing medicines, and contacting relevant healthcare professionals [7]. Previous studies showed that the pharmacist-participated warfarin therapy management (PPWTM) provided significantly better anticoagulation control by preventing bleeding and thromboembolic events when compared with the usual care [8,9].

Though several economic evaluation studies are being conducted to evaluate pharmacists' services at anticoagulation, no review of cost-effectiveness of PPWTM [10,11] has been undertaken so far.

This chapter aims to fill this gap by evaluating the literature on economic evaluation studies of a PPWTM. This is done in comparison with usual care, which is defined as less warfarin monitoring services or using physician management alone.

METHODS

Databases and Search Strategy

The following databases were systematically searched: MEDLINE, EMBASE, and Cochrane. Databases were searched from their inception to August 31, 2015.

For the search strategy, the Medical Subject Headings of "warfarin" and "cost benefit" were used to combine with the following keywords "incremental cost-effectiveness ratio," "Quality-Adjusted Life Years," "cost utility," "economic," "cost effectiveness," "pharmacy service," "pharmacist-provided," or "pharmacist-managed," "anticoagulant." Appendix A shows the search strategies.

There was no language and study design restriction. References of initially identified articles were examined to identify additional studies that met the selection criteria.

Eligibility Criteria

Two investigators independently reviewed all abstracts and screened all potentially relevant, full-text articles for inclusion criteria. The inclusion criteria were studies which: (1) used warfarin as an anticoagulant, (2) evaluated both cost (in monetary units) and effectiveness outcomes (i.e., life-years, quality-adjusted life years (QALYs), or incremental cost-effectiveness ratio (ICERs)), (3) had a control group (with healthcare professionals other than pharmacist as service providers), and (4) had an anticoagulant clinic with PPWTM as an intervention group. Studies, which were not original articles such as comments, letters, case reports, surveys, or editorials, were excluded. Studies from the same population (duplicate studies), studies not reporting economic evaluation findings, or studies with insufficient information to compute the effect estimates were also excluded.

Appraisal of Individual Studies

Two investigators assessed the quality of each included study independently. This was done by using the following three tools: First, a 10-item critical appraisal by Drummond et al. [12] was utilized to evaluate methodology and reporting of studies. Each item carries a nominal scale with the possible answers of "yes," "no," and "can't tell." A greater number of answers with "yes" represent a higher quality of a study. Second, the Quality of Health Economic Studies (QHES) Instrument was employed to assess appropriateness of methods, validity and transparency of results, and comprehensiveness of result reporting in each study [13]. Possible answers for each item are "yes" and "no." A question with a "yes" answer will be shown with a weighted point value; each item has a different point value generated from a regression method. The maximum score is 100 representing the perfect quality. Lastly, unlike the former two instruments, Consolidated Health Economic Evaluation Reporting Standards (CHEERS) [14] focuses only on what should be reported in a study. CHEERS checklist includes 24 main recommended items.

It is expected that an anticoagulation clinic, which include pharmacists as part of the team would manage warfarin therapy. As a result, the warfarin dose would be managed and optimized and no bleeding or any thromboembolic events would occur.

RESULTS

Study Selection

There were 494 articles found from the databases (Fig. 9.1) and after removing duplicates and screening by titles and abstracts, and on the basis of eligibility 15 articles were included. Eleven articles were excluded. The reasons include, no cost analysis ($n = 1$), comparing a PPWTM intervention with other medicines ($n = 2$), no cost—utility analysis ($n = 7$), and no discussion ($n = 1$). Four articles met the criteria and were included in the final analysis. Key features of these articles are summarized in Table 9.1.

Study Characteristics

All included studies were single-country studies. Two studies were conducted in the United States [15,16], while the other two studies were in Asia including Hong Kong [17] and Thailand [18]. All four studies evaluated cost-effectiveness of two or more warfarin therapy management strategies. All studies compared a more frequent monitoring provided by healthcare professionals including pharmacists [15—17] or physicians [16,17] or either a combination of physician and pharmacist [18]. The comparators in these studies were either usual care with less time being spent on monitoring or either care provided by physicians alone. In the study by Lafata et al. [15]

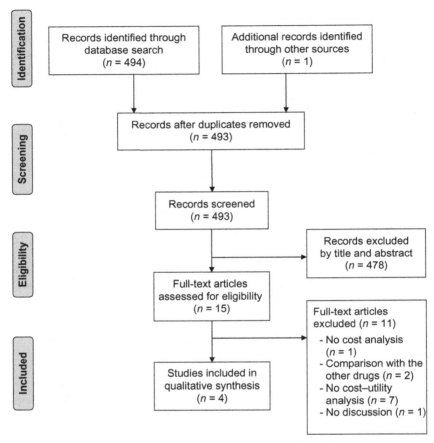

FIGURE 9.1   Flow diagram of study identification, inclusion, and exclusion.

patient self-tested INRs at home by using capillary monitors. These patients then reported these results to an anticoagulation clinic.

You et al. [17] focused on Asian adult population aged 18 years or older, while Sullivan et al. [16] focused on elderly patients with atrial fibrillation who were at high risk of stroke and were at the age of 70 or older. Saokaew et al. [18] specified the age of 45 years for the patients with the indications requiring warfarin therapy.

All studies used Markov cohort simulation technique. Economic models in all studies (i.e., Refs. [15–18]) used a combination of a decision tree of warfarin therapy strategies and a Markov model for repeated health states. Each study portrayed distinct model scenarios and health outcomes. However, in general, all models allowed recurrence of health outcomes related to bleeding and embolism, with the different types or levels of bleeding.

TABLE 9.1 Design and Study Characteristics

Study	Lafata et al. [15]	You et al. [17]	Sullivan et al. [16]	Saokaew et al. [18]
Publication year	2000	2003	2006	2013
Country/region	USA	Hong Kong	USA	Thailand
Study type	CEA	CEA	CEA, CUA	CUA
Intervention	UC, AC, and patient self-testing	Routine medical care and AC	UC and anticoagulation management service	UC and PPWTM
Population	Warfarin users	Warfarin users	Atrial fibrillation	Warfarin users
Perspective	Society, health care	Health care	Society	Society, health care
Model	Markov	Markov	Semi-Markov	Markov
Base case (age)	57 years	58 years	70 years	45 years
Time horizon (years)	5	10	10	Life long
Cycle length (month)	12	12	1	3
Discount rate (%)	C:3, B:3	NR	C:3, B:3	C:3, B:3
Cost data	H: all direct medical costs (including nurse home or AC were the cost of equipment, supplies, and staff time) S: incurred by medical providers, patients, and	H: direct medical cost (medical record of the outpatient clinic between January 1, 1999 and June 30, 2001 included medication, laboratory and diagnostic tests, clinic visits, emergency room visits, hospitalization, and surgery)	The frequency and cost of clinic visits and laboratory testing in the anticoagulation clinic at the university medicine group practice anticoagulation clinic	Direct medical cost: cost of TE event, cost of bleeding event. Cost of pharmacist service, cost of sequelae Direct nonmedical cost: cost of transportation, food cost

(Continued)

TABLE 9.1 (Continued)

Study	Lafata et al. [15]	You et al. [17]	Sullivan et al. [16]	Saokaew et al. [18]
	caregivers in receipt of care			
Costing year	1997	NR	2004	2012
Outcome	The UC to AC testing results in a cost-effectiveness ratio of $31,327 per avoided event and $232,226 per QALYs	The AC group was prevented of events in so far as the number of events per 100 patient-years and direct medical cost was lower by 9.9 (51%) and $339 (29%) when compared to UC group	The AC group improved effectiveness by 0.057 QALYs and reduced cost by $2100 compared with UC group	S: PWTM increase QALY by 0.79 and increase costs by $3083 compared with UC H: PWTM also results in 0.79 QALY and increase costs by $3093 compared with UC
ICER	H: $31,327	Cost saving	Cost saving	H: $3882.3
	S: $232,226			S: $3894.7
Funding	Boehringer Mannheim Corp.	School of Pharmacy, The Chinese University of Hong Kong	The Bristol Myers Squibb Company	The program Strategic Scholarships for Frontier Research Net Work

AC, anticoagulation clinic; B, benefits; C, costs; CEA, cost-effectiveness analysis; CUA, cost–utility analysis; H, health care perspective; NR, not reported; PWTM, pharmacist-participated warfarin therapy management; QALYs, quality-adjusted life years; S, societal perspective; TE, thromboembolism; UC, usual care.

The study perspectives were slightly different in four studies. Lafata et al. [15], Sullivan et al. [16], and Saokaew et al. [18] used societal perspective. You et al. [17] utilized public health perspective, while Saokaew et al. [18] also used a health care system perspective. Time horizons tended to be long term for all studies. Studies by Lafata et al. [15], You et al. [17], Sullivan et al. [16], and Saokaew et al. [18] were performed using the simulations of 5 years, 10 years, 10 years, and lifetime, respectively. An annual discount rate of 3% was used in the studies conducted by Lafata et al. [15], Sullivan et al. [16], and Saokaew et al. [18]. You et al. [17] did not discount the outcomes or costs of the future to the present value.

Cost-effectiveness measures were incremental costs per QALYs gained in studies by Lafata et al. [15], Sullivan et al. [16], and Saokaew et al. [18]. Lafata et al. [15] and You et al. [17] also showed differences in costs and number of health events between the intervention and usual care, and incremental costs per avoided event.

PPWTM efficacy or effectiveness was estimated by different methods such as efficacy to control patients' INRs in the therapeutic range [15] or efficacy on health events (i.e., bleeding and thromboembolic events) taken from trials [16–18]. Two studies [16,17] performed a search for efficacy data, while one study [18] cited efficacy based on a previously published systematic review and meta-analysis [9]. To derive the rate of bleeding and thromboembolic events, two studies clearly specified the trials data [16,17], while one study [16] adjusted the value to reflect real-world setting. This was done by using a numerical factor, which was based on the opinion of an expert. The other two studies [15,18] used longitudinal cohort study to derive the event rate. All studies obtained utility from literature except the study [17] which did not use utility in their analysis.

Studies by Lafata et al. [15] and You et al. [17] did not state the cost-effectiveness thresholds. Sullivan et al. [16] used $50,000 per QALY as a cost-effective threshold for an intervention. While in Saokaew et al. [18] study, two different figures: 150,000 Thai Baht ($5000) and 450,000 Thai Baht ($15,000) were used as cost-effective threshold.

All studies performed one-way sensitivity analysis to assess which parameter affected the results. Three studies (i.e., Refs. [15,16,18]) did multi-way or probability sensitivity analyses with Monte Carlo simulation technique. Sullivan et al. [16] also conducted bivariate sensitivity analysis. However, no study performed scenario analysis.

Overall Quality Assessment

All studies had items checked according to Drummond's checklist (Table 9.2). Studies by Lafata et al. [15], You et al. [17], Sullivan et al. [16], and Saokaew et al. [18] have scored 82 points, 87 points, 89 points, and 93 points, respectively, according to QHES criteria (Table 9.3). The results by applying CHEERS are also displayed in Table 9.4.

TABLE 9.2 Quality Assessment by Drummond et al. [12]

	A Checklist for Assessing Economic Evaluations	Lafata et al. [15]	You et al. [17]	Sullivan et al. [16]	Saokaew et al. [18]
1	Was a well-defined question posed in an answerable form?	Yes	Yes	Yes	Yes
2	Was a comprehensive description of the competing alternatives given (i.e., can you tell who did what, to whom, where, and how often)?	Yes	Yes	Yes	Yes
3	Was there evidence that the program's effectiveness had been established?	Yes	Yes	Yes	Yes
4	Were all the important and relevant costs and consequences for each alternative identified?	Yes	Yes	Yes	Yes
5	Were costs and consequences measured accurately in appropriate physical units?	Yes	Yes	Yes	Yes
6	Were costs and consequences valued credibly?	Yes	Yes	Yes	Yes
7	Were costs and consequences adjusted for differential timing?	Yes	Can't tell	Yes	Yes
8	Was an incremental analysis of cost and consequences of alternatives performed?	Yes	Yes	Yes	Yes
9	Was allowance made for uncertainty in the estimates of costs and consequences?	No	Yes	Yes	Yes
10	Did the presentation and discussion of study results include all issues of concern to users?	Yes	Yes	Yes	Yes

TABLE 9.3 Quality Assessment by QHES [13]

No.	Question	Points	Lafata et al. [15]	You et al. [17]	Sullivan et al. [16]	Saokaew et al. [18]
1	Was the study objective presented in a clear, specific, and measurable manner?	7	Yes	Yes	Yes	Yes
2	Were the perspective of the analysis (societal, third-party payer, etc.) and reasons for its selection stated?	4	No (no reason to for selection)	Yes	No (no reason to for selection)	Yes
3	Were variable estimates used in the analysis from the best available source (i.e., randomized control trial—best, expert opinion—worst)?	8	Yes	Yes	Yes	Yes
4	If estimates came from a subgroup analysis, were the groups prespecified at the beginning of the study?	1	Yes	Yes	No	No
5	Was uncertainty handled by (1) statistical analysis to address random events and (2) sensitivity analysis to cover a range of assumptions?	9	Yes	Yes	Yes	Yes
6	Was incremental analysis performed between alternatives for resources and costs?	6	Yes	Yes	Yes	Yes
7	Was the methodology for data abstraction (including the value of health states and other benefits) stated?	5	Yes	Yes	Yes	Yes
8	Did the analytic horizon allow time for all relevant and important outcomes? Were benefits and costs that went beyond 1 year discounted (3–5%) and justification given for the discount rate?	7	Yes	No	Yes	Yes

(Continued)

TABLE 9.3 (Continued)

No.	Question	Points	Lafata et al. [15]	You et al. [17]	Sullivan et al. [16]	Saokaew et al. [18]
9	Was the measurement of costs appropriate and the methodology for the estimation of quantities and unit costs clearly described?	8	Yes	Yes	Yes	Yes
10	Were the primary outcome measure(s) for the economic evaluation clearly stated and did they include the major short term, was justification given for the measures/scales used?	6	Yes	Yes	Yes	Yes
11	Were the health outcomes measures/scales valid and reliable? If previously tested valid and reliable measures were not available, was justification given for the measures/scales used?	7	Yes	Yes	Yes	Yes
12	Were the economic model (including structure), study methods and analysis, and the components of the numerator and denominator displayed in a clear, transparent manner?	8	Yes	Yes	Yes	Yes
13	Were the choice of economic model, main assumptions, and limitations of the study stated and justified?	7	Yes	Yes	Yes	Yes
14	Did the author(s) explicitly discuss direction and magnitude of potential biases?	6	No	No	No	No
15	Were the conclusions/recommendations of the study justified and based on the study results?	8	No	Yes	Yes	Yes
16	Was there a statement disclosing the source of funding for the study?	3	Yes	Yes	Yes	Yes
	Total points	100	82	87	89	93

TABLE 9.4 Quality Assessment by CHEERS [14]

Item No.	Recommendation	Reported on Page No./Line No.				
		Lafata et al. [15]	You et al. [17]	Sullivan et al. [16]	Saokaew et al. [18]	
1	Identify the study as an economic evaluation, or use more specific terms such as "cost-effectiveness analysis" and describe the interventions compared	Title	Title	Title	Title	
2	Provide a structured summary of objectives, perspective, setting, methods (including study design and inputs), results (including base-case and uncertainty analyses), and conclusions	31/1–26 (no setting and perspective)	1106/18–24 and 1106/7–12 (column 2)	1021 and 1022 (abstract)	437 (abstract)	
3	Provide an explicit statement of the broader context for the study. Present the study question and its relevance for health policy or practice decisions	N	1106/17–19 and 1107/1–20	N	438/3–8 (column 2)	
4	Describe characteristics of the base-case population and subgroups analyzed including why they were chosen	33/5–12	1108/15–19 (column 2)	1024/9–11	438/15–18 (column 2)	
5	State relevant aspects of the system(s) in which the decision(s) need(s) to be made	N	N	N	N	
6	Describe the perspective of the study and relate this to the costs being evaluated	34/15–20	1108/8–10 and 22–25 (column 2)	1023/11–15 (column 2)	439/2–3	

(Continued)

TABLE 9.4 (Continued)

Item No.	Recommendation	Reported on Page No./Line No.				
		Lafata et al. [15]	You et al. [17]	Sullivan et al. [16]	Saokaew et al. [18]	
7	Describe the interventions or strategies being compared and state why they were chosen	31/31−44 (column 2)	1107/9−10	1023/11−15 (column 2)	438/18 (column 2) and 439/1−2	
8	State the time horizon(s) over which costs and consequences are being evaluated and say why appropriate	32/10−12	1107/5−9	1025/21−23	439/2−3	
9	Report the choice of discount rate(s) used for costs and outcomes and say why appropriate	34/20−23	N	1027/6−7	439/3−6	
10	Describe what outcomes were used as the measure(s) of benefit in the evaluation and their relevance for the type of analysis performed	33/9−13 (column 2)	1108/5−22	1027/16−22 (column 2)	439/41−42 (column 2)	
11a	Single study−based estimates: Describe fully the design features of the single effectiveness study and why the single study was a sufficient source of clinical effectiveness data	N	1108/15−21	1024/37−42	N	
11b	Synthesis-based estimates: Describe fully the methods used for the identification of included studies and synthesis of clinical effectiveness data	N	N	N	439/39−48	

12	If applicable, describe the population and methods used to elicit preferences for outcomes	N	N	1027/16–24 (column 2) and 1028/1–12	439/41–62 (column 2) and 440/1–2
13a	Single study–based economic evaluation: Describe approaches used to estimate resource use associated with the alternative interventions. Describe primary or secondary research methods for valuing each resource item in terms of its unit cost. Describe any adjustments made to approximate to opportunity costs	34/9–11	1108/9–12 (column 2)	1025/43–45 (column 2) and 1027/1–3	439/59–60 and 1–40 (column 2)
13b	Model-based economic evaluation: Describe approaches and data sources used to estimate resource use associated with model health states. Describe primary or secondary research methods for valuing each resource item in terms of its unit cost. Describe any adjustments made to approximate to opportunity costs	34/9–11	1108/9–12 (column 2)	1025/43–45 (column 2) and 1027/1–3	439/59–60 and 1–40 (column 2)
14	Report the dates of the estimated resource quantities and unit costs. Describe methods for adjusting estimated unit costs to the year of reported costs if necessary. Describe methods for converting costs into a common currency base and the exchange rate	34/20–22	N	1027/4–5	439/3–6
15	Describe and give reasons for the specific type of decision-analytic model used. Providing a figure to show model structure is strongly recommended	32/9–10	1107/5–9	1023/11–15 (column 2)	438/9–13 (column 2)

(Continued)

TABLE 9.4 (Continued)

Item No.	Recommendation	Reported on Page No./Line No.			
		Lafata et al. [15]	You et al. [17]	Sullivan et al. [16]	Saokaew et al. [18]
16	Describe all structural or other assumptions underpinning the decision-analytic model	32/15–23	1107/10–13	1023/11–15 (column 2)	438/9–13 (column 2)
17	Describe all analytic methods supporting the evaluation. This could include methods for dealing with skewed, missing, or censored data; extrapolation methods; methods for pooling data; approaches to validate or make adjustments (e.g., half-cycle corrections) to a model; and methods for handling population heterogeneity and uncertainty	32/25–27 (column 2) 33/1–3	1108/5–7	1024/9–11 (column 2)	439/8–58
18	Report the values, ranges, references, and if used, probability distributions for all parameters. Report reasons or sources for distributions used to represent uncertainty where appropriate. Providing a table to show the input values is strongly recommended	34/23–25 and 34/29–31 (column 2)	1108/17–21 (column 2)	1026	438
19	For each intervention, report mean values for the main categories of estimated costs and outcomes of interest, as well as mean differences between the comparator groups. If applicable, report ICERs	35/17–28 (column 2)	1109/32–34 and 1109/1–5 (column 2)	1028/16–22 (column 2)	440/4–11 (column 2)

20a	Single study–based economic evaluation: Describe the effects of sampling uncertainty for estimated incremental cost, incremental effectiveness, and incremental cost-effectiveness, together with the impact of methodological assumptions (such as discount rate, study perspective)	N	N	N	439/42–48
20b	Model-based economic evaluation: Describe the effects on the results of uncertainty for all input parameters, and uncertainty related to the structure of the model and assumptions	35/29–32 (column 2) and 36/1–3	1109/6–14	1028/23–38 (column 2), 1029/43 and 1–3 (column 2)	440/12–23 (column 2)
21	If applicable, report differences in costs, outcomes, or cost-effectiveness that can be explained by variations between subgroups of patients with different baseline characteristics or other observed variability in effects that are not reducible by more information	35/8–14	1109/32–33	N	N
22	Summarize key study findings and describe how they support the conclusions reached. Discuss limitations and the generalizability of the findings and how the findings fit with current knowledge	36/14–32, 36/33–49 (no generalizability and current knowledge)	1109/29–36 (column 2), 1111/13–22 and 1–17 (column 2), 1111/1–12	1029/4–21, 1030/1–27 (column 2), 1031/32–36 (column 2) (no current knowledge)	441/3–10, 442/18–49 and 59–66 (no current knowledge)

(Continued)

TABLE 9.4 (Continued)

Item No.	Recommendation	Reported on Page No./Line No.			
		Lafata et al. [15]	You et al. [17]	Sullivan et al. [16]	Saokaew et al. [18]
23	Describe how the study was funded and the role of the funder in the identification, design, conduct, and reporting of the analysis	37/1–6	1106	1032/3–4	442/7–13
	Describe other nonmonetary sources of support				
24	Describe any potential for conflict of interest among study contributors in accordance with journal policy. In the absence of a journal policy, we recommend authors comply with International Committee of Medical Journal Editors' recommendations	N	N	1032/6–7	442/6

In general, all included studies were rated with high scores. All of them had well-defined questions and comprehensive description of the competing alternatives. All studies performed cost-effectiveness analysis by using appropriate modeling techniques. These studies described all relevant costs and consequences for intervention and usual care.

Study Results

Two studies [15,17] reported the number of events prevented from PPWTM, while the other two studies [16,18] did not. When costs and outcomes were evaluated Lafata et al. [15] and Saokaew et al. [18] showed that PPWTM was more expensive than usual care; in contrast, You et al. [17] and Sullivan et al. [16] demonstrated that the anticoagulation clinics were less costly than usual care.

Lafata et al. [15] estimated that the total cost in the intervention group to be higher than that of the usual care; by $139.54 (1997 US dollar value) per patient (calculated from ($419,514−405,560)/100 patients) if only medical care cost is considered, and by $1159.34 (calculated from ($645,671−529,737)/100 patients) if considering medical care and patient costs as well as caregiver costs.

According to Saokaew et al. [18], the intervention was more expensive than the usual care by $3126.26 (2012 US dollar value) (calculated from $93,787,655.73/30/1000 patients), when counting only medical care cost, and by $3083.03 (calculated from $92,490,794.78/30/1000 patients) when including medical care and patient costs both. Conversely, You et al. [17] described that the intervention was less costly than usual care, by $339 (US dollar value approximately between 1999 and 2001) over the period of 10 years. Sullivan et al. [16] revealed that the intervention was less expensive by $2085 (2004 US dollar value) (calculated from $8661−10,746) over 10 years. All three studies evaluating QALYs showed that the intervention increased QALYs for patients. Incremental QALYs gained per person by the intervention were 0.005 per 5 years in Ref. [15], 0.058 per 10 years in Ref. [16], and 0.7941 for lifetime in Ref. [18].

All studies concluded that PPWTM either cost-saving or it was cost-effective. Lafata et al. [15] showed that the intervention compared with the usual care saved the cost. When societal perspective was used, it appeared to be cost-effective as the intervention incurred additional cost of $2322.26 per QALY per person. In this scenario $50,000 per QALY was used as a threshold. You et al. [17] stated that the intervention saved the cost as it lowered the costs and decreased the number of bleeding and thromboembolic events. Sullivan et al. [16] concluded that the intervention was cost-saving because it lowered the costs and increased the QALYs. Saokaew et al. [18] demonstrated that the intervention was cost-effective because the ICERs were less than the cost-effective threshold of $5000. Using Thai health care system's perspective, the ICER was recorded as $3894.7 per QALY and by using the societal perspective, the ICER was $3882.3 per QALY.

One-way sensitivity analyses from all studies showed that several distinct parameters influenced the cost-effectiveness results. Lafata et al. [15] reported that the influential parameters were the difference in time spent on therapeutic range between two groups and difference in annual testing frequency (e.g., an addition of five tests for the comparison between patient self-testing and anticoagulation testing clinic). You et al. [17] reported that the risk of bleeding was the key factor. Saokaew et al. [18] found that if older patients (i.e., 65 years) received the intervention for long-term use of warfarin, the intervention may not be cost-effective; as opposed to the base case where starting age of patients was 45 years. The most influential parameter in this case was discount rate.

Multivariate probabilistic sensitivity analyses confirmed that the intervention by pharmacists was either considered cost saving or cost-effective. Lafata et al. [15] reported that the intervention reduced the number of events with 88% certainty, increased life years with 79% certainty, and decreased disabled life years with 80% certainty. Sullivan et al. [16] suggested that 91% of the time the intervention would improve QALYs and reduce costs, if a $50,000 per QALY threshold to be considered. Saokaew et al. [18] showed that around 50% of the time, the intervention was cost-effective when using a $5000 per QALY threshold, and 65% of the time, the intervention was considered cost-effective if a $15,000 per QALY threshold has to be used.

DISCUSSION

This review summarized existing evidence on the cost-effectiveness of an anticoagulation monitoring service, which included pharmacists providing services compared with the usual care or physician management alone for long-term warfarin therapy (i.e., 5 years and longer). Our findings demonstrated that a PPWTM intervention was either cost-effective or it could save the cost when compared with the usual care.

However in these studies, some of the important methodology considerations were found missing. For example, You et al. [17] did not report discount rates, also cost-effectiveness threshold was missing in the studies of Lafata et al. [15] and You et al. [17]. This may be because as the guidelines, such as CHEERS [14], were not published when these studies were conducted.

Another important point for discussion is the challenges in selecting input parameters to be used in the model. Some studies [17,18] used input parameters, which may not have represented their target population, as the data was not related to their target population. You et al. [17] used probabilities of clinical events (i.e., bleeding and thromboembolism) derived from European and American population, however they clearly mentioned this as a limitation and a source of potential bias. They also explained that Chinese populations tend to be more sensitive to warfarin than the Western populations. Saokaew et al. [18] used parameters from the non-Thai population and weighted this with the proportions of Thai patients. This was an attempt to produce parameters close to Thai population. Using data from similar settings such as Southeast Asian countries for Thai population could be another viable option.

There is a potential of patient self-testing to manage warfarin monitoring as shown in Lafata et al. [15] study. By keeping in view the societal perspective and including patient/caregiver costs and medical care costs, patient self-testing was found to be more effective than the PPWTM intervention. However, this conclusion is sensitive to the frequency of tests.

This is also observed in another patient self-testing study, which has shown benefits in terms of improved patient satisfaction and better anticoagulation control [19]. However, further studies are warranted to understand the cost-effectiveness of patient self-testing in different settings.

CONCLUSIONS

This chapter illustrates the use of systematic review to summarize cost-effectiveness studies evaluating a PPWTM intervention compared with the usual care. All studies adopted Markov model to estimate the cost-effectiveness of the interventions. The effect of PPWTM on outcomes (e.g., time spent on therapeutic range, the probabilities of developing events including thromboembolic events and bleedings) is generally reported to be the key influential parameter. Even though the studies were conducted in various countries with slight differences in methodology, all of them consistently showed that the use of PPWTM was either cost-effective or resulted in saving costs. Given the increasing recognition of the importance to consider economic evidence as part of policy decision making, researchers in other countries might be interested to perform similar studies. However, it may possible that they may consider adopting or modifying some model, parameters, which are being used in the present studies.

REFERENCES

[1] Pirmohamed M. Warfarin: almost 60 years old and still causing problems. Br J Clin Pharm 2006;62(5):509–11.

[2] Stehle S, Kirchheiner J, Lazar A, Fuhr U. Pharmacogenetics of oral anticoagulants: a basis for dose individualization. Clin Pharmacokinet 2008;47(9):565–94.

[3] Kearon C, Akl EA, Comerota AJ, et al. Antithrombotic therapy for VTE disease: Antithrombotic Therapy and Prevention of Thrombosis, 9th ed: American College of Chest Physicians Evidence-Based Clinical Practice Guidelines. Chest 2012;141(2 Suppl): e419S–494.

[4]   Wittkowsky AK. Warfarin and other coumarin derivatives: pharmacokinetics, pharmaco-dynamics, and drug interactions. Semin Vasc Med 2003;3(3):221−30.

[5]   Linkins LA, Choi PT, Douketis JD. Clinical impact of bleeding in patients taking oral anticoagulant therapy for venous thromboembolism: a meta-analysis. Ann Int Med 2003;139(11):893−900.

[6]   Willey ML, Chagan L, Sisca TS, et al. A pharmacist-managed anticoagulation clinic: six-year assessment of patient outcomes. Am J Health Syst Pharm 2003;60(10):1033−7.

[7]   Damaske DL, Baird RW. Development and implementation of a pharmacist-managed inpatient warfarin protocol. Proc (Bayl Univ Med Cent) 2005;18(4):397−400.

[8]   Saokaew S, Sapoo U, Nathisuwan S, Chaiyakunapruk N, Permsuwan U. Anticoagulation control of pharmacist-managed collaborative care versus usual care in Thailand. Int J Clin Pharm 2012;34(1):105−12.

[9]   Saokaew S, Permsuwan U, Chaiyakunapruk N, Nathisuwan S, Sukonthasarn A. Effectiveness of pharmacist-participated warfarin therapy management: a systematic review and meta-analysis. J Thromb Haemost 2010;8(11):2418−27.

[10]   Anderson RJ. Cost analysis of a managed care decentralized outpatient pharmacy anticoa-gulation service. J Manag Care Pharm 2004;10(2):159−65.

[11]   Gallagher J, Mc Carthy S, Woods N, Ryan F, O'Shea S, Byrne S. Economic evaluation of a randomized controlled trial of pharmacist-supervised patient self-testing of warfarin therapy. J Clin Pharm Ther 2015;40(1):14−19.

[12]   Critical assessment of economic evaluation. In: Drummond M, Sculpher M, Stoddart G, O'Brien B, editors. Methods for the economic evaluation of health care programmes. 3rd ed. Oxford: Oxford University Press; 2005.

[13]   Ofman JJ, Sullivan SD, Neumann PJ, et al. Examining the value and quality of health eco-nomic analyses: implications of utilizing the QHES. J Manag Care Pharm 2003;9(1): 53−61.

[14]   Husereau D, Drummond M, Petrou S, et al. Consolidated Health Economic Evaluation Reporting Standards (CHEERS)—explanation and elaboration: a report of the ISPOR Health Economic Evaluation Publication Guidelines Good Reporting Practices Task Force. Value Health 2013;16(2):231−50.

[15]   Lafata JE, Martin SA, Kaatz S, Ward RE. The cost-effectiveness of different management strategies for patients on chronic warfarin therapy. J Gen Intern Med 2000;15(1):31−7.

[16]   Sullivan PW, Arant TW, Ellis SL, Ulrich H. The cost effectiveness of anticoagulation management services for patients with atrial fibrillation and at high risk of stroke in the US. Pharmacoeconomics 2006;24(10):1021−33.

[17]   You JH, Chan FW, Wong RS, Cheng G. Cost-effectiveness of two models of management for patients on chronic warfarin therapy—a Markov model analysis. Thromb Haemost 2003;90(6):1106−11.

[18]   Saokaew S, Permsuwan U, Chaiyakunapruk N, Nathisuwan S, Sukonthasarn A, Jeanpeerapong N. Cost-effectiveness of pharmacist-participated warfarin therapy manage-ment in Thailand. Thromb Res 2013;132(4):437−43.

[19]   Rose AJ, Phibbs CS, Uyeda L, et al. Does distance modify the effect of self-testing in oral anticoagulation? Am J Manag Care 2016;22(1):65−71.

APPENDIX A   SEARCH STRATEGIES

Cost-effectiveness

1. pharmacist/	(25918)
2. pharmacy/	(252429)
3. pharmacist participated/	(610)
4. pharmacist-managed/	(253)
5. pharmacist-provided/	(138)
6. pharmacy service/	(63458)
7. (((((1) OR 2) OR 3) OR 4) OR 5) OR 6/	(297356)
8. warfarin/	(22913)
9. warfarin therapy/	(16688)
10. warfarin management/	(4441)
11. anticoagulant/	(206338)
12. anticoagulant therapy/	(104441)
13. anticoagulant management/	(17030)
14. (((((8) OR 9) OR 10) OR 11) OR 12) OR 13/	(210373)
15. cost—effectiveness/	(93120)
16. cost—benefit/	(82252)
17. cost—utility/	(10688)
18. economic/	(724945)
19. financial impact/	(45789)
20. quality of life/	(249971)
21. Quality-Adjusted Life Years/	(12284)
22. Incremental cost-effectiveness ratio/	(3521)
23. (((((((15) OR 16) OR 17) OR 18) OR 19) OR 20) OR 21) OR 22/	(973769)
24. ((8) AND 16) AND 18/	(265)
25. ((7) AND 14) AND 23/	(494)

Chapter 10

Economic Evaluation of a Medicines Management Model in New Zealand: A Proposal

Z.-U.-D. Babar[1,2] and R. Edlin[2]
[1]Lahore Pharmacy College, Lahore, Pakistan, [2]University of Auckland, Auckland, New Zealand

Chapter Outline

BACKGROUND

Medicines continue to be the most common treatment offered to patients and represent a major component of the healthcare budget; it is acknowledged that in many instances medicines are used less than optimally, resulting in both poor health outcomes and unnecessary costs [1,2]. In New Zealand, as elsewhere, there is growing recognition of the importance of medicines management services [3]. Community pharmacy is taking a central role in medicines management, with an emergent evidence base supporting the importance of these services in improving patient adherence [4]. However, just because a program or service has been shown to demonstrate positive outcomes for patients in a trial setting does not mean it will be easily implemented in practice [5]. Changes in the role and relevance of medicines management provide a scope and need for alternative models of care. Hence, this proposal outlines the effectiveness and cost-effectiveness of alternative models of medicines management in New Zealand.

Economic Evaluation of Pharmacy Services.

The pharmacy profession is undergoing considerable change and the concept of clinical pharmacy has evolved to include a strong emphasis toward patient-orientated care [6]. This is of particular importance due to the impact of aging populations, multiculturalism, and the health disparities observed among minority ethnic communities in most developed countries [7]. Technological change has also led to an increased use of technology including: automation at community pharmacies, e-prescribing, e-communication, and use of robotics, as well as pharmacists' access to integrated patient records—all are directly related to how patients and consumers are accessing and using medicines [8].

The traditional role of pharmacists—to prepare and dispense medicines—does not reflect the current range of activities within the profession. The 2006 National Framework for Pharmacist Services in Primary Care defined five new pharmacist services to be offered to benefit the New Zealand (NZ) public: health education, medicine and clinical information support, medicine-use review and adherence support (MUR), medicine therapy assessment (MTA), and comprehensive medicine management (CMM) [9]. In addition, the Pharmacy Council of New Zealand set up the Pharmacist Prescriber Scope of Practice in 2011, and a number of experienced clinical pharmacists have undertaken the required educational program and registered as designated prescribers [10].

There is limited research in the NZ context on the implementation of medicines management services, and generally they have not been widely adopted. While one NZ study has shown that Medicine Use Review (MUR) had positive effects on patients' knowledge and adherence to medicines, the overview of such services did not report significant results on patients' clinical outcomes [11]. A recent UK study on MUR services has shown that the success of any new patient–pharmacist model of interaction will depend on a range of factors [12]. These included the patients' understanding of the pharmacists' role; the perceived hierarchy and position held by pharmacists and other medical professionals including general practitioners (GPs); and experience of what actually occurs during the MUR interaction. It is anticipated that MURs and other forms of medicines management services will increasingly be required to deliver effective patient care. Within these initiatives, it is expected that pharmacists will work collaboratively with GPs, nurses and other healthcare professionals [8].

Despite recent and ongoing research, there remains a paucity of knowledge on the quality of services delivered by pharmacists and a lack of evidence in terms of patient outcomes and value for money [13]. It is recognized that poor medicines adherence could lead to poor health outcomes, increases in prescribing costs, and higher incidences of adverse drugs events. Hence, medicines management policies have become increasingly important [14–15]. In England alone, the gross annual cost of National

Health Service (NHS) primary care prescription medicines wastage is estimated at £300 million/year, including £90 million worth of unused prescription medicines [16]. In a bid to improve patients' adherence to medicines, the NHS in the United Kingdom is involving health professionals so that medicines management services can be formalized [17−18]. Benefits promoting effective use of medicines are evident; however, there are challenges to better understand patients' needs to facilitate approaches that allow collaboration between pharmacists, other health professionals and patients [19]. To enable such a shift, significant rethinking is required to develop models of care through which medicines are delivered.

The overall goal of this research is to build a relevant, evidence-based model of care through which we could foster greater collaboration within primary care, obtain better use of prescribed medicines, and improve patient health outcomes!

AIM AND OBJECTIVES

The overall goal of this research is to build a relevant, evidence-based model of care through which we could foster greater collaboration within primary care, obtain better use of prescribed medicines, and improve patient health outcomes.

Here are key objectives:

- To explore medicine management policies in New Zealand
- To identify stakeholders perspectives regarding current model of medicines management in New Zealand
- To explore identify and build alternative models and approaches in managing medicines in NZ
- To build a decision-analytical exemplar model for assessing cost-effectiveness of medicines management in New Zealand. The sub objectives are
  - To identify whether it is possible to build an exemplar model of care
  - To identify which specific issues/parameters in exemplar model are associated with decision uncertainty (i.e., "Which option is most efficient?")

Building a cost-effectiveness medicines management model could provide value for money and the best model of care.

PROPOSED RESEARCH DESIGN AND METHODS

Stage 1: Identifying Stakeholder Perspectives

In order to identify which approaches are likely to be feasible in a New Zealand setting, it is critical to understand the views of stakeholders and the role of pharmacists. This stage would report on discussion/questions in New Zealand context from stakeholder perspectives (six interviews).

This will also include views regarding the acceptability of current and future technologies, the response to societal challenges of inclusiveness, and perspectives on how medicines will be managed in the future. Critically, this will also consider the feasibility of alternative relationships between pharmacy and other primary care practitioners.

Once we have identified what would be useful (i.e., the decision problem) then further evidence base would be identified.

Stage 2: Identifying the Evidence Base and Alternatives

It will be identified what can be taken from the literature and what would need to be identified from the experts within New Zealand. There is also scope to look at specific questions, their answers and previous models being discussed in the literature.

Once a range of feasible approaches has been identified, the project can summarize the existing evidence base around management strategies and models of care. This will require meta-analyses and systematic reviews of a series of feasible, relevant interventions identified out of Stage 1 to provide a summary of the existing evidence base. There will also be a review of previous economic studies dealing with the medicines management.

Stage 3: Identifying Alternative Models of Medicines Management

In order to provide greater clarity, both a specified clinical area (e.g., diabetes care or hypertension) and alternative models of care will be identified. This step is important in order to allow for more specific, quantitative investigation in the exemplar modeling (Stage 4). Both the clinical area and alternatives will be selected based on both the likely acceptability within a New Zealand context and the quality of evidence available from the international literature. Where a conflict exists between these two criteria, acceptability within New Zealand will be the determining factor as the relevance of alternatives must be the key criterion.

We expect that there are likely to be multiple alternatives identified at the end of this process, and two alternatives would be screened for further scrutiny.

Stage 4: Building an Exemplar Economic Model

Within the scope identified at Stage 3, a model will be constructed to represent the broad effects of interactions within community pharmacy. For example, the model may consider the effectiveness of pharmacists in influencing GP recommendations and in influencing patient adherence with medications. An indicative economic model will be constructed for a NZ setting to identify the effects that models of care might have on disease processes. As an example, the model might consider costs from a DHB perspective and health as quality-adjusted life years (QALYs), so that alternatives can be compared in terms of an incremental cost-effectiveness ratio that can allow changing models of care alongside other types of expenditures in health. At this stage, many elements of the exemplar model are likely to lack specific information; where no or very poor evidence exists, this will be noted. In nutshell, a couple of candidate interventions would be identified early on, and the exemplar model could consider the cost-effectiveness between these options.

The exemplar model will be "firmly" set into a context. A model based on expert judgment would provide findings of relevance. It is argued that it's not the quality of the evidence but the uncertainty about the best ways to move forwards will define the model. If there is poor data but no uncertainty about the right thing to do, then there is a policy-relevant finding in the absence of good data. If there is uncertainty about the right thing to do, then there is scope to ask which questions are the model important to deal with.

In this exemplar model, techniques and theories discussed in Chapters 4, 5, and 6 can be used.

Stage 5: Using Stakeholder Judgments to Build a NZ Evidence Base

Stakeholders will again be contacted and Delphi methods will be used to obtain expert judgment where evidence gaps exist. Consensus values will be used to fill the evidence gaps in the model and the potential cost-effectiveness model (of care) assessed based on these data. Results from this model will be investigated further to identify which specific issues/para-meters are associated with decision uncertainty (i.e., "Which option is most efficient?") in order to identify future research priorities.

Evaluating the process would facilitate identifying future steps and knowledge transfer. The process of the feedback would also serve as a validation exercise.

RESEARCH IMPACT

At a District Health Board level, effective uptake and use of medicines has the potential to both increase the effectiveness of existing expenditures and reduce significant wastage within the health system. As a consequence of reducing this wastage, this could also free up additional resources to provide for healthcare needs of other patients. It is also likely that better models of care may also disproportionately benefit older people, which will become of increasing importance in light of demographic change. At a profession level, the study may also impact on funding decisions on future service delivery, policy development, and around the future roles of pharmacists. The models of care considered within the study will also have implications for pharmacy education and for professional relationships within primary care.

ACKNOWLEDGMENT

The authors would like to acknowledge the contribution of Prof. John Shaw (at University of Auckland) for his input in the earlier version of this chapter.

REFERENCES

[1] Babar ZU, Francis S. Identifying priority medicines policy issues for New Zealand: a general inductive study. BMJ Open 2014;4:e004415. Available from: http://dx.doi.org/10.1136/bmjopen-2013-004415.

[2] Edlin R, Round J, Hulme C, McCabe C. Cost-effectiveness analysis and the efficient use of the pharmaceutical budget: the key role of clinical pharmacologists. Br J Clin Pharmacol. 2010;70:350—5.

[3] New Zealand Ministry of Health. Medicines New Zealand. Wellington, New Zealand: Ministry of Health; 2007; <http://www.pharmac.health.nz/assets/moh-medicines-nz.pdf>.

[4] Edmund J, Calnan MW. The reprofessionalisation of community pharmacy? An exploration of attitudes to extended roles for community pharmacists amongst pharmacists and general practitioners in the United Kingdom. Soc Sci Med 2001;53:943—55.

[5] Fixsen DL, Naoom SF, Blase KA, Friedman RM, Wallace F. Implementation Research: A Synthesis of the Literature. National Implementation Research Network 2005; <http://ctndisseminationlibrary.org/PDF/nirnmonograph.pdf>.

[6] Pharmaceutical Society of New Zealand Focus on the Future: Ten Year Vision for Pharmacists in New Zealand: 2004—2014. http://psnz.org.nz/public/home/documents/10_yea_plan.pdf.

[7] Ling MA, Panno NJ, Shader ME, Sobinsky RM, Whitehead HN, et al. (2009) The Evolving Scope of Pharmacy Practice: Perspectives from Future Pharmacists http://www.pharmacy.ohio-state.edu/forms/outreach/intro-to-pharmacy/Evolving_Scope_of_Pharmacy_Practice.pdf.

[8] Smith J, Picton C, Dayan M. Now or never: shaping pharmacy for the future, the report of the Commission on future models of care delivered through pharmacy November 2013. London: United Kingdom Royal Pharmaceutical Society of Great Britian; 2013; <http://www.rpharms.com/promoting-pharmacy-pdfs/moc-report-full.pdf>.

[9] Pharmacy Council of New Zealand (2006) Medicines Management. Definition, Levels, Competence Framework http://www.pharmacycouncil.org.nz/cms_show_download.php?id_44.

[10] Shaw J, Duffull S, Print A. Development of a postgraduate educational program for pharmacist prescribers in New Zealand. J Pharm Pract Res. 2013;43(2):122—7.

[11] Hatah EMD. Investigating medication review services provided by community pharmacists. PhD Thesis. New Zealand: University of Otago. Dunedin; 2013.

[12] Latif A, Boardman HF, Pollock K. Understanding the patient perspective of the English community pharmacy Medicines Use Review (MUR). Res Social Admin Pharm. 2013;9:949—57.

[13] Ambler S, Sheldrake L. Pharmacy practice research: challenges and opportunities. Prim Health Care Res Dev. 2009;10(1):4—6.

[14] Horne R, Weinman J, Barber N, et al. Concordance, Adherence and Compliance in Medicine Taking. London: National Co-ordinating Centre for NHSService Delivery and Organisation; 2005; <http://www.academia.edu/877439/Robert_Horne_J_Weinman_N_Barber_et_al._Concordance_adherence_and_compliance_in_medicine_taking_Executive_summary>.

[15] Osterberg L, Blaschke T. Adherence to medication. N Engl J Med 2005;353:487−97.

[16] Trueman P, Taylor DG, Lowson K, et al. Evaluation of the Scale, Causes and Costs of Waste Medicines. York Health Economics Consortium and the School of Pharmacy. University of London; 2010; <http://discovery.ucl.ac.uk/1350234/1/Evaluation_of_NHS_Medicines_Waste__web_publication_version.pdf>.

[17] Department of Health (2008) Pharmacy in England: Building on Strengths − Delivering the Future. http://www.dh.gov.uk/en/Publicationsandstatistics/Publications/Publications PolicyAndGuidance/DH_083815.

[18] Blenkinsopp A, Bond C, Raynor DK. Medication reviews. Br J Clin Pharmacol 2012;74:573−80.

[19] Pound P, Britten N, Morgan M, et al. Resisting medicines: a synthesis of qualitative studies of medicine taking. Soc Sci Med 2005;61:133−55.

Index

Printed in the United States
By Bookmasters